Management of Professionals

Management of Professionals

Insights for Maximizing Cooperation

Desmond D. Martin
Department of Management

Richard L. Shell
*Department of Mechanical
and Industrial Engineering*

*University of Cincinnati
Cincinnati, Ohio*

Marcel Dekker, Inc.   **New York and Basel**

ASQC Quality Press   **Milwaukee**

230238

Library of Congress Cataloging-in-Publication Data

Martin, Desmond D.
 Management of professionals: insights for maximizing coopera-
tion / Desmond D. Martin, Richard L. Shell.
  p.   cm.
 Includes bibliographies.
 ISBN 0-8247-7847-2
 1. Professions. 2. Personnel management. I. Shell, Richard L.
 II. Title.
 HD8038.A1M376 1988
 658.3'044--dc19

 87-30682
 CIP

MARCEL DEKKER, INC.
270 Madison Avenue, New York, New York 10016

Current printing (last digit):
10 9 8 7 6 5 4 3 2 1

Printed in the United States of America

To SueAnn Shell and Nicole and Michael Martin

Preface

This book is an outgrowth of the success of an earlier book entitled *What Every Engineer Should Know About Human Resources Management* (Marcel Dekker, 1980). It was apparent from the response to that earlier work that a need existed for an updated and expanded volume designed to provide managers and professionals with tested management concepts and techniques that can be applied to increase individual and organizational effectiveness.

The American work environment is increasingly composed of well-educated men and women who consider themselves professionals. Clearly, these employees have unique needs and expectations regarding how they manage and how they are managed in their working environment. The presence of global competition threatens the American industrial base and offers new and greater challenges for management. The professional employee will often hold the key to whether or not these challenges are successfully met, which may in fact determine individual firm survival. Thus, it is imperative that both professionals and their managers gain a greater understanding of their mutual dependency. This book has been developed to address that need. Relevant research and concepts directed at the professional work environment have been crystallized into a practical, "no-nonsense" approach to improving organizational effectiveness and bottom-line profitability.

We wish to thank our many friends and acquaintances from the business world, and our academic colleagues and students, who have influenced and shaped many views expressed in this book. Our experience has been greatly enriched by the association with these individuals. Special thanks is expressed to Ms. Barbara Reckers from the Institute of Advanced Manufacturing Sciences for the magnanimous word processing effort required to complete the manuscript.

Desmond D. Martin

Richard L. Shell

Contents

Management of Professionals

1

Successfully Managing The Professional: The Challenge

I. INTRODUCTION AND OVERVIEW

This book is about management, but more importantly it is about managing a growing and vital part of American organazations, namely the professional employee. In addition, this book provides a concentrated overview of effective management practice for the person trained as a professional (e.g., engineer, scientist, physician, or other health specialist) who is or suddenly finds himself or herself thrust into a managerial position. It is clear that professionally trained persons continue to present new and greater challenges to their bosses and organizations, and that many older more traditional management practices simply do not work. In fact, incorrect "management knowledge" more often that not is worse than no knowledge at all. One can *not truly learn about management* by just reading about the unique super star manager or the top most successful corporations, or while searching for excellence, or in one minute. The authors believe that management skills are earned not given, thus it requires work and individual effort (an old-fashioned idea). This book is written in a most condensed form to minimize reading and study time. Examples and theories are cited only when deemed essential for clear understanding or necessary reinforcement. It is important to remember . . . In addition to having correct knowledge about management, *success is only realized by the skillful application of that knowledge!*

The objective of this book is to provide the latest management concepts and knowledge that can be used to manage professionals in such a way that organization effectiveness will be maximized. In order to establish a proper prospective for realizing this objective, Chapter 1 examines what management is, and briefly reviews how management theory and thought has evolved over time. Characteristics of the professional work environment will be identified as well as the unique problems of professionals in managerial roles. It is the author's contention that a large gap exists between the knowledge and application of management skills. Managers can make substantial contributions to the effectiveness of their organizations by concentrating and learning from selected management research and then making an on going effort to insure proper application. Thus the link between theory and practice.

II. WHO IS A PROFESSIONAL?

During the past several decades the term professional has been used to characterize an increasing number of employees. In fact, many employees want to be considered "professionals" by their colleagues and co-workers. Years ago Mary Parker Follett defined a professional in strict terms as one who maintains a loyalty to a code of ethics that transcends his or her loyalty to the rest of the organization.[1] According to this strict usage of the term, very few employees would quality as a professional. In more popular terms, professionals are likely to be defined as employees with specialized or technical education who utilize that knowledge in performing their regular work. More recently John Naisbitt defied a professional as one who creates, processes, and distributes as his or her primary job.[2] Under these two categorizations many organizations are staffed primarily by professionals. In fact, according to Naisbitt, the second largest group of workers in the United States is professional.[2]

The demand for professionals (knowledge workers) has increased dramatically since the 1960s. Professional workers and managers are primarily "information people" which include lawyers, teachers, engineers, physicians, computer programmers, systems analysts, architects, accountants, librarians, newspaper reporters, social workers, nurses, and clergy. Of this example group, the health professionals exhibit another dimension. In addition to being "information people," they also incorporate a fairly high level of physical work in their normal activities, i.e., they are usually subjected to both mental and physiological fatigue.[3] Many of today's professionals have a specific code of ethics and formalized licensing procedures. Examples are physicians, lawyers, accountants, nurses, school teachers, engineers, and members of the clergy. There are other specialized employee groups that may not have strict or formalized licensing procedures, but do assume many of the same characteristics as licensed professionals. Some examples are various types of building trades people (some of which are licensed), computer programmers and operators, personnel administrators, and other groups that engage in specialized support activities within the organization. In fact, any attempt to comprise a comprehensive list of today's professionals becomes very voluminous.

Does managing these professionals differ from non-professionals? In almost all cases this question should be answered affirmatively. Professionals as a group tend to have a strong sense of self worth and often possess high mobility. Thus they put pressure on management to manage effectively. Effective management to the professional tends to follow modern human relations guidelines. They expect considerable freedom and autonomy in performing their work. Also, they expect and respond well to interesting and challenging assignments.

This book is concerned with the complex problem of managing professional employees in a way to obtain maximum productivity. Since perceptions determine reality, managers need to be both competent and perceived to be competent. These two occurrences are not always linked together. Since many professionals are often promoted into management positions they must be prepared to face these managerial challenges (opportunities). However, a large percentage of these employees have little or no management skills training and are often unprepared to function as an effective manager. This book is designed to provide basic managerial skills to the professional newly appointed to a management position and focuses on professionals managing other professionals. Several recent best selling books have had a people management theme, and the trend clearly promotes managing and viewing employees as a highly valued human resource. In spite of all the literature on the subject, only traditional approaches are still widely practiced by today's managers. They often seem easier to apply but in reality do not obtain results for the professional work force.

III. THE SPECIAL CHARACTERISTICS OF PROFESSIONALS

As stressed throughout this book, professionals exhibit specific needs that place demands on their managers beyond that of normal supervision. Many of these needs are associated with autonomy, recognition and the desire for interesting work assignments and are common among all professionals. Some differences however can be observed when specific professional work environments are viewed more closely. In order to provide insight into these differences it is useful to briefly examine a few of the major types of professionals as well as the changing role of women in the work place.

A. The Scientist and Engineer

Often one of the major functions of this group is to provide directed creativity within the organization to develop new products, processes, and services. Successful management in this setting requires the establishment of a work climate that fosters free expression and encourages independent thought. Reward systems are needed that evaluate the methodology utilized to produce innovation as well as actual achievements. For example, scientists and engineers who engage in the conduct of experiments for development should be positively recognized even though their efforts do not always result in a meaningful end product. Appraisal systems that recognize only the end results are not appropriate for this group. These types of employees usually work best in an environment where managerial control over their work is minimized. Good managers of creative scientists and engineers concentrate their efforts in attaining high levels of support and removing obstacles to effective performance. This managerial climate results in high levels of motivation because good scientists and engineers tend to be high achievers and are almost always internally motivated.

B. The Health Professional

Health professionals often work in a more credentials oriented status conscious environment than most other professionals. The elevated position that the physician has historically occupied in America adds complexity to this professional work environment. Physicians often need recognition of their superior status position for continued cooperative effort with other professional groups. Problems that ensue when this recognition is not realized have increased in recent years with the upgrading of other professionals in the health field, e.g., nurses, laboratory specialists, and administrators. Consequently, effective managers in this environment should be skilled in conflict reduction techniques as well as understanding unique needs of each professional employee group they manage.

As previously mentioned, many health professionals such as nurses have both mental and physical demands in their normal work activities. Consequently, the manager must be sensitive to the needs of the knowledge worker as well as the needs of workers who perform jobs requiring a substantial amount of physical energy expenditure.

C. The Staff Specialist

There are many kinds of staff specialists in every large organization. One example is the modern personnel administrator. As with most other staff specialists, personnel directors must be particularly skilled at boundary spanning because their work permeates the entire organization. Also, the personnel administrator and other staff managers should strive to develop this skill among the other members of their support departments. Elements of successful boundary spanning are developed in Chapter 3.

D. Women As Professionals

In 1965 *Harvard Business Review* polled its readers to determine their attitudes about women in business — how they viewed their managerial characteristics and their suitability for top corporate positions. The results of this survey revealed that 54 percent of the men and 50 percent of the women thought that women rarely expect or desire positions of authority.

Twenty years later, the authors of this article reported what they found when they sent the same survey to another sample of 1900 male and female executives.[4] In the interim, of course, Title VII of the Civil Rights Act, the women's movement, and the growing number of women in business have greatly changed actual situations and perceptions about women. In 1985, only 9 percent of the men and 4 percent of the women surveyed think that women don't want top jobs. And men, in general, are far more willing to accept women as colleagues and to see them as competent equals. However, more than half of the respondents don't think women will ever to be totally accepted in business.

According to this study, women held 33 percent of all managerial and administration positions in 1984. Twenty years ago, they held only 14 percent of the executive jobs. But as women have progressed, have attitudes toward female executives changed accordingly? Response to the 1984 *HBR* survey which was a duplicate of the 1965 survey revealed several other important changes. The more important findings are summarized below:

> Men, in particular, are much more likely today than 20 years ago to see women as desiring positions of authority.
>
> More people today believe that EEO laws can expedite women's progress in business.
>
> The percentage of executives who think women are uncomfortable working for other women rose during

the 20-year period. Fewer, however, think that men
are uncomfortable working for women.

Overall, men's attitudes have changed more than women's.

Male and female executives disagree to a great extent on
the issue of pay inequity.

Even when equal pay levels are justified by experience,
male executives in our survey earn much more than
their female counterparts.

The professional woman is required to make several challenging and sometimes difficult decisions early in her career. The
superwoman myth was exposed several years ago, and many professional women realize they cannot assume full responsibility for
all traditional family roles in addition to growing career pressures.
Women professionals can maintain solid personal relationships
and have well adjusted families, but it may mean delaying child
bearing and applying effective time management techniques to
personal life activities. There is a trend among working couples to
postpone children until their 30s in order to establish themselves in
their profession, and to attain increased financial resources to improve their quality of life.

In the context of the professional work environment, one successful professional woman offers the following tips to women attempting to move ahead:[5]

1. Keep track of your organizational structure and top
   management changes, and try to identify and be visible to emerging leaders.
2. Keep most of your discussions at work confined to
   professional topics and avoid extended discussions of
   personal items.
3. Avoid negative informal evaluations of your managers. It is particularly undesirable to make enemies in
   high places.
4. Since most company sponsored charitable campaigns
   involve and are supported by upper level management, it is desirable to actively participate in them.

5. Maintain a conservative style of dress. Communicate through both behavior and dress, strong commitment to both your firm and your profession.
6. Continually monitor your professional environment for opportunities for visibility, new learning opportunities, and promotion. If you're being passed over repeatedly in these important areas, it may be time for a career change.

It is clear from examining a few typical groups of professionals that managers in these work environments need greater managerial knowledge and skill than ever before. This need will likely intensify in the future.

IV. THE PROFESSIONAL AS A MANAGER

It is usually a difficult transition when an employee is promoted from a doer to planner and organizer. This transition is often most difficult for the professional. An employee who has a large personal investment in academic and/or specialized training is likely to see the application of those acquired skills as the most vital part of their life. When promoted into the management hierarchy many of these employees tend to feel that their greatest contribution can still be made through the application of their acquired specialized skills. As a result, the greater portion of their work time is devoted to performing non-managerial tasks. Generally, when a manager does this, the organization suffers.

Managerial effectiveness is usually increased as more time is spent on managerial functions, particularly planning, organizing and facilitating the work of their subordinates. New managers need to shift their work focus away from operative and technical activities and toward the development and application of current "state of the art" management skills. If the individual can not do this then he or she should not be a manager.

V. MANAGEMENT DEFINED

Management may defined as the establishment and realization of goals through the cooperative efforts of all concerned persons.

To further explain this definition, additional discussion is useful. The word goals usually implies the collective goals of the organization and certain personal goals of participating individuals. Both types of goal realization are required for organizational success. The term cooperative efforts implies that management must be able to obtain the cooperation of persons, and direct their efforts toward goal realization. Management must also be able to measure, evaluate, and control the efforts of all persons and functions within the organization. In addition to individuals within the organization, the term concerned persons means that management must be able to properly interface and benefit from individuals outside of the organization that bear influence on ultimate goal realization. Indeed, management is complex in its structure and activities. It consists of people and physical things. Consequently, the key to successful management is obtaining the proper balance between the theory, principles, and practices of management, and human behavior in organizations. It may be said, the world is management.

VI. MANAGEMENT: AN ART AND SCIENCE

Is management an art? Is management a science? Considerable opinion has been set forth concerning the answer to these questions without definitive agreement. An examination of the fundamentals of science and art will be helpful in the understanding of management.

Science relates to knowledge developed from experimentation conducted to determine underlying principles. Commonly, this development of knowledge involves physical experimentation or empirical observation to generate, classify, and analyze data, and formulate statistically valid conclusions. Berelson and Steiner have summarized the important characteristics of science in the outline below:[6]

1. The procedures are public: There is made available to the scientific community a minutely detailed description of the procedures and findings.

2. The definitions are precise: Each important term is clearly delineated, so that common meanings can be universally applied.
3. The data collecting is objective: Regardless of whether data confirm or refute hypotheses or personal preferences, they are accurately measured and treated without bias.
4. The findings must be replicative: Other scientists must be able to reproduce the study and reach the same finding before a hypothesis is generally accepted as validated.
5. The approach is systematic and cumulative: Ultimately the goal is to construct an organized system of verified propositions, a body of theory; individual research projects should be related to existing theory to achieve an overall theoretical structure; new studies may be indicated by gaps or apparent inconsistencies among findings.
6. The purposes are explanation, understanding, and prediction; the growth of understanding and certainty, the decisions concerning control, creation, or change of conditions are applications of a science; they become part of the science only as they assist in meeting the six criteria discussed herein.

While it is unlikely that management will ever exactly match the characteristics of science, it appears that more science is being incorporated into the ongoing practice of management. A possible reason for this trend is the ever-increasing complexity of most business operations. The scientific approach helps solve management problems relating to productivity and quality enhancement, meeting environmental requirements, technology development, computerization, and cost control, just to mention a few.

Art is defined by Webster as "skill in performance acquired by experience, study, or observation." By this definition a large part of management can be classified as an art. Certainly it is true that managers are many times evaluated on their skill in performance, and managers enhance that skill by experience, study, and observation.

It can be concluded that for most organizations, management today should be a combination of art and science. Management should be a mixture of scientific method and analytical techniques, integrated with intuition and judgment derived from experience. In most situations, this combination is necessary to effectively manage change constantly occurring within the organization.

VII. MANAGEMENT THEORY AND THOUGHT

Management can be further explained and better understood by briefly reviewing the major theory and thought appraoches developed over the past several decades. Practicing managers and researchers have developed their own views and ideas about management. In some cases overlay and similarity has occurred, causing reinforcement, while at other times a totally different concept was created. This development of different "schools" of management was apparent a number of years ago and has been summarized by Harold Koontz as follows:

> There are the behaviorists ... who see management as a complex of the interpersonal relationships and the basis of management theory the tentative tenets of the new and underdeveloped science of psychology. There are also those who see management theory as simply a manifestation of the institutional and cultural aspects of sociology. Still others, observing the central core of management is the decision making, branch in all directions from this core to encompass everything in organization life. Then, there are mathematicians who think of management expressed in symbols and the omnipresent and ever revered model. But the entanglement of growth reaches its ultimate when the study of management is regarded as one of a number of systems and subsystems, with an understandable tendency for the researcher to be dissatisfied until he has encompassed the entire physical and cultural universe as a management system.

The subsections that follow summarize the thought and theory of the classic schools of management, and mention a few authors that have substantially contributed to the history of management. It is interesting to note that several individuals initially trained in a professional specialty were among these early pioneers.

A. Scientific Management

The first structured school of management theory and thought, defined as scientific management, evolved from the industrial revolution. An early developer of scientific management was Frederick W. Taylor in his work at Midvale Steel Company during the late nineteenth century.[8] He believed that management should define specific tasks for every worker to complete in a specified time, select the worker best suited for each task, and be concerned with worker motivation. In short, he believed that management should solve problems with logical study and scientific research as opposed to relying on rules of thumb and trial and error methods.

A number of others worked to enlarge the practice of scientific management. Henry L. Gantt, an associate of Taylor, worked to improve the scheduling of manufacturing operations, and Frank B. and Lillian E. Gilbreth developed techniques for studying human motions and improving methods (micromotion study).[9] In addition to time study and methods analysis, the early scientific management school fostered several useful and commonly accepted industrial practices including job evaluation, worker training, and personnel and industrial relations.

B. Process/Functional Management

The management process school or functional management treats management more as a profession than does probably any other school of management. This theory states that the basic management function is consistent and independent of the nature of the organization. The theory assumes that once the manager's functions have been defined, knowledge of practical methods of implementing these functions can be systemically observed, evaluated, and taught.

The beginning of functional management was intitated by a French engineer, Henry J. Fayol, who in 1861 published *Administration industrielle et generale*. This book was not published in the

United States until 1949.[10] Based on his own career, Fayol observed that all industrial activities could be grouped into the following six major categories: Technical, Commercial, Financial, Security, Accounting, and Managerial. The first five categories were relatively well known and encompassed the activities of manufacturing, buying, selling, and record keeping. Consequently, Fayol was most concerned with managerial activities and formulated a number of general principles relating to authority, responsibility, division of work, remuneration, centralization, discipline, and unity of command.

A number of other authors helped structure functional management. These included Mooney and Reiley[11] and Dennison[13] for their work in organization, and Tead[13] for his work in leadership.

Another early proponent of the management process theory, Davis, proposed three organic functions of a manager as follows:[14]

Planning: The exercise of creative thinking in the solution of business problems. It involves the determination of what is to be done, how and where it is to be done, and who shall be responsible.

Organizing: The process of creating and maintaining the requisite conditions for the effective and economical execution of plans. These conditions are principally concerned with morale, organizational structure, procedure, and the various physical factors of performance.

Controlling: The regulation of business activities in accordance with the requirements of business plans. The control process included three principal phases: (a) The assurance of proper performance as specified by the plan; (b) the coordination of effort in conformity with the requirement of the plan; (c) the removal of interferences with proper execution of the plan.

C. Human Relations

The practice of scientific management during the 1920s and 1930s, while successful in fulfilling workers' economic needs, failed to consider psychological needs. Much of the early work in industrial psychology was based on a book by Lillian Gilbreth.[15] The first major study to examine the psychological factors relating to worker productivity was the Hawthorne experiments conducted by Mayo and Roethlisberger.[16] The most interesting results of this study was that worker output increased no matter what change was made in physical condition, e.g., noise or lighting levels. The fact that the workers perceived they were a "select" group and were under observation caused increased ouput. In short, the psychological factors outweighed the actual physical environment considerations. Human relations knowledge added to scientific management and functional management theories and thought, but there were still shortcomings — the more complete understanding of human behavior. While the detailed topics relating to behavior in organizations are discussed in later chapters, a historical overview of the behavioral science school of management follows.

D. Behavioral Science

A number of persons have contributed to the early theory and thought of behavior as it relates to management. These include Maslow,[17] Bakke,[18] Dalton,[19] Stogdell,[20] Likert,[21] Sayles,[22] Leavitt,[23] Vroom,[24] Herzberg,[25] Argyris,[26] McGregor,[27] and Bennis.[28] These behaviorists focus on the development of individual and group needs, and the interaction of these needs with the organizational environment. When this approach is integrated into the broader "socio-technical" system, it has become widely recognized as an important part of the effective management of professionals. One of the major purposes of this book is to provide managers with proven managerial and applied behavioral tools that will help increase the effectiveness of their organizational units. Bottom line, a good manager must produce results.

E. Social Systems

The social system approach views workers from a much less flexible viewpoint than the behavioral theorist. Where as in behavioral science, motivation is contingent upon each worker's needs and aspirations, the social system theorist relates more to basic motivators relevant to the present culture. The social system school looks at a corporation as basically an input-output model, with the employees working only when they feel the inducements received equal or outweigh their contributions.

March and Simon[29] and Simon and coworkers[30] have outlined the major characteristics of an organization following the input-output model:

1. An organization is a system of interrelated social behaviors of a number of persons whom we shall call the participants in the organization.
2. Each participant and each group of participants receives from the organization inducements, in return for which he or she makes contributions to the organization.
3. Each participant will continue participation in an organization only so long as the inducements offered are as great or greater than the contributions he or she is asked to make.
4. The contributions provided by the various groups of participants are the source from which the organization manufactures the inducements offered to the participants.
5. Hence, an organization is "solvent" — and will continue in existence — only so long as contributions are sufficient to provide inducements in large enough measure to draw for these contributions.

F. Management Science

The management science approach has also been defined as the mathematical school, the decision theory school, quantitative methods, and operations research. The modern day foundation for management science began during World War II when mathematical models were developed to solve problems relating to the management of war operations.

The mathematical school attempts to approach each management situation with a parallel mathematic model (either deterministic or probabilistic). The problem is then solved using the precise logical structure of mathematics. If the model does indeed match the business problem at hand and the computations can be completed, the mathematical approach has value. The wide spread use of computers throughout business and industry have increased the usefulness of this approach.

The decision-making process has probably received more attention than any other subject among management scientists. Traditional decision theory stresses rational thinking, the acquisition of valid data, and quantitative models to arrive at a proper decision. Examples of different business situations may be developed to produce several alternate solutions to a particular problem. There is also an emphasis on objectivity in evaluating different alternatives.

G. Systems and Contingency

Management has borrowed the systems concept from the physical and natural sciences. This approach requires the interrelatedness of all activities within an organization. Norbert Weiner contributed much theory and thought to modern day systems concepts through his work in cybernetics.[31]

The contingency approach came into being because of the individual shortcomings of previously developed schools of management. For example, the behavioral approach works well in many situations involving people problems, but it does not produce results in operations problems requiring the techniques of management science for solution. Similar statements could be made concerning the other management schools. The first authors to observe the need for a contingency approach included Woodward,[33] Fiedler,[34] and Lorsch and Lawrence.[34]

The contingency approach requires that the practice and application of management theory should be contingent upon the needs of a specific management situation. Consequently, behavioral and scientific techniques should be applied along with selected principles and practices from each school or management to solve existing problems. The successful manager must have the ability to recognize which management approach(es) to use in a given situation at a particular point in time.

VIII. EMPHASIS OF THIS BOOK

The major thrust of this book is to familiarize today's professional with current "state of the art" management skills that will help assure personal success (and success for their organizations) when they become new or are prospective managers. This is an important challenge because studies show that many technically trained people assume managerial positions within ten years after their first career job assignment. In the case of engineers, it has been found that about two-thirds have managerial assignments within ten years after receiving their bachelors degree.[35] The book stresses principles and practices of effective management that professionals need to understand. Particular emphasis is placed on behavioral patterns associated with professionals and their work environment.

Chapter 1 has focused on introducing fundamental concepts of management theory and thought. The professional's needs are summarized along with the role of the professional as a manager. Characteristics of professionals were examined broadly, with some discussion devoted to the needs of specific professional groups.

Chapter 2 is devoted to planning and forecasting. Effective management must begin with planning, and to plan one must be able to forecast the future. Aspects of long-range (strategic) and operational (short-term) planning are discussed. In addition, a number of commonly used forecasting techniques are reviewed.

Chapter 3 addresses the management functions of organizing and staffing. An historical background is included to give the reader a prospective on how and why today's organizations came into being. The principles of "unity of command" and "division of labor" are discussed. The proper roles for line and staff are identified. Span of management concepts are defined along with the methodology necessary for correct organizational design. The final section of the chapter provides insight into the importance and nature of good employee selection.

Chapter 4 highlights the principles of directing and controlling. Responsibility and authority are discussed and suggestions for delegation are offered. Ideas for salary administration and performance measurement are important management concerns. The relationship of budgets to control is reviewed along with the importance of management information systems. Finally, suggestions are offered for the application of critical path scheduling to enhance project direction and control.

Chapter 5 is devoted to the important management activity of decision making. The nature of the decision-making process is summarized, followed by a recommended systems analysis technique to aid decision making. In addition, the concepts of "utility theory" and "expected value" are discussed as they relate to decision making.

Chapter 6 contains a concise development of the emergence and importance of individual and group needs. An understanding of these needs is the cornerstone of modern behavioral management, and the significant impact of individual needs on group development and organizational effectiveness is covered. Specific attention is given to the needs of professional personnel, and what the unique nature of these needs imply to their bosses.

Chapter 7 analyzes the number one management concern, namely, building effective communication. The major types and dimensions of organization communication are classified. The importance of informal and nonverbal communication is explained in a practical context. Several techniques and tools to improve the level of understanding within the professional environment are provided. Attention is given to major problem areas including tips on overcoming defensiveness, increasing communication feedback and participation, and building an overall organization climate that is characterized by mutual trust.

Chapter 8 focuses on the motivational problems that face managers of professionals. These managers are encouraged to confront the motivation problem directly, and six basic steps are outlined that will help to make this confrontation successful. The most practical motivational models are identified and explained and are specifically put in the professional work environment. The overall emphasis of this chapter is to provide a basic no-nonsense approach to motivating professionals.

Chapter 9 emphasizes the importance of strong leadership in effective management. Several leadership styles are developed and critiqued. Common leadership problems such as delegation, participation, and the facilitative role of the manager are discussed in a simple and practical manner. Situational leadership is emphasized as a practical solution to the leadership problem. Several leadership models are offered and criteria are provided for choosing an appropriate leadership style.

Chapter 10 discusses the complex problem of organizational change. This chapter also looks at managerial behavior in time of crisis, and suggests common pitfalls to avoid. Three phases of change that are related to managerial effectiveness are explained. An analysis is made of the factors that lead to resistance to change. Since resistance to change often leads to reduced motivation, it can be an extremely costly management problem. Several tips are provided on how managers of professional staff can properly implement change and alleviate resistance. While employee participation is often very useful in reducing resistance, it sometimes is either inappropriate or insufficient, and in these latter cases alternatives are suggested.

Chapter 11 explains the difficult and challenging issues of managing conflict and stress. Leading causes of conflict are identified, and both the functional and dysfunctional aspects of it are examined. The complex nature of stress is analyzed and both conflict and stress reduction techniques are offered.

Chapter 12 provides a detailed look at the new trend toward higher involvement management. Attention is given to the appropriateness of involvement management to the professional work environment, and challenges in moving an organization from more traditional practices to the high involvement mode.

Chapter 13 summarizes the impact of the major managerial factors covered throughout the book on organizational effectiveness. Comments are included concerning the changing attitudes and values of the American work force and career development in the professional organization. particular attention is given to the career needs of professionals and a career development model is provided.

Enjoy your reading and learning. Remember, management can make the difference.

REFERENCES

1. M. P. Follett, "How Must Business Management Develop in Order to Possess the Essentials of a Profession," in H. C. Metcalf and L. Vwik, eds., *Dynamic of Administration, The Collected Paper of Mary Parker Follett,* London: Sir Isaac Pitman & Sons, 1941, pp. 117-145.

2. J. Naisbitt, *Megatrends,* New York: Warner Books, 1982, p. 5.

3. O. Geoffrey Okogbaa, and Richard L. Shell, "The Measurement of Knowledge Worker Fatigue," *IIE Transactions,* Vol. 18, No. 4, December 1986, pp. 335-342.

4. C. D. Sutton and K. K. Moore, "Executive Women — 20 Years Later," *Harvard Business Review,* September-October, 1985, pp. 42-43.

5. Victoria L. Stadler, "Can Women Have It All," University of Cincinnati College of Business Administration, 1987 (mimeograph).

6. B. Berelson and G. A. Steiner, *Human Behavior,* Harcourt, Brace & World, New York, 1964, pp. 16-17.

7. H. Koontz, "The Management Theory Jungle," *Academy of Management Journal,* Vol. IV, No. 3, December 1961, pp. 174-175.

8. F. W. Taylor, *The Principles of Scientific Management,* Harper & Brothers, New York, 1911.

9. F. B. Gilbreth and L. E. Gilbreth, *Applied Motion Study,* Macmillan, New York, 1971.

10. H. J. Fayol, *General and Industrial Administration,* Sir Isaac Pitman & Sons, London, 1949.

11. J. D. Mooney and A. C. Reiley, *Onward Industry,* Harper & Brothers, New York, 1931; and *The Principles of Organization,* Harper & Brothers, New York, 1939.

12. H. Dennison, *Organization Engineering,* McGraw-Hill, New York, 1931.

13. Ordway Tead, *The Art of Leadership,* McGraw-Hill, New York, 1935.

14. R. C. Davis, *Industrial Organization and Management,* Harper & Brothers, New York, 1940, pp. 35-36.

15. L. M. Gilbreth, *The Psychology of Management,* Macmillan, New York, 1914.

16. E. Mayo, *The Human Relations of an Industrial Civilization,* Harvard University Press, Cambridge Mass., 1933.

17. A. Maslow, *Motivation and Personality,* Harper & Brothers, New York, 1954.

18. E. W. Bakke, *Bonds of Organization,* Harper & Row, New York, 1950.

19. M. Dalton, *Men Who Manage,* John Wiley & Sons, New York, 1959.

20. R. M. Stogdell, *Individual Behavior and Group Achievement,* Oxford University Press, London, 1959.

21. R. Likert, *New Patterns of Management,* McGraw-Hill, New York, 1961.

22. L. Sayles, *Managerial Behavior,* McGraw-Hill, New York, 1964.

23. H. J. Leavitt, *Managerial Psychology,* University of Chicago Press, Chicago, 1964.

24. V. H. Vroom, *Work and Motivation,* John Wiley & Sons, New York, 1964.

25. F. Herzberg, *Work and the Nature of Man,* World Publishing Co., Cleveland, 1966.

26. C. Argyris, *Integrating the Individual and the Organization,* John Wiley & Sons, New York, 1964.

27. D. McGregor, *The Human Side of Enterprise,* McGraw-Hill, New York, 1960.

28. W. Bennis, *Changing Organizations,* McGraw-Hill, New York, 1966.

29. J. G. March and H. A. Simon, *Organizations,* John Wiley & Sons, New York, 1958.

30. H. A. Simon, W. Smithburg, and V. A. Thompson, *Public Administration,* Alfred A. Knopf, New York, 1950.

31. N. Wiener, *Cybernetics,* The MIT Press, Cambridge, Mass., 1948.

32. J. Woodward, *Industrial Organization,* Oxford University Press, London, 1965.

33. F. E. Fiedler, *A Theory of Leadership Effectiveness,* McGraw-Hill, New York, 1967.

34. J. W. Lorsch and P. R. Lawrence, *Studies in Organizational Design,* Irwin-Dorsey, Homewood, IL, 1970.

35. Richard L. Shell, "Engineers Ten Years After Graduation," Unpublished survey University of Cincinnati, 1985.

2

Planning and Forecasting

I. INTRODUCTION

Planning and forecasting are processes which should precede all future action. These processes ensure that management continually looks forward and works to maximize the resources of the business. The planning activity asks the questions of what has to be done, when, and how. Forecasting supports the planning activity by utilizing data from the past to calculate numerically based projections of the future. Consequently, forecasting must be an integral part of planning. Planning also tests the quality and coherence of managements objectives and helps to develop a common understanding of them.

Planning can be viewed as a method of determining desirable future conditions and then setting goals and objectives to obtain this desired state. Typical questions that must be answered by the planner include the following: What is our business? What should be our business? How can we maintain profitability? Who are our customers? What customers should be sought? What products or services should be added? These are just a few of the many questions that must be answered.

Historically, the most formal planning efforts focused upon tactical or short-term operational type problems. Strategic or long-range planning was accomplished using intuitive approaches common with entrepreneurs. Today, successful organizations must be able to correctly plan for short-term operations as well as the formal development of strategic plans to aid in obtaining desired performance for the longer-term future.

II. THE PLANNING PROCESS

Applications of strategic and tactical planning are varied over many industries including manufacturing, service sector companies, and government. Within each of these at least three basic operating levels are present: the business unit level, the corporate level, and the institutional level.[1] Some common application areas of strategic and tactical planning include:

> Productivity improvement programs
> Department activities (personnel, production, design)
> Quality management and improvement
> Manufacturing and production
> Management policies
> Information and decision support systems
> Production and inventory control
> Acquisitions and mergers
> Technology transfer
> Health care benefits
> Financial needs

The planning process for each of these areas have basically identical activities associated with them, and are characterized as elements or stages of formulating and enacting the plan. These include defining the current position, defining goals and objectives, establishing a planning horizon, developing and monitoring performance measures, and the continual update and review of the entire process.

The planning process in the organization may be classified into three types: Bottom-up, top-down, and interactive. The distinction between the types relates to where the plan is presented, reviewed, and decided.

The bottom-up approach requires the operating unit or division to gather information and set goals. Planning for this approach is decentralized and corporate planning departments are relatively small. Only high level key long-range planning is made at the corporate level. Many larger firms in the United States use this type of planning.

The top-down approach, as opposed to bottom-up, has all planning done at the corporate level. Divisions are assigned goals and guidelines to follow. Large corporate planning offices are required.

Interactive planning is a cross between the bottom-up and top-down approach. There is interaction between top management and the operating unit or division. The planning department functions to gather information which it submits to top management. They then develop goals and broad directives. These are submitted to the divisions or units which then devise guidelines and formulate direct goals. The interactive approach is recommended for the greatest long-range planning effectiveness.

The planning event or start of the process may also be conducted in a variety of ways. Many planning activities utilize off site retreats for develolpment of strategic plans. This methodology was traditionally used for top management only, but today the trend is towards more participative and interactive planning systems. In interactive planning each element of the organization that is affected by a strategic decision is included in the development of that decision.

The evolution of the activity and nature of planning in the United States has progressed as follows:

1950's - top management only
1960's - rigid plans still applying the top down approach
1970's - delegation to staff, development of planning departments

1980's - distributed and participative

1990's - increased flexibility, adaptability, and scope

Whatever type of planning process is used there are key points critical to every planning effort. These include effective leadership, top management commitment, good communication, clear understanding of objectives at all levels, links to staff levels, realistic goals, performance measures, and continual review and control.

III. STRATEGIC PLANNING FOR LONG-RANGE SUCCESS

Strategic planning is the continuous, systematic process of making present time decisions, based on knowledge and insight of their potential; organizing the efforts needed to enact these decisions; and measuring the results of these decisions against the expected performance.[2] The strategic planning system is thus a tool by which resources are dedicated to activities which are expected to achieve a pre-defined set of goals and objectives.[3]

The use of strategic planning in the United States first began in the 1950's and was primarily concerned with financial data and budget control. Common planning horizons were in the range of 5-20 years. During the 1960's a common approach was that of "portfolio planning". This type of planning was especially useful in determining acquisitions, divestitures, and the overall nature of the business.

The first use of computer models in planning began in the 1970's with the increased availability and affordability of computers. As may be expected, today the use of computer models is widespread and continues to have potential and growth. With the energy crisis during the early 1970's many companies began to shorten planning horizons, redirect attention towards cost cutting and conversation, and increased emphasis on productivity and manufacturing competitiveness.[4,5]

Today these applications of strategic planning take on even greater significance due to new technologies, shortened product cycles, the demand for lower costs, increasing competition, and the global marketplace. The most modern factories, sometimes referred to as "factories with "economy of scale" to factories with "economy of scope". These factories are thus more flexible, efficient, responsive, and capable.

Current trends place an even greater importance on the ability of manufacturing as a strategic component of the business. Without investment in new technology and management techniques, market share, profit margin, and cash flow will most likely decline. Continual deferment will only place the laggard companies further behind the leaders in the field.[6]

Strategic planning is one of the more difficult tasks corporate executives must perform. Not only are they asked to plan a course for the business to follow in an uncertain future, they also must forecast technology and economic conditions, as well as the social and political environments outside the business. In addition to all of these, responsibility for a long-range plan is enormous — the survival of the corporation is totally dependent on the long-range plan. For this reason, long-range planning must be the responsibility of top management and receive high priority in the organization.

Although formal long-range planning is relatively new in the field of management, more than 80 percent of the large corporations in the United States have some kind of long-range planning. The requirements for obtaining lead time also demands that firms make decisions long before the real need exists to fill vacant areas or implement necessary change.

Long range planning is most commonly given distinct identification and attention in larger firms in high technology industries. Professionals are likely to value planning and to consider it an important factor in success. Consequently, managers in the professional environment should pay specific attention to the planning function. A recent survey of Fortune 500 companies indicates the most probable characteristics of the strategic planning function as follows[7]:

A small (less than six professionals) corporate planning department and additional planning at the divisional level.

The planning function is relatively new to the corporation (eight years or less).

Strategic plans are developed in meetings of the corporation's top managers on an annual basis.

The annual strategic plan is integrated with the annual financial plan.

This same study indicates that one-third of the companies use the planning process to manage extensively. Executives of several companies surveyed offered specific examples of improved management as a result of formalized strategic planning. This improved management usually has increased the short-term profitability of the firm and many executives predict that it is likely to make a greater contribution in the future. The Paul and Taylor study cited two general areas of strategic planning that need attention and improvement.[7] First, formal planning needs to be spread more widely throughout the organization. Namely, managers of professionals need to integrate the planning process as an important aspect of their job. Second, a tighter linkage is needed between planning and execution. All too often, time and money is spent on developing an outstanding plan, but because staff planners and line executives do not work well together on planning, the plan is never implemented. Managers at all levels need to appreciate the vital contribution of good planning to firm success. Experiences, in the early eighties, that United States manufacturing firms had with foreign competition clearly illustrates this fact.

IV. TACTICAL PLANNING FOR OPERATIONAL SUCCESS

Operational plans are usually more narrow in scope than long-range plans and short term in their impact. An operational plan is often used by lower and middle level managers because they are more familiar with the plan's functions and operations. Also, the responsibilities are fewer. An operational plan will not have the overall effect on a company as will a long-term plan.

Questions addressed by an operational planner are more restrictive and specialized than those of the long-range planner. Examples of these questions might be: How many and what skill type of technical personnel are required for a product development? What inventory levels should be maintained? What replacement policy should be used with regard to a certain type of equipment? How much of a product should be produced over a period of a year or six months' time. What level of tooling and test equipment should be designed to support planned production? Since the planning period is short, present trends and market position are often assumed to be relatively unchanged; thus, operational planning lends itself to the use of recent past data. Comparatively little forecasting is done before preparing an operational plan. Mathematical models, exponential smoothing, and the program evaluation and review technique (PERT) are frequently used for short-range planning.[8]

In general, a short-term plan should be completed concurrently with long-term planning. For example, if an organization has a one-year time horizon for operational planning and a five-year period for long-range planning, the operational plan becomes the first year of the long-range plan. Independent of the planning horizon time period, it is recommended that both operational and long-range planning be updated at least annually. Following initial planning efforts, a long-range plan only requires complete planning for the last year, with the other years being appropriately updated. At the very least, goals established in short-term planning should be set to enhance the long-term goals. If a tight linkage exists between the long-range and operational planning, it will make long-range planning seem more action oriented and more credible to the members of the organization. Tight linkage does have a negative side; it often hinders creativity and is likely to cause managers to avoid risks. Future-oriented companies will often want a loose linkage, while conservative cash-generating firms may choose the former.

V. EVALUATION OF PLANNING SYSTEMS AND THEIR RESULTS

The evaluation of decisions made by planning systems is becoming increasingly common. This may be a direct result of many companies previous failures with strategic planning, the increased scope and importance of the plan to the business, or the cost effectiveness necessity to evaluate the outputs of the system and forecasting models it uses.

One set of guidelines top evaluate planning is based upon assessments of performance in the areas listed below[9]:

Effectiveness of planning
Relative worth of the strategic planning system
The role and impact of the strategic planning system
The performance of the plans
The relative worth of the strategy
Adaptive value of the system
Relative efficiency of the system
Adequacy of resources
The allocation of planning resources
The appropriateness of the planning goals

Another approach for evaluation is to look at specific criteria such as the extent of which the plan has fostered organizational learning and the range of alternatives which it has generated.

The idea of productivity measurement has also been applied to the evaluation of strategic plans, not only on the goal or production level, but at the efforts and results of the entire system. This seems to be part of a trend to include productivity improvement at all levels of the business as a goal of strategic plans.[10] The authors strongly recommend that planning to improve productivity be a major component of the overall planning process.

VI. BASIC FORECASTING METHODS

As mentioned earlier, most firms use more than one method of forecasting in both long-range and short-range planning. The variety of methods are extensive. Methods used mainly for tactical operational planning differ from those used for strategic long-range planning because of the uncertainty involved in predicting farther into the future. Selection of the right technique can be almost as important as the planning itself. Use of the wrong method, insufficient or incorrect data collection, or improper analysis may leave the planner and top management with a very poor prediction about the future.

Forecasting for planning is concerned with all aspects of descriptive statistics including methods for collecting, organizing, analyzing, summarizing, and presenting data, in addition to formulating valid conclusions. In a more narrow sense, the term statistics denotes only the data or the numerical solutions of the data, e.g., calculations of means and standard deviations. Planning is concerned with making reasonable decisions or arriving at meaningful conclusions on the basis of analysis of the forecasting data. A number of commonly used deterministic and probabilistic forecasting methods are briefly discussed in the sections that follow. These methods are included to remind readers with forecasting experience of the commonly used techniques, and to suggest that readers with minimum forecasting background consult a basic forecasting text to become familiar with the fundamental techniques.

A. Linear Regression

The least-squares method is commonly used to fit a straight line through a group of data points. The principle of least squares requires that if a dependent variable y is a linear function of an independent variable x, the best location of the $y = a + bx$ will exist when the sum of the squares of deviations of all data points from that location is minimized. The values of a and b may be obtained by solving the normal equations.

$$a = \frac{\Sigma x^2 \Sigma y - \Sigma x \Sigma xy}{n\Sigma x^2 - (\Sigma x)^2}$$

and

$$b = \frac{n\Sigma xy - \Sigma x \Sigma y}{n\Sigma x^2 - (\Sigma x)^2}$$

Forecasting commonly requires that the independent variable x is time. A regression line or curve y on x is often termed a trend line in time-series forecasting.

The method of least squares permits the computation of sampling errors and provides for the determination of the estimates' reliability. Confidence limits can be determined by computing the variance of y from the estimated value of y by the regression line with the following equations:

$$S_y^2 = \frac{\Sigma \epsilon_i^2}{v}$$

where

S_y^2 = confidence interval
ϵ_i^2 = square of the deviation
= $y_i - (a + bx_i)$
v = degrees of freedom

Additional confidence limits and significance tests may be determined for the regression equation depending on the forecast requirements.

For two or more independent variables, multiple linear regression may be used as expressed by the following equation:

$$y = a + b_1x_1 + b_2x_2 + \bullet \bullet \bullet + b_mx_m$$

where

a = a constant
b_i = partial regression coefficients

Single or multiple independent variable linear regression requires the following assumptions:

1. The regression of y on x_i is linear.
2. The data are taken from a representative forecasting population.
3. There are no extraneous variables.
4. The deviations from y are mutually independent and have the same variance for any value of x_i.
5. The deviations are normally distributed.

B. Curvilinear Regression and Curve Fitting

Many situations in the planning process require forecasting from nonlinear data. Calculations for nonlinear regression are best performed with computerized assistance. The following are examples of curvilinear relationships useful in forecasting for planning:

Exponential or logarithmic: $y = ax^b$

Semilogarithmic: $y = ae^{bx}$

Reciprocal y: $y = \dfrac{1}{a + bx}$

Reciprocal x: $y = a + \dfrac{b}{x}$

Hyperbolic: $y = \dfrac{x}{a + bx}$

Polynomial: $y = a + b_1 x + b_2 x^2 + \bullet \bullet \bullet + b_m x^m$

A number of nonlinear relationships may be transformed to linear expressions. For example, nonlinear data points following the exponential form, $y = ax^b$, on Cartesian coordinates may be transformed to a linear relationship on logarithmic coordinates with the following equation:

$$\log y = \log a + b \log x$$

All of these functions can be statistically evaluated for their fit to the data. Commonly used measures include the standard error of y, correlation coefficient, and confidence limits.

C. Correlation

For linear regression, the coefficient of correlation explains how well the variables are satisfied by a given relationship. Fig. 2.1 depicts data point diagrams with associated values of correlation. The correlation coefficient, r, may be computed as shown below:

$$r = \frac{n\Sigma xy - \Sigma x \Sigma y}{[n\Sigma x^2 - (\Sigma x)^2]\,[n\Sigma y^2 - (\Sigma y)^2]^{\,1/2}}$$

The value of r must be in the range $0 \leqslant |r| \leqslant 1$. The magnitude of the correlation coefficient indicates the strength of the relationship between variables. It should be noted that the correlation coefficient is a measure of relationship strength and is purely mathematical. It does not determine any cause or effect implications.

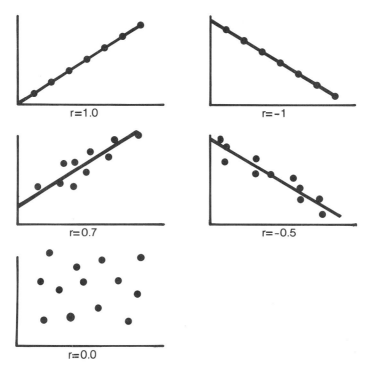

Figure 2.1 Data point diagrams with associated values of correlation coefficient.

D. Moving Averages and Exponential Smoothing

Most forecasting requirements for planning are concerned with time-series data and projections. Figure 2.2 depicts examples of commonly encountered time-series models. If the planner assumes the forecast should place equal weight on all past data points, then the moving average, A_m, may be computed with the following equation:

$$A_m = \frac{x_t + x_{t-1} + \bullet\,\bullet\,\bullet + x_{t-n+1}}{n}$$

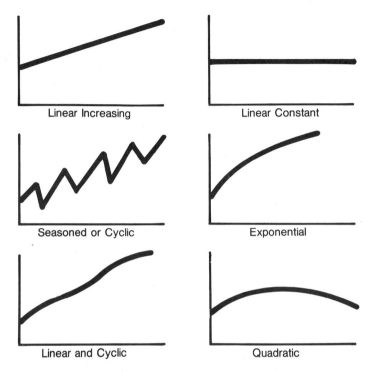

Linear Increasing   Linear Constant

Seasoned or Cyclic   Exponential

Linear and Cyclic   Quadratic

Figure 2.2 Common models for time-series forecasting.

If the forecast should reflect historical data and current trends, the exponential smoothing function is recommended. This function may be expressed as follows:

$$S_t(x) = \alpha x_t + (1 - \alpha) S_{t-1}(x)$$

where

$S_t(x)$ = smoothed value of the function

α = smoothing constant

The value of the smoothing constant must lie between $0 \leqslant \alpha \leqslant 1$. When the value of the smoothing constant is small, the function $S_t(x)$ is strongly influenced by past data. When the value of the smoothing constant is large, $s_t(x)$ is influenced mostly by the current trend. It is recommended that smoothing constant values be developed from experience for specific planning and forecasting requirements.

E. Simulation

Up to this point, several deterministic methods of forecasting have been reviewed. In addition to these methods, certain probabilistic methods are useful.

Simulation techniques are generally used with longer-term forecasting, because they frequently require a great deal of time and effort to develop. A model must be created that represents a situation which will react the way a real system would. Various input is fed into the model which produces an output modeling the outcome of the real issue. Managers should use these models to answer "what if" questions that develop in many planning situations.[11]

Another modeling approach useful in planning is the Monte Carlo technique. This technique uses random variables selected from a probability distribution to input into the model. Ouput from this type of model is in the form of a distribution of the end results. From this, a manager can determine the most likely end result and decide whether it is acceptable.

VII. COST AND ACTIVITY INDEXES

In addition to internal data, most forecasts for planning should consider outside factors. Index numbers have been used in planning for a long time. For example, in the mid eighteenth century, an Italian, G. R. Carli, developed an index to evaluate the effects of the discovery of America on the purchasing power of money in Europe.[12] During more recent years, numerous indexes have been developed. Examples of these include wholesale and retail prices, productivity, wages, and building construction. In addition to their main point of concern, most indexes apply to a time and place, namely a given year for a certain geographic region.

VIII. SUMMARY

Problems of planning that face organizations today are probably more complex than ever before. In the midst of changing economic times, severe competition which is often global, business failures, rapidly changing technologies, and political upheaval, the activity of corporate planning becomes extremely difficult. Without planning and forecasting, a firm's chance of survival becomes questionable if not improbable. It is important that managers of professional staff realize that planning serves to give an organization guidelines to follow and a standard to gauge its progress.

REFERENCES

1. Richard G. Hamermesh, "Making Planning Strategic", *Harvard Business Review,* July-August 1986.

2. Robert S. Mankin, "Strategic Planning: An Overview", *Managerial Planning,* September/October 1984 Vol. 33 No. 2, pp. 14-21.

3. Daniel H. Gray, "Uses and Misuses of Strategic Planning". *Harvard Business Review,* January-February 1986, pp. 89-97.

4. Robert H. Hayes, "Strategic Planning - Forward in Reverse?", *Harvard Business Review,* November-December 1985, pp. 111-119.

5. Wickham Skinner, 'The Productivity Paradox", *Harvard Business Review,* July-August 1986, pp. 55-59.

6. Robert S. Kaplan, "Must CIM Be Justified by Faith Alone?", *Harvard Business Review,* March-April 1986, pp. 87-95.

7. R. N. Paul and J. W. Taylor, "The State of strategic Planning: A Survey of Fortune 550," *Business,* January-March 1986, p. 43.

8. Barry Render and Richard L. Shell, "Forecasting Techniques for Production Planning and Control," *Proceedings, Annual Systems Engineering Conference,* American Institute of Industrial Engineers, 1975, pp. 279-303.

9. King, William R., "Evaluating the Effectiveness of Your Planning," *Managerial Planning,* September-October 1984, Vol. 33, No. 2, pp. 4-8.

10. Carl G. Thor, "The Role of Productivity Measurement in Strategic Planning", *Industrial Management,* March-April 1986, pp. 24-25.

11. Richard L. Shell and S. Chandra, "Simulation for Automated Job-Shop Development," *Proceedings, Annual Systems Engineering Conference, American Institute of Industrial Engineers, 1975, pp. 16-25.*

12. Phillip F. Oswald, *Cost Estimating for Engineering and Management,* Prentice-Hall, Englewood Cliffs, N.J., 1974, p. 148.

3
Organizing and Staffing

I. HISTORICAL DEVELOPMENT

In general, an organization may be defined as a social invention developed by persons to accomplish things otherwise not possible. It is a social invention that takes a variety of people, knowledge, materials, and equipment and gives them structure and purpose to become an interrelated effective unit with common goals. An organization may also be described as a structured system by which decisions are transmitted from management to subordinate levels, taking into account communication, influence, authority, responsibility, and loyalty. Staffing supplies the people to operate the enterprise through the organizational structure.

Why have organized structure? In today's economic and business environment things are constantly changing; therefore, it becomes necessary for an organization to be flexible enough to identify the need for change, and through internal manipulation make the change as smoothly as possible. In essence, organizational structure is a tool of effectiveness, and if groups of people were more effective without organizational structure, it would not be needed. But as organizations increase in size, structure becomes necessary for both effectiveness and efficiency.

Historically, organizations have tended to be structured with all authority coming from a few individuals or in some cases only a single individual. Examples of this are early family enterprises in which only the father and his children governed all phases of the business. Technical and management skills were of little importance in the early days before the industrial revolution because industries were small and lacked the competition of today's world marketplace. The structure of this early organization was very simple. It was a huge subordinate group connected by a thin link to an extremely small management group on top. There was room in this system only for authority directed to subordinates through middle managers who enacted all decisions made from above. With little technical or scientific advancement going on in most markets, this system managed quite well up until the industrial revolution.

During the time of thriving technical achievement, businesses found it necessary to augment their organizational structure and improve upon their managerial strategies to keep pace with the emerging changes. No longer were organizations centrally staffed. Span of management, the number of individuals reporting directly to one superior, was contracted to better coordinate all functions of management. Organizations tended to decentralize power in contrast to prerevolutionary times. The newer structure of the organization began to take the shape of a pyramid. No longer could corporations sit idle and hope that the family, or central body, would dictate all directives no matter how minute. Authority began to be delegated downward, with improved rewards granted to all managers. This tended to develop energetic involved subordinates at lower levels of management.

As business complexity and technology advanced further, there became a need for even more specialists for each phase of management. A marketing manager, personnel supervisor, engineering director, and other specialists began to be represented in upper management. In today's dynamic technical-business society, management requirements have been met by a newer formation or organizational structure. It resembles a large pyramid with a smaller pyramid balanced directly on top of it. Specialists are given higher authority positions ranging from advisors to direct supervision in the area of their expertise. It is commonplace to have a person trained and working in a specialized professional area assigned supervisory responsibilities.

Organizational structures will always have to be redefined and augmented to meet the *ever-changing* management requirements and marketing needs for the corporation's services or products. In addition, the organizational structure is modified to some extent to take advantage of particular strengths of key employees. With this brief historical view of the organization, a more detailed discussion of the components and interactions of the organization may be pursued.

II. UNITY OF COMMAND

The concept of unity of command was established by Henri Fayol.[1] He stated that "no member of an organization should report to more than one supervisor." This was and is today a very controversial idea. Followers of Fayol stated that confusion, loss of productivity, conflict, and poor morale were all symptoms of having subordinates answer to more than one supervisor. In actual practice this rule need not be absolutely rigid, prohibiting all but unified command. There are problems associated with unity of command in that subordinates must technically receive a flow of command or influence through only one supervisor. Since most managers usually lack expertise in every detailed aspect of their operation, specialist's skills may be passed by for lack of availability, time, pride, or various other reasons. The solution of the unity of command problem lies in the proper utilization of staff personnel, possible use of the matrix organizational structure, and the informal organization to be discussed later in this chapter.

III. DIVISION OF LABOR

The concept of assigning elements of a task to different workers is as old as human civilization. Cicero, for example, called it the very basis for civilization. In 1776, Adam Smith in his book *The Wealth of Nations* discussed the division of labor in detail by using examples of manufacturing.[2] He observed that several persons each manufacturing a steel pin produced considerably fewer pins during a work period than did the same number of persons working as specialists on assigned elemental tasks. This was the first reported progressive manufacturing line. The division of labor creates the need for coordination and therefore impacts organizational structure.

In a macro sense, there are two ways of classifying the division of labor. The first is by division or ranking of hierachy of authority based on status within the company as shown in Figure 3.1. The second is to divide horizontally according to function as shown in Figure 3.2. In this form, the type of labor is the primary factor in determining how the work is divided. This is apparent if one considers, for example, the personnel, accounting, and engineering departments, which do not perform detail work together but must at some point be interconnected.

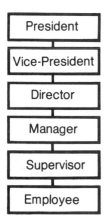

Figure 3.1 Vertical division of labor.

Examples of today's application of the Adam Smith division of labor concept would include the basic manufacturing process of most high-volume produced products, e.g., automobiles, appliances, and food. As a total manufacturing work task is more

Figure 3.2 Horizontal division of labor.

finely divided, the cycle time for each work station decreases, namely, more division of labor. Figure 3.3 depicts the general relationship between productive effort, that is, the percentage of labor expended that adds real value to a product, and the manufacturing cycle time. Cycle time is inversely proportional to the application of the division of labor. Conceptually, this same increase in productive effort as related to the division of labor for hourly workers also extends to professional level employees. The optimal cycle time, however, is considerably longer for the professional performing knowledge based tasks that require mostly mental processing.

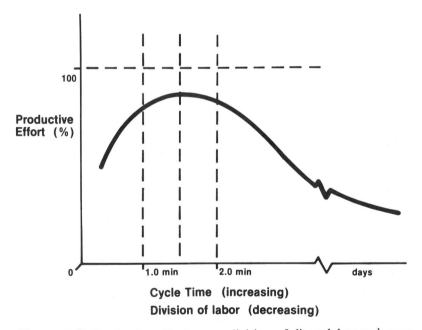

Figure 3.3 Productive effort versus division of direct labor and manufacturing cycle time.

The major benefit resulting from the division of labor is increased productivity. When efficiency is increased, output is increased, which means that operating costs are lower and profits higher.

Negative effects of division of labor are also present.[3] Output may increase, but product quality often will be lowered. This goes hand in hand with another problem—job dissatisfaction. Many people, both professional and direct hourly employees working on specialized jobs, have low job satisfaction that tends to lower concern for quality. A third negative effect, also related to the first two, is high personnel turnover. The hiring and training of new personnel is expensive, but the cost of replacing a person who leaves a subdivided job is less, since there is less to learn and as a result training costs are lower. The strategies to overcome the negative effects of division of labor as well as its specific effects on professionals working as managers are discussed in later chapters.

IV. LINE AND STAFF

Another way to divide jobs in an organization is by separating them into the *doer's* and the *advisors.* Management groups responsible for performing the main objectives of the organization are classified as *line,* and all others as *staff* or support personnel.

Staff groups perform three basic functions. First, they provide a service to the organization by performing certain tasks which are needed but not absolutely necessary on a day-to-day basis for continuing operation of the organization, such as the design of new products or services. Second, staff gives advice on matters that fall within that group's area of knowledge, such as suitability of substituting material in the manufacture of a product, economic justification of new capital equipment, or the development of a profit sharing plan. Third, staff acts as a control function. The staff tries to keep uniformity of policy administration in all organizational groups. In order to further clarify the rather complex nature of line-staff relationships, it is useful to look at a typical manufacturing firm. In this type of organization, the *line management* usually is composed of those managers who direct units that are involved in the fabrication or assembly of the product. Line people are, in effect, those individuals who are involved with the major thrust of the business.

Staff people, on the other hand, are those individuals whose major responsibility is to serve the line and provide advice that is necessary or useful in producing products or services. Thus, in most manufacturing organizations, personnel, material management, industrial engineering, design engineering, and financial units are staff. For example, engineers (staff) tend to focus on their specialty, and have a strong desire to excel in the application of both new ideas and technical knowledge. Line people tend to focus on shorter-term profits and those developments that are less risky or offer higher probabilities of success. Since line managers usually have the final authority with regard to product decisions, it is not unusual to find a bright young engineer who feels that his or her good ideas or developments are not being utilized effectively.

The above example reflects the differing set of needs, values, and expectations between these two groups. In fact, several factors lead to line-staff conflict. Staff personnel usually come from different backgrounds than line personnel. Persons working in staff positions are usually university trained and have a professional specialty. The second factor is a different set of task objectives and responsibilities. This is due to the fact that staff people strive to develop the most comprehensive solutions which are not always understandable by line personnel. Third, the two groups have different ways of gaining recognition. Staff personnel are judged by the thoroughness of their plans, which will be seen by top executives, while the line people are concerned with high output and the workability of plans. Fourth, staff and line groups sometimes have different time goals. Staff is usually concerned with long-term results, but the line manager is most concerned with short-term output.

Historically, conflict between line and staff was intensified because of lines' resentment of staffs' superior education and tendency to assume line atuhority. In recent years the educational gap has narrowed substantially between these groups, and the willingness of line managers to accept professional staff as an integral part of the organization has increased. Thus, the problem of line-staff conflict is not as great today as it was in the 1950s and 1960s. Supportive line-staff relationships and effective intergroup communications are vitally important to professionals.

V. SUCCESSFUL BOUNDARY SPANNING TECHNIQUES FOR PROFESSIONALS

Line managers may feel that staff will take all the credit for successful projects. Also, line insecurities may affect the relationship to the extent that all staff suggestions or proposals are viewed as a threat. In order to be effective, staff professionals need to accomplish successful boundary spanning, i.e., they must integrate activities. This is particularly true for personnel professionals whose specialties must permeate the entire organization; it is also true that many project teams must move information to other well defined organizational units. Excellent examples of needed information flow across professional boundaries are found among research and development groups in industry, and research teams in the health professions. Studies show that successful boundary spanning is often associated with a special type of leadership labeled gatekeeping which is needed to effectively link professional teams to outside sources.[4] Gatekeepers are essential to effective boundary spanning which has been recognized as one of the more important elements of effective leadership and managerial behavior.[5] These leaders, who are usually managers, gather internal information in professional groups and exchange this information with relevant outside units and individuals. According to research, effective gatekeepers have many positive effects on professional groups.[5] Gatekeeping supervisors are technically competent, interpersonally active, and identify with young professionals. This emerging close relationship works to reduce turnover among competent young professionals.[5] Also, young skilled professionals reporting to gatekeeping managers are likely to attain a significantly higher rate of promotion to management than professionals working for non-gatekeeping managers. Young professionals need to interact with their colleagues and managers to learn expectations and how to be high performing contributors.

Effective boundary spanning has many other positive effects on the entire professional group. One of the most beneficial is the ability of the gatekeeper to integrate needs of the professional with the presence of outside environmental constraints. The boundary spanning activity should be viewed as an important part of both strategy and implementation for professionals.[6] Boundary spanning managers improve the technical performance of professional groups and directly affect the personal growth and development of individual members.

The following summary points are offered for the manager of professional workers in order to improve boundary spanning and line-staff relationships:

1. Be sure a gatekeeping supervisor is selected.
2. With regard to line relationships for professional staff

    Be sure line personnel are given credit for their accomplishments; remember that the staff role is basically advisory.

    Do not usurp line authority. This kind of activity will cause line managers to become defensive, and impede the development of a constructive relationship. In fact, the end result will be less staff influence in the future.

    Help line people solve their problems. This will pay large dividends in building future line-staff relationships.

    Understand the nature and impact of interpersonal communication. The information on improving interpersonal communication skills contained in Chapter 7 will be useful in working with line personnel. Specifically, it is important for professional staff managers to avoid communicating personal superiority when working with line employees.

    Be cost conscious and assume a practical orientation concerning problems in which expertise is sought.

3. With regard to other professional groups
   Keep communications open with outside professionals.
   Use gatekeepers to help develop young professionals within the group to reduce turnover and build self-esteem.
   Use internals (staff group employees) to keep gatekeepers informed of pertinent intra-group matters.

VI. PROFESSIONALS AS LINE MANAGERS

Many professionals experience difficulty in moving into managerial decision making positions. A basic problem often unique to the managerial role relates to the fact that much of their success depends on the work and accomplishments of others. This is a marked contrast to seasoned professionals that have gauged their contributions and well being by how well they have applied their acquired training and expertise to produce results. Movement into management requires a shift in work emphasis from doer to planner which can be a difficult transition for the typical professional. Two basic changes that professionals as line managers need to make are increased delegation of operational assignments, and facilitation activities for employees that report to them in their new role. Specific guides to successful delegation are contained in Chapter 4 and the facilitation motivation issue is developed in detail in Chapter 8. Newly promoted supervisors in the professional work environment need to acquire superior delegation and motivation skills if they are to be effective as line managers.

VII. PROFESSIONALS AS STAFF ADVISORS TO LINE MANAGERS

As mentioned, a major role associated with many professionals in the corporate work environment is the staff advisory position. For example, human resource professionals typically advise line management or the president/CEO may have a scientific advisor. Effective performance in advisory staff positions is directly related to a well managed relationship with the line organization. Staff professionals may be very knowledgeable in their field and perform their specialized tasks well. However, without line management support, application of their specialized knowledge may not occur.

VIII. SPAN OF MANAGEMENT

Span of management may be defined as the number of subordinates directly reporting to a manager. The term *span of management* is used instead of *span of control* because as Koontz and O'Donnell point out, "the span is one of management and not merely of control."[7] There is no exact rule for determining the correct span for any particular situation. In the 1930s V.A. Graicunas analyzed the problem of superior-subordinate relationships and developed the following mathematical expression:[8]

$$R = n \left[\frac{2^n}{2} + (n - 1) \right]$$

where

R = the number of all types of relationships that might concern management
n = the number of subordinates

The Graicunas expression considers not only the direct relationship between a superior and his or her immediate subordinates, but also the relationships with different groupings and the cross-relationships among subordinates. In practical application, very few managers engage in all relationships theoretically possible.

A more useful span of management expression can be developed to relate the total number of employees in the organization with the number of levels of management and the individual span of each manager. This expression is

$$N = \sum_{i=1}^{j} L_i (SC_i) + 1$$

where

N   = the total number of personnel in the organiza-
        tional structure
L_i = the number of managers at each organizational
        level
SC_i = the average number of subordinates reporting to
        each manager
i   = summing index = 1, 2, ..., j
j   = the number of management levels

Figure 3.4 depicts a flat organization with only two levels of management above the nonsupervisory personnel. Figure 3.5 shows a more vertical organization with four levels of management above the nonsupervisory personnel. Solving for the total number of personnel for the vertical organization (Figure 3.5) yields

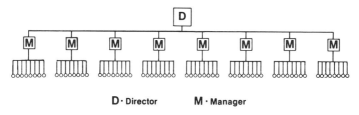

D· Director   M · Manager

Figure 3.4   Broad span of management with horizontal organization

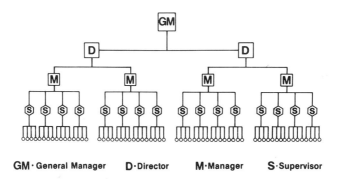

GM· General Manager   D·Director   M·Manager   S·Supervisor

Figure 3.5   Narrow span of management with vertical organization

$$N = \sum_{i=1}^{4} L_i (SC_i) + 1$$

$$= 16(4) + 4(4) + 2(2) + 1(2) + 1$$

$$= 87 \text{ employees}$$

This organization contains 64 nonsupervisory employees and 23 managers with spans ranging between 2 and 4. A similar calculation for the flat organization (Figure 3.4) yields 73 total personnel. The number of nonsupervisory employees totals 64, the same as the more vertical organization. Obviously, the difference is that the vertical organization contains 14 more managers.

An important aspect of the span of management relationship is that once any two of the three variables are determined, the third is set. For example, if we require a given number of nonsupervisory personnel and desire to limit the span of management, then the number of management levels is fixed along with the total number of employees in the organization or if we require a given number of nonsupervisory personnel and desire to limit the number of management levels, then the span of management is fixed along with the total number of employees in the organization.

There is no clear agreement on how size (number of individuals supervised), routineness of task, and the number of different specialties influence the span of higher level management. Obversely, if spans are too small, management time is not efficiently utilized and supervisors at other levels may be overloaded. Conversely, if spans are too large, management control and effectiveness will likely deteriorate because of being overloaded. A study by Dewar and Simet reported that specialization of workers supervised is an important determinant. They could not however resolve whether size or technology is the primary cause of spans.[9]

In most organizations, the number of nonsupervisory personnel is determined by the enterprise operations. Consequently, the span of management decision is critical in determining the number of management levels and total organizational size. In a technically oriented department, a smaller span is normally more desirable. Where mass production and job specialization occurs, a manager

Table 3.1 Number of Executives Reporting to the President in 100 Large and 41 Medium-Sized Companies

No. of executives reporting to president	No. of large companies	No. of medium-sized companies
1	6	3
2	-	-
3	1	2
4	3	2
5	7	4
6	9	8
7	11	7
8	8	5
9	8	2
10	6	4
11	7	1
12	10	-
13	8	1
14	4	1
15	1	-
16	5	-
17	-	1
18	1	-
19	-	-
20	1	-
21	1	-
22	-	-
23	2	-
24	1	-
Totals	100	41

Source: Reprinted from Ernest Dale, *Planning and Developing the Company Organization Structure*, Research Report no. 20, American Management Association, New York, pp. 77-78.

can supervise a larger number of persons, especially if they perform similar tasks and their output is easily determined. In general, the acceptable span of management *decreases* with

Less predictable work demands.
Greater discretion allowed to the subordinates.
Technically demanding specialties among subordinates.
Greater job responsibility, as measured by the length of time between a decision and its review or results.
Greater task interdependence among subordinates. When subordinates work on simple, repetitive, and easily measured tasks, the span of control can be larger.

As a guideline, four to seven subordinates is typical for professional problem-solving groups, while 20 to 25 or more may be managed at the first-level manufacturing or clerical supervisory position. Experience indicates that in most organizations the top manager has a span too large for the best operating effectiveness. Table 3.1 summarizes the results of a study to determine the number of executives reporting to the president in 100 large and 41 medium-sized companies. The average (arithmetic mean) number of executives reporting to the president was 9.64 in large companies and 7.00 in medium-sized companies. It is important to note, even with this modest sample, the wide variation that exists in large and medium sized companies.

IX. ORGANIZATIONAL DESIGN

An organizational structure is the framework within which management and the operations of an organization are performed. The structure establishes formal authority as opposed to informal authority. This formal network of authority is the framework of who reports to whom and is usually documented on a diagram that shows the relative locations and reporting relationships of the units and management positions in the organization. If a sound organizational structure can be developed, it will improve performance and make the people in the organization more work oriented, as their positions are clearly defined.

The right kind of organizational structure should provide an entrepreneurial spirit that is flexible, innovative, and market responsive. During design, the manager should keep in mind that the organizational structure is fundamental to the productive utilization of human resources. The organization should permit individuals and groups to work together as needed to complete assignments. It should effectively integrate human resources, computer based business systems, and advanced technologies useful for business improvement.

Correct organizational design can substantially shorten throughput for major projects. The traditional practice of sequentially accomplishing work activities is no longer acceptable. For example, moving new product development step-by-step through progressive stages with little contact among involved groups will not produce the timely results of getting new products or services to the market place. The need for simultaneous activities is critical for quick reaction capability. This can be accomplished by integrating key individuals with critical skills from various organizational components.

Organizational structure should provide communication and coordination by grouping jobs and people; the structure aids the communication between people working on the same or similar job activities. An organizational structure determines the location of decision making within the organization. By varying the number of intermediary levels between the president or chief executive officer and each individual department in an organization, the focus of decision making is determined.

An organizational structure should create the proper balance and emphasis on activities. Activities considered important to a firm's success should be placed at higher levels in the organization in order to stress their importance. By being placed higher in the organization, there are less managers to interfere with and slow down communication, and the time required for decision making is greatly reduced. Activities of relatively equal ranking should be placed at similar management levels in the structure in order to insure that they will receive about equal emphasis. This equalization will prevent one department's domination of another, a necessity for the firm's successful operation.

The organization, if possible, should focus on common products or services. The following statement summarizes other design objectives for most organizational structures:

> The organizational structure (1) must be logical and systematic and definitely fix responsibility and authority; (2) must be personal to the extent of taking into account the aspirations and needs of individual members; in this way the employee's good will is obtained; their best efforts are utilized and their business relations made pleasant; (3) must provide for cooperation between various divisions and levels of the undertaking; (4) be capable of modifications as may become necessary; and (5) facilitate decision making.[10]

X. ORGANIZATIONAL CONFIGURATIONS

There are several standard organizational structures. Each of these have different characteristics that may fit the specific product or service and people needs of an organization. In actual practice, a firm's formal organization is usually a hybrid of two or more of the standard structures.

The fundamental structure has a pattern of departmentalization by major functions such as engineering, manufacturing, quality assurance, and marketing, as shown in Figure 3.6. This structure allows each manager to specialize in one area of activity, enabling them to gain knowledge and expertise in that particular area. In a functional organization, if someone develops a new process or idea, it is easily implemented in all areas since it was created for a particular problem solution possibly common to more than one product line. An example of an engineering department's organizational structure is also shown in Figure 3.6.

A limitation of functional organization is that one group may lose touch with another area. To prevent this it is necessary for a good network of communications to exist. Also, the coordination

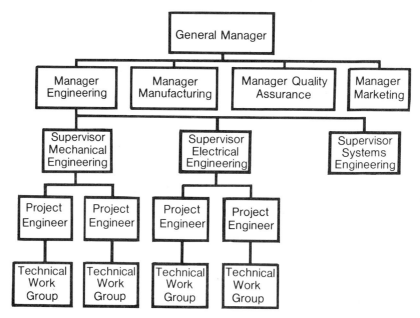

Figure 3.6 Functional organization

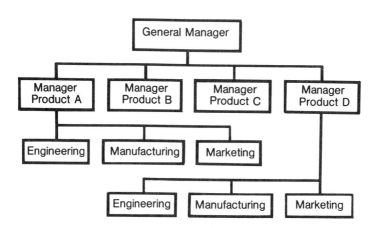

Figure 3.7 Product organization

between groups may become difficult and conflict may arise; therefore, a higher level manager may be required to alleviate differences among departments.

The product structure divides an organization by product line. This is depicted in Figure 3.7. The manager of each product is given the responsibility of all phases of operation from product design and manufacturing through all marketing functions. There are two general advantages of a product organization. The first is that the members have a tendency to feel they are in competition with other groups and may increase productive output to impress superiors and out perform other product lines. Secondly, a person is able to learn more as he or she is given a broader responsibility as compared to the relatively narrow knowledge requirements of the functional organization. This learning allows a manager to be more adaptable and qualified as promotional opportunities develop within the organization.

The disadvantages of product organization may have serious effects on the profitability of the enterprise. An example of a major possible problem is that two different product lines may have the exact or at least a similar problem and both groups will assign personnel to correct the problem. This is a waste of precious time and money due to the repetition of efforts.

A structure by territory as shown in Figure 3.8 divides the organization by regions or areas. This may be necessary if the product line varies or customer needs differ as the geography or other factors change. Also, an organization may have plants in different parts of the country, and operating conditions vary considerably from one area to another. In this type of situation, the area decentralization organization has advantages.

A client-oriented organizational structure is advantageous when each client is a large enough consumer to devote personnel and time to a specific interest group. An example of this type of organization (Figure 3.9) is one that does work for marketing to the general public and also the government or other mass buyers.

The last organization to be mentioned is the *matrix structure*. This structure involves departmentalization by function and by product. The dotted lines in Figure 3.10 represent a special organization

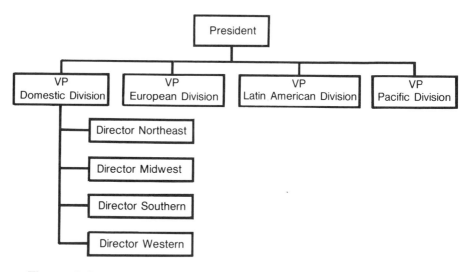

Figure 3.8   Organization by territory

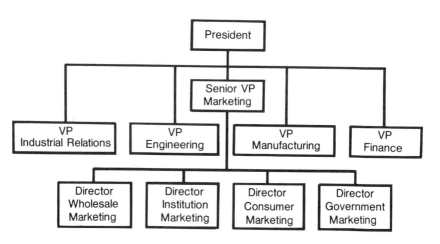

Figure 3.9   Organization by client

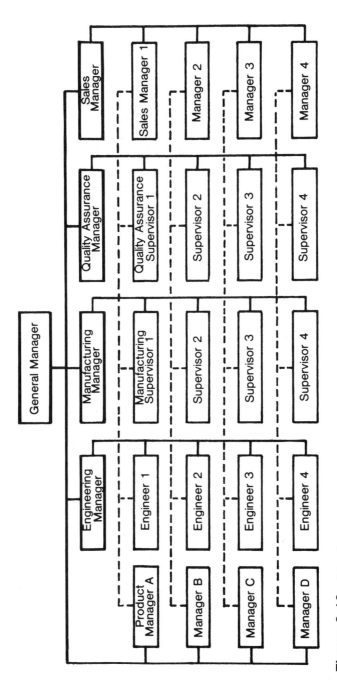

Figure 3.10 Matrix structure

clustered around product A and comprising personnel who are members of various functional departments. They are permanently assigned to engineering, manufacturing, quality assurance, and sales, but apply their effort to product A and work for the manager of product A. It is important to note that the functional managers of engineering, manufacturing, quality assurance, and sales are still involved with their permanently assigned personnel. They have the responsibility of providing information relative to their functional areas to each employee. In addition, the functional manager assists the product manager with employee evaluation. While the two managers should agree on the major evaluation factors, the authors strongly urge that the product manager has the final recommendation to higher management. This is particularly important for merit salary increases. Without this authority, the product managers influence over the various functional specialists that are only assigned for the duration of the product is greatly reduced.

Some researchers evaluating the matrix organizational structure have reported that it increases capacity for information handling and decision making by establishing formal, lateral channels of communications that supplement and complement existing functional channels.[11,12] The authors have found the matrix organization very effective with managers trained as professionals. This experience is supported by Delbecq and Filley who suggest that matrix structures provide opportunities for "advanced work and collegial interaction with a prestigeful set of colleagues."[13] A study by Joyce tested the effects of matrix structure on organizational processes, role perceptions, and work attitudes. He found that the matrix structure caused predicted increases in the quantity of communications, but decreased the quality of those communications. Negative effects were reported on relevant role perceptions, work attitudes, and coordination. It is important to note, however, that two work groups were studied: engineers and draftspersons. The engineers (professionals) experienced only minimally negative effects, while the draftspersons (technicians) experienced much greater negative effects.[14]

While the matrix organization violates the strict unity of command, the concept will work if the product manager and the various functional managers interface well, especially as related to employee evaluation and recommendations for salary increases.

XI. SELECTION OF PERSONNEL

It is both proper and functional for managers to select those new people who will work for them. Managers who work in organizations that have an effective personnel/human resources department can and should obtain assistance in the selection process. Personnel/human resources departments usually can provide help with preemployment screening which includes interviews, reference checks, and selective testing.

A. Federal Law and Discrimination Court Decisions

In recent years it has become necessary for managers to be more concerned with women and minorities among their applicants. Specifically, Title VII of the Civil Rights Act of 1964 as amended by the Equal Employment Opportunity Act of 1972 with later amendments clearly prohibits employment discrimination against any individual or group because of race, color, religion, national origin, sex, sex orientation, handicap, status as disabled veteran or veteran of the Vietnam war, or age. Several agencies of the federal government including the Equal Employment Opportunity Commission and the Office of Federal Contract Compliance are given the responsibility of enforcing the provisions of this legislation.

Several hiring practices have been subject to legal interpretation through the courts in recent years, and it is beyond the scope of this book to analyze the impact of these decisions in detail. Personnel or legal departments can provide insight to management during the hiring process so that discrimination problems can be avoided. A few of the landmark decisions that have implications in selecting professionals are summarized below:

In McDonnell Douglas Corporation versus Green (1973), the court specified four criteria for establishing a prima facie case of unfair discrimination. These criteria have been cited often in subsequent cases, and include the following elements: (*1*) *complainant belongs to a racial minority;* (*2*) *she/he applies for and is qualified for a job for which the employer is seeking applicants;* (*3*) *she/he is rejected despite the qualificiations; and* (*4*) *after the rejection, the position remained open and the employer continued to seek applicants from persons of the complainant's qualifications.*

In *Griggs versus Duke Power* a case which involved the requirement of both a high school diploma and a satisfactory score on an aptitude test, the decision established two major points. First, it is not enough to show a lack of discriminatory intent if the selection discriminates against one group more than another. Second, it is the employer's responsibility to prove that all employment requirements are directly job related.

The *Albermarle versus Moody* case decision reaffirmed the idea that any test used for selecting or promoting employees must be a valid predictor or performance measure for a particular job. In a related decision involving the case *Washington versus Davis* the court implied that if a test is clearly related to the job and work tasks performed, it is not illegal simply because a greater percentage of minorities or females do not pass it.

Finally, the much publicized case *Bakke versus the University of California* involved the issue of reverse discrimination. Bakke, a white male argued that although he had superior qualifications he was denied admission to the University of California Medical School at Davis because of guarantees given to minority applicants. The Supreme Court ruled in a narrow five to four decision that he should be admitted, but admission plans that consider race as a factor are not illegal. Thus, the Bakke decision did not clearly answer the question of the existence of "reverse discrimination" in affirmative action plans used in selection. Managers need to be aware of these important issues in the selection of professional employees.

Technical managers who work for companies that do a large amount of business with the federal government should be particularly concerned with avoiding charges of discrimination in their hiring practices. Federal contracts may be withheld or canceled in cases where an investigating agency finds that discriminatory hiring practices are being used. It is important to note that the *result* of the hiring practices rather than *intent* is the real test. In other words, a manager may have no intention of discriminating in his or her hiring practices, but if these practices actually result in discrimination against women or minorities, the law is being violated. Again, personnel/human resources or legal departments can provide a considerable amount of help and insight to these kinds of hiring problems.

B. Hiring the Right Person

The major objective in the selection process is to get a good match between candidates and jobs. Managers should be concerned with a given candidate's skills and aptitudes, his or her personality type, and general level of social development. While skills and aptitudes determine what can be accomplished on the job, personality and social factors often determine motivation and more importantly what will be accomplished. It is also essential to consider the prospective employee's perception of future promotions and compensation increases, and determine if they are consistent with the company's plans. An accurate appraisal of these factors is necessary for good selection to take place, and to minimize employee turnover.

The manager either independently or with the aid of the personnel department has available several tools that can help evaluate potential job candidates. The four most commonly used tools are the *interview, application form, tests,* and *references.* One study completed in the 1970s indicated that the interview was the most preferred and widely used selection tool.[15] According to this study managers prefer the interview because they believe that the interview is most effective in evaluating the "will do" job factors, namely, motivation, personality, and social development. The authors' experience indicates this is still true today. Also, there is a general consensus among a majority of managers that these later factors are the most difficult to assess in the hiring process.

Managers, however, should be aware there are several weaknesses associated with the interview. For example, it may be biased, and decisions tend to be made early in the interview and are often based on incomplete information. Structured interviewing which uses predetermined questions conducted by two or more interviewers is a useful means of counteracting personal bias and increasing the accuracy of the appraisal. While for lower level jobs these additional interviews may be too costly and time consuming, for higher level positions the improved results usually more than offset this additional cost.

Application forms and testing can also be useful in selection. However, in using each of these tools, the manager must be careful that they do not result in discrimination against any group specified by federal legislation. For example, certain types of information regarding sex, race, and marital status can no longer be used legally in making hiring decisions *unless* such factors can be shown to be a basic functional requirement of the position. Also, test results should be validated when used in hiring. Specifically, the employer should be able to show a correlation between test scores and job performance. References can be of some help in establishing character and previous employment record, and many organizations routinely contact them. A candidate's immediate past supervisor is a most preferred reference.

An accurate, up-to-date job description is extremely useful (essential) when selecting candidates for a given job. This description should include an identification of the duties of the job, performance requirements, and the general level of difficulty associated with performing the assigned duties. A good description of this latter group of factors is very helpful in attaining a suitable match between the personality and social makeup of the candidate and the intrinsic content of the job. It is usually wise to solicit input from current incumbents in developing accurate job descriptions which include stating performance requirements for these positions. This is particularly useful for professional employees. In addition to improving the quality of selection, performance requirements or standards are an effective basis for evaluating the new employee on the job.

Any special managerial attention given to the hiring process will pay large dividends in the future. Absenteeism, turnover, and motivation problems are costly to both the managers in time and effort, and to the organization in "bottom line" results. A good selection program reduces absenteeism, turnover, and can substantially improve employee performance; consequently, the proper selection of new employees is a vital managerial function. While a thorough understanding of the later chapters of this book which are concerned with the behavioral aspects of management is crucial in improving selection skills, a knowledge of the material contained in Chapter 6 on individual and group needs is particularly beneficial.

XII. SUMMARY

In choosing a structure the manager has to select the one that best meets the requirements for the total organization. There are several factors to consider in making this decision. These include environment, tasks and technology, people available, and coordination requirements.

Two important variables in an organization's environment are its stability and diversity. Some companies may face a relatively stable, predictable demand for their products or services, while others face rapid and unpredictable changes. Examples of areas that must be monitored for stability include labor markets, reliability of suppliers, technology, and political and economic conditions. These are all areas that the organization and manager must adapt to if the firm is going to be successful.

Functional organizational structures provide the greatest institutional commitment to permanence. They help the firm establish routines and patterns suited to predictable environments. A major disadvantage is that because they are more suited to stable environments, they often hamper a firm's ability to cope with instability in the outside environment.

Product, territory, and client-oriented organizations are by definition more flexible. They allow the addition or subtraction of a structure unit as conditions change. Structural flexibility inside the organization helps cope with instability outside of the organization.

The coordination between various groups must be considered when choosing a structure and designing its component parts. Cooperation must exist between different departments; if there is little cooperation or coordination, the organization will suffer. An example would be the need for coordination between sales and product development. Because of their field contact the personnel in sales are likely to have substantial knowledge of customer needs and wants. A high level of cooperation will allow product development to meet customer demands without wasting time on low priority activities.

The educational level of the employees in an organization is a clue to choosing the best structural type. People of modest education may often be hired to fill jobs that have well established routines, while those of higher intellect and education most often are hired to fill jobs where competence and flexibility are required. In organizational design, one must be careful to maintain organizational structure in relation to the educational levels of available personnel. As more individuals obtain higher education (usually associated with professionals), rigid structures often "cramp their style."

A flexible structure like the product-oriented type will easily allow the addition or deletion of units. The type of structure that an organization chooses will have a great effect on its overall productivity. An examination of the company's environment, the tasks within the operation, and the characteristics of the personnel are of paramount importance in choosing a structure. The choice must be made with one central consideration in mind: *Given the firm's goals and strategy, which structure will help it cope most effectively with its environment?* This question should be kept in the executive's mind when it is time to make or change an organizational structure.

The structure can be defined graphically with a formal outline of the organization. This outline indicates the names of departments and individuals with job titles and the relationships among all units. In addition to the graphical outline, an organizational manual is useful. The manual should include the duties and responsibilities of each job. It has been stated that this manual is the final documentation of the organizational design process. It clearly delineates the objectives of each organizational unit, the scope of authority of the manager of each unit, and its relationship to other units. If relationships to organizations outside the company are part of a particular job, these relationships should also be defined. The organizational manual is also very useful for orienting new personnel to their jobs.

This chapter highlights the problems and importance of good employee selection. It is clear that many useful tools are available to improve the match of individuals and jobs. Managers can improve their unit's performance by understanding the nature of these tools which includes their strengths, weaknesses, and applicability. The hiring of a new employee should be considered an opportunity to gain a quality human resource and improve the organization's ability to excel.

REFERENCES

1. Henri J. Fayol, *General and Industrial Administration,* Sir Isaac Pitman and Sons, London, 1949.

2. Adam Smith, *The Wealth of Nations,* Clarendon Press, Oxford, 1776.

3. Ronald Boyer and Richard L. Shell, "End of the Line at Lordstown," *Business and Society Review,* No. 3, Autumn 1972, pp. 31-35.

4. R. Katz and M.L. Tushman, "A Longitudinal Study of the Effects of Boundary Spanning Supervision on Turnover and Promotion in Research and Development," *Academy of Management Journal,* Vol. 26, No. 3, September 1983, pp. 437-456.

5. G. Graen and S. Ginsburg, "Job Resignation as a Function of Role Orientation and Leader Acceptance," *Organizational Behavior and Human Performance,* Vol. 19, 1977, pp. 1-17.

6. M.J. Dollinger, "Environmental Boundary Spanning and Information Processing Effects on Organizational Performance," *Academy of Management Journal,* Vol. 27, No. 2, June 1984, pp. 351-368.

7. H. Koontz and C. O'Donnell, *Principles of Management,* 4th ed., McGraw-Hill, New York, 1968, p. 241.

8. V.A. Graicunas, "Relationship in Organization," reprinted in L. Gulick and L. Urwick (eds.), *Papers on the Science of Administration,* Institute of Public Administration, New York, 1937, pp. 181-187.

9. Robert D. Dewar and Donald P. Simet, "A Level Specific Prediction of Spans of Control Examining the Effects of Size, Technology, and Specialization," *Academy of Management Journal,* Vol. 24, No. 1, March 1981, pp. 5-24.

10. John A. Logan, Harry Rubey, and Walker W. Milner, *The Engineer and Professional Manager,* 3rd ed., Iowa State University Press, Aimes, Iowa, 1970.

11. S.M. Davis and P.R. Lawrence, *Matrix,* Addison-Wesley, 1977.

12. L.G. Hrebiniak and William F. Joyce, *Implementing Strategy,* Macmillan, 1984.

13. A. Delbecq and A.C. Filley, *Program and Project Management in a Matrix Organization: A Case Study,* Graduate School of Business, University of Wisconsin (Madison), 1974.

14. William F. Joyce, "Matrix Organization: A Social Experiment," *Academy of Management Journal,* Vol. 29, No. 3, September 1986, pp. 536-561.

15. Desmond D. Martin, William J. Kearney, and George D. Holdefer, "The Decision to Hire: A Comparison of Selection Tools," *Business Perspectives,* Vol. 7, No. 3, Spring 1971, pp. 11-15.

4

Directing and Controlling

I. INTRODUCTION

Direction and control are two essential aspects of management. Early approaches considered planning, organizing, and controlling the three fundamental parts of management, but through the influence of the behaviorists, directing is now considered equally important. Controlling is concerned with *the regulation of business activities in relation to the original plan.* Directing can be defined as *the guiding of work toward the accomplishment of organizational objectives.* The importance and use of directing and controlling for managers can be shown by examining the following: responsibility, authority, delegation, managing the relationship with your boss, work measurement and wage incentives, salary administration, control systems, system and individual performance, budgeting, information systems, and critical path scheduling.

II. RESPONSIBILITY

Responsibility is considered to be the foundation of control and direction. It may be defined as the *obligation to execute functions* or *work*.

The division of responsibility must be decided upon so that a company can operate properly. First the work must be divided among available personnel. Hopefully, a person with the right skills and abilities can be found for each job. Once this is done, jobs with similar objectives and requirements are grouped together to form a section. A manager with the right qualifications is then selected to supervise the section of workers. In this simple arrangement the supervisor is responsible for the output of the entire group. The guide to this kind of grouping is called *functional similarity*. This is simply the process of putting like functions together. Functional similarity usually leads to specialization.

The concept of functional similarity is basic to the process of dividing responsibility and delegating authority. However, functional similarity cannot always be used. For example, quality control activities to monitor product output or service delivery is similar to many manufacturing operations, yet it should be kept separate to insure that it will not be biased or compromised. Often it may be advantageous to create internal competition and keep similar operations separate. In a small organization it is not uncommon to have two dissimilar operations in the same group. Typical examples are the grouping of product design and prototype building and testing, shipping and receiving, and the grouping of computer operations and finance.

It is important to note that ultimate responsibility cannot be delegated but authority can be delegated by managers to their subordinates who are then held accountable.

There are three other important guidelines to follow in dividing responsibility and delegating authority: Avoid gaps, overlaps, and delegation of authority for work that is not part of the objective. Overlap is when two or more people are responsible for the same function. This is usually caused by unclear boundaries or vague directions and orders from higher level management. Large firms usually have overlap problems when duplicate work is done in different parts of the organization. Overlap creates controversy and sometimes leads to groups fighting about the overlap area. When this occurs the overlap area is usually desired by both groups to enhance their power. More often than not, when the work is extremely difficult or where the effort may go unnoticed by higher management, the overlap area will be neglected by both parties. A gap is the failure to foresee all requirements for the effective accomplishment of goals. A gap is usually created when an area is unforeseen in the original plan or any updated plan. The dangers of this are that the function may never get done, and if it is done it may be attempted by someone not qualified for the job.

III. AUTHORITY

As stated earlier, authority is derived from responsibility. Authority can be defined as *the power to decide, to command, and to perform.* It can also be defined as formal power to act or power freely granted. Authority has been traditionally thought of as being obtained from the high levels of management and passed on to lower levels. However, with the development of the informal authority concept and acceptance theory, the traditional view must be modified.

Informal authority is the *authority an organization does not plan.* It exists in the lower levels of the organization and generates upward instead of downward. It may or may not follow the formal structure of the organization.

An important idea concerning authority is the Barnard-Simon theory, often referred to as *acceptance theory.*[1] This theory states that authority exists only when subordinates accept the commands as authoritative. The theory is also consistent with the traditional idea of authority by reasoning that when individuals accept authority from above, they do so because they recognize the support of top management. The value of this theory is that it recognizes the individual's decision to accept authority as the key to the existence of authority. In order to get the individual to accept authority it may be necessary to use positive rewards or negative sanctions.

The theory also emphasizes the importance of leadership qualities. The leadership style of a manager can determine how much of his or her authority will be accepted by subordinates. Thus, the Barnard-Simon theory shifts the emphasis from the traditional thought of authority existing merely because it comes from above to the theory where the support and acceptance of authority by subordinates determines its existence. There are six basic types of authority:

Authority from outside
Authority from expertise and position
Authority from personal attributes
Line authority
Staff authority
Functional authority

Although authority rests in a position, its source may be external to the organization to which it belongs. For example, a local law enforcement person is given certain authority by laws passed by the city council. The council in turn is elected by the people, who are defined as the ultimate source for all authority. If a person does not feel that "the people" are the ultimate source of authority, he or she will not accept this source and will probably act differently from those who do.

Authority from expertise and position is based on the notion that in most organizations and social situations certain individuals become recognized for being skilled, capable, and competent. Their advice is sought and their instructions are accepted, provided that the complying person believes that the expertise is being used to his or her advantage.

Authority from personal attributes is authority that resides in a person and comes from what is often called charisma, which is usually projected by appearance and behavior.

Line authority is the formal power to act over and command all operations and functions within a particular part of the organization. Examples of this include an assembly supervisor who has control over certain parts of the production line, or a head nurse in charge of a hospital ward. Staff authority is the ability to advise line management on the performance of line functions.

Staff authority carries no power to give orders directly or make decisions. It usually exists in special areas and should only be used to advise or consult with line managers. An example would be an industrial engineer assigned to study the problems of a manufacturing process. When the study is completed the engineer has no power to alter the process; he or she can only present the findings and recommendations to the line manager for a decision. Another example would be the product designer recommending a specific vendor for material procurement.

The power to command within a certain area of expertise is called *functional authority* which is usually associated with professionals. Examples of these areas include maintenance, law, medicine, accounting, and computer systems.

Authority is one of two sources of power; the other is force. The threat of force alone is usually enough to make most people yield. Professionals are seldom fired for displeasing the boss; the fear of being humiliated or considered incompetent is perhaps the most common threat for professionals in the managerial role.

The power of authority can be divided into three categories: office, knowledge, and character. As previously discussed, the authority of office is the power given to someone simply because he or she is the boss. The authority of knowledge is the power delegated because one is an expert in a particular field. Managers may be given this power even though they are less able to perform certain tasks as well as subordinates. An example would be the manager of a research laboratory. The manager may know less about a test procedure than a lower level technician, yet it is the overall knowledge of that specific experiment and all the other experiments being conducts that gives the manager the power of authority. Perhaps the most important power is authority of *character.* This power has to be earned. Its major components are honesty of purpose, truthfulness, openness, good will, and good manners. Charm in this case is unimportant. It may be stated that "no one trusts a smoothy." Reliance on the authority of character as the chief ingredient in managerial leadership excludes the use of force and the generation of fear. Fear may be the worst enemy of managerial productivity. The development of power and a power base is an important part of leading professionals, and is discussed in greater detail in Chapter 9.

IV. DELEGATION

Delegation is the *distribution of responsibility and authority* within an organization. Stated another way, delegation is the decentralization of decision making.

As alluded to earlier, authority is delegated from a manager to a subordinate. The superior creates a relationship based on obligation between the superior and the subordinate; although the superior delegates authority, he or she is not relieved of the responsibility. It must be remembered that delegation only allows for someone else to do the work.

Whenever a manager delegates authority, a *risk* is created. The risk is that the subordinate may fail, leaving not only the subordinate to take the blame, but also the person who delegated the authority. Some managers attempt to avoid this risk by limiting delegation and retaining all responsibility. Usually this is a poor policy because even in the smallest organization one manager cannot handle the total work load volume. Delegation also becomes necessary when the work load of a management position exceeds the physical and psychological capacity of one person. While delegation reduces the manager's work load in one respect, it adds to the work load by increasing the span of management.

Another argument for greater decentralization is the need to develop initiative and self-reliance among subordinates. Many successful executives believe that subordinates should be constantly challenged. The personality of the executive may also effect the extent of delegation. The psychological makeup of some executives inhibits their willingness to delegate decision-making prerogatives. A refusal to delegate may also be promoted by the degree of risk involved. Hard times and increased business competition for the organization may foster centralization. The organization's ability to absorb a mistake by a subordinate may be greatly reduced under these circumstances.

Managers trained in a professional specialization are often reluctant to release authority. One reason for refusing to delegate authority is that no one in the organization is qualified to handle it. Another reason is that many managers enhance their indispensability to the enterprise by retaining authority. The most *undesirable* reason for not delegating authority is that a manager may not have sufficient delegating skills.

The ability and willingness to delegate authority to others is the essence of being a manager. Not to delegate should be considered a management *failure*. Delegation is, in fact, one of the most critical aspects of managing professionals effectively.

Delegating authority properly is a complex process. Many managers are actually just making assignments when they think they are delegating. One of the best ways to distinguish between assignment and delegation is to look at the nature of the communication between the manager and subordinate regarding the task. If the manager communicates "how to do it" he or she is usually giving an assignment rather than delegating. Since the reward system in most organizations favors "pleasing the boss", even the slightest suggestion of how to do the job is likely to be followed by the employee. Many of the positive motivational and development aspects of delegation are not present in assignment. When delegation is present, the manager's communication usually specifices "what needs to be done," but avoids any reference to preference for method. The authors have worked closely with one chief executive of a major corporation that always tells his new VP's before a staff meeting "I expect you to bring potential or alternative solutions to problems to our meeting rather than to bring me the problem(s) and to ask for solutions". This is an excellent approach to decision making through increasing delegation in managing professionals. It fosters creative problem solving among key managers, increases commitment, and frees up valuable executive time.

A manager's communication suggesting "whatever" rather than "how" or "what" is indicative of abdication. While abdication can be an effective management tool in a few unusual situations, it fails in most. Highly skilled professionals such as MD or PhD scientists who have a large investment in themselves and their work may move forward toward organizational goal accomplishment with little or no direction. These situations are rare, however, and most managers need a clear cut focus on objectives so some periodic evaluation can be made of the professional employees progress.

The presence or absence of agreement between manager and subordinate on objectives and methods effects the delegation process. Figure 4.1 illustrates ways to handle delegation in specific cases that involve agreement or disagreement. The most effective delegation occurs in Quadrant A. Managers should attempt to enlarge this quadrant by increasing the number of situations where there is substantial agreement with subordinates on both means/methods and objectives. In order to reduce the size of Quadrant B, the manager must convince the subordinate of proper objectives, and in Quadrant C, the emphasis should be on reaching agreement on techniques. Several of the tools developed in Chapter 10 on change can be utilized. It is important to emphasize selling and gain commitment through democratic processes as opposed to telling or

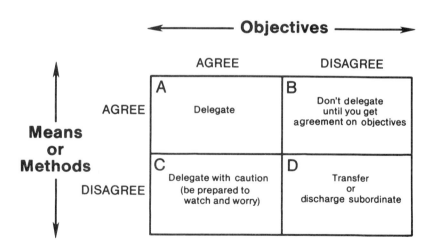

Figure 4.1 The delegation window—relationships between managers and subordinate. (Adapted from R.T. Riley, presentation at Executive Program, University of Cincinnati, Cincinnati, Ohio, April 20, 1987.)

placing demands on subordinates. Quadrant D calls for definite steps that involve a change in personnel. Disagreement on both means/methods, and objectives is likely to result in destructive conflict.

V. MANAGING THE RELATIONSHIP WITH YOUR BOSS

All managers are not only bosses but also subordinates (everyone has a boss somewhere). The relationship between you and your boss is important both for you *and* the organization. Among the more important factors that emerge from this relationship are the timing and content of your work assignments, mutual satisfaction of personal needs, and prospects for advancement.

There are two major aspects to managing this relationship effectively. First, you need to understand the boss and his or her context. Understand what your bosses objectives and priorities are and then try to make them congruent with your own. As developed in Chapter 8, a basic part of the motivation process is to attain mutual agreement on job expectations. Thus, there are many positive benefits to the manager, boss, and subordinates in achieving this congruence. There is evidence which indicates that managers who work effectively with their bosses seek out information about the boss's goals, problems, and pressures.[2] It is also important to be alert for cues that indicate possible changes in the boss's priorities. You also need to understand your *own* management style. More specifically, what is it about you that impedes or facilitates working with your boss. Those things that are facilitative to a constructive relationship should be nurtured. Obviously, things that impede the relationship should be corrected.

People sometimes react in one of two extremes to their bosses. Counterdependent behavior is characterized by *opposition* to the boss's decisions. The boss is naturally seen as an institutional enemy and a conflict laden relationship ensues. Conversely, the overdependent subordinate tends to see the boss as an all-wise, all-knowing parent who should train, develop, and protect him or her. As Gabarro and Kotter suggest, both counterdependence and overdependence leads managers to hold unrealistic views of what a boss is . . . *Bosses are neither perfect nor always wrong.*[2]

Good working relationships are based on accommodations of differences in *work style*. Assess both your and your boss's strengths and weaknesses. In your communications with superiors be aware of overreactions associated with your style. Moreover, understanding your bosses' reactions are useful in choosing approaches that help to build a constructive relationship.

VI. WORK MEASUREMENT AND WAGE INCENTIVES

A. Work Measurement Techniques

Work measurement may be defined as *the application of techniques designed to estimate the time for* a *qualified worker to conduct a specified task at* a *defined level of performance to produce* a *minimum acceptable quality output.* Properly practiced, the field of work measurement encompasses correct methods definition that specifies the human interface with all necessary tools and equipment. In addition to determining *how and with what to perform the task*, it is important that the work place meets acceptable standards of ergonomic design and occupational safety and health. A final requirement of professional work measurement is to ensure worker cooperation in the measurement process and involvement in the creation of the total job environment. The importance of applying interpersonal skills by the work measurement engineer or analyst cannot be over valued; labor standards are not psychologically limiting if the worker is involved and motivated.[3]

There are five fundamental work measurement techniques:

1. Judgement estimating
2. Historical data which includes accounting records and self logging
3. Direct observation timing with performance rating
4. Work sampling
5. Predetermined time systems

In addition to these five fundamental techniques, standard data systems and mathematical applications are also utilized to determine production time standards and cost. While judgement estimating and historical data are often used to approximate standard time values, both techniques have little underlying theory or standardized procedures and consequently produce poor estimates of standard times. Therefore, they are not considered engineered work measurement practices.[3]

B. Government Involvement

The United States Department of Defense for many years has shown great interest in work measurement, primarily through the efforts of the Air Force Systems Command. This is perhaps best evidenced by the establishment of MIL-STD-1567 (USAF), Work Measurement, released June 30, 1975, and superseded by MIL-STD-1567A, released March 11, 1983. More recently, the Application Guidance and Verification Plan was initiated in 1984, drafted during 1985, and finalized May 3, 1986, as MIL-STD-1567A Work Measurement Guidance Appendix. The military standard requires the application of a disciplined work measurement program as a management tool to improve productivity on those contracts to which it is applied. It establishes criteria which must be met by the contractors work measurement programs and provides guidelines for using the techniques to assure cost-effective development and production of systems and equipment.

The military standard defines Type I Engineered Labor Standards as those established using a recognized technique such as time study, standard data, a predetermined time system, or a combination thereof to derive at least 90 percent of the normal time associated with the labor effort covered by the standard and meeting specified requirements. All Type I standards must reflect an accuracy of plus or minus 10 percent with a 90 percent or greater confidence at the operation level. For short operations, the accuracy requirement may be better met by accumulating small operations into super operations whose times are approximately one-half hour. Type I standards must also include:

1. Documentation of an operations analysis.
2. A record of standard practice or method followed when the standard was developed.

3. A record of rating or leveling.
4. A record of the standard time computation, including allowances.
5. A record of observed or predetermined time system values used in determining the final standard time.

All other work measurement standards are defined as Type II and have no specified accuracy requirements.

C. Benefits of Work Measurement

A comprehensive, professionally developed work measurement program has considerable value to any manufacturing or service organization. MIL-STD-1567A outlines the following benefits of employing such a program:

1. achieving greater output from a given amount of resources;
2. obtaining lower unit cost at all production levels through more efficient operations;
3. reducing the amount of waste time in performing operations;
4. reducing the number of operations and the amount of equipment needed to perform these operations;
5. encouraging continued attention to methods and process analysis because of the necessity of achieving improved performance;
6. improving the budgeting process and providing a basis for price estimating, including the development of government cost estimates and "should cost" analyses;
7. providing a basis for long-term planning of manpower, equipment, and capital requirements;
8. improving production control activities and delivery time estimation;
9. focusing continual attention on cost reduction and cost control;
10. helping solve layout and materials handling problems by providing a relevant data base;

11. providing an objective and measured base from which management and labor can project piece work requirements, earnings, and performance incentives.

D. Wage Incentives

Often times workers will not give extra or sustained effort without some form of incentive. In one form or another, incentives have been used for many years. For example, from the *Bible*, II Timothy 2:6 (from Paul) "It is the hard-working farmer who ought to have the first share of the crops." Today, most organizations are striving to improve productivity and quality in order to maintain or improve their position in the world market place. Properly designed and implemented wage incentive programs can help. Before any incentive program is implemented, some measure of performance must be established. All incentive programs can be categorized as follows:

Direct financial
Indirect financial
Intangible (non-financial)

Direct financial programs may be applied to individuals or groups of workers. For individuals, each employee's compensation is governed by his or her performance to standard during a given time period. Group plans are applicable to two or more individuals working as a team on tasks that are usually interdependent. Each employee's compensation is based on his or her base rate and the group performance during the incentive period.

The motivation to sustain higher output levels is usually greater for individual incentives as compared with group incentive programs. Therefore, individual incentives are recommended wherever feasible. In addition to overall lower productivity, group programs may cause employees to question the same pay for individuals who in reality worked above or below the group average. Also, it may be difficult to justify different base rates within the group. On the plus side, group programs are easier to implement and administer.

Several incentive programs that share gains in output with the employees have been developed during the past several years. In fact, current emphasis on involvement management (Chapter 12) has provided additional impetus to their use. One program developed by Mitchell Fein has obtained excellent success since its initiation in 1974. The program's name, Improshare, was derived from "improved productivity through sharing". Improshare productivity measurements use traditional work measurement standards and practices modified to a selected base period. Productivity gains above the base are shared on an equal 50-50 basis between employees and the company.[6]

Indirect financial programs are usually less effective than direct financial programs. The principle advantage of indirect plans is that they require less detailed and accurate production standards. Organizational policies that favorably impact morale, result in increased productivity, and provide some financial benefit to employees are considered indirect incentive programs. It is important to note that for indirect financial programs no exact relationship exists between employee output and incentive pay. Examples of indirect incentive programs include relatively high base rates, generous fringe benefits, year end bonuses, and profit sharing.

A profit sharing plan properly designed and implemented is an old idea that may increase worker efficiency, improve quality, decrease cost, and enhance employee morale. However, profit sharing has the same limitations as other indirect incentive programs and some additional ones. For example, in addition to no direct relationship between performance and incentive pay, other limitations include allowing too much time between output and payment, and the employee becomes accustomed to the extra pay or benefits and fails to realize that the incentive is conditional on continued high performance.

One of the most successful profit sharing programs in the United States which is supportive of the involvement management concept (Chapter 12) resides at the Lincoln Electric Company in Cleveland, Ohio. Since 1934, this company has paid more in annual bonuses than regular wages. James F. Lincoln, Past President and Founder of the company, offered the following suggestions to organizations considering profit sharing:[5]

1. Determine that the system is going to be adopted and decide that whatever needs to be done to install it will be done.
2. Determine what plan and products the company will make that will carry out the philosophy of "more and more for less and less."
3. Get the complete acceptance of the board of directors and all management involved in the plan, together with their assurance that they will continue to take whatever steps are necessary for a successful application of it.
4. Arrange a means whereby management can talk to the men and the men can talk back. That means full discussion by all.
5. Make sure of co-operative action on the agreed plan of operation. This will include the plan for progressively better manufacturing by all people in the organization and the proper distribution of the savings that result from it.
6. Set your sights high enough. Do not try to get just a little better efficiency with the expectation that such gain will be to the good and expect to leave the matter there.
7. Remember, this plan for industry is a fundamental change in philosophy. From it new satisfactions will flow to all involved. There is not only more money for all concerned, there is also the much more important reward—the satisfaction of doing a better job in the world. There is that greatest of all satisfactions, the becoming a more useful man.

Other than Mr. Lincoln's referral to the masculine gender, it would be difficult to determine when these suggestions were written. They are as valid today as they were in the 1930s. The Lincoln plan clearly ties employee bonuses to individual and company performance which Lincoln employees regard as a performance incentive.

Intangible incentive programs include rewards that do not have any influence on employees salary or wages. These programs however when viewed as desirable by the employees can improve productivity. Examples of intangible incentive programs include job enrichment, job enlargement, nonfinancial suggestion plans, employee involvement groups, and time off without any reduction in pay.[6]

Payment by results is not always the best incentive system. A poorly developed set of production standards and controls can upset internal consistency, which results in actual and perceived wage inequities among employees and increased stress on management. A number of studies conducted by the authors involving workers in manufacturing have indicated that *lower output* may result if inconsistent production standards are in-place. Workers sometimes develop the habit of performing at slower rates for each job so that output standards are not changed. Another alternative is to record a lower production output and then apply the surplus time to a more difficult task. Most workers make little effort to reach bonus levels on difficult jobs. A result of this situation is that many workers have surplus time which is spent not working at all. Consequently, work standards are distorted and production is generally less efficient. The solution to this problem lies in the establishment of correct and fair output standards with proper employee incentives.

Special incentive allowances for waiting, process, and development activities can be used to obtain a more consistent salary administration program. Waiting allowances are used where frequent delays occur due to material shortages, breakdowns, or other problems. Process allowances can be paid to workers who only control their own rate of working for a portion of the time, the rest being machine-paced. Development allowances can be paid to workers whose jobs are being modified or have just been introduced. Many firms such as General Electric use special incentives to modify behavior in desirable directions. Examples include issuing actual dollars or "tokens" that can be exchanged for valuable products to individual employees for good safety, absenteeism, or quality records over specified time periods. While all incentives of this type do not achieve their desired results, in most cases they are quite successful.

Some salary administration plans provide a fixed bonus rate. Under this system bonus pay is fixed and is related to an agreed level of work output (similar to the gain sharing plans previously mentioned). The management and workers together must accept the responsibility for ensuring that output targets are achieved. Management should also encourage workers to contract for higher levels of output and pay.

When a successful incentive program exists, there also exists harmony between workers and management. One of the requirements for successful incentives is that the pay/effort/output relationship is clearly understood by all concerned personnel, both workers and management.

When a company's incentive system is failing, it leads to poor management-worker relationships and causes morale problems. A common cause of failure is that the rewards are too remote or ill-defined for an individual to increase his or her work commitment.[7] As suggested previously, many incentive plans of various types are a significant part of newer "involvement" management practices that are discussed in Chapter 12.

VII. WAGE AND SALARY ADMINISTRATION

All managers are concerned with wage and salary administration. At the very least for their subordinates and themselves. It is common for organizations to have policies governing wage and salary scales for three levels of employees. One for non-exempt employees, i.e., those workers that are hourly paid and receive time and one half for overtime work beyond forty hours weekly. A second scale for exempt employees, i.e., those management and professional employees that are paid a salary and generally are not compensated for overtime hours worked. A third scale will usually exist for executive employees that includes higher salaries.

While the policies governing wage and salary administration and the scales themselves vary considerably for hourly, salaried, and executive employees, many of the job analysis and evaluation concepts are very similar. Total monetary remuneration for all employees should be commensurate with levels prevailing in the local geographic area for similar positions (external consistency). In some cases to obtain a specialized professional, his or her salary offer may have to be commensurate with regional or even national pay levels. In general, pay rates must allow adequate and fair differentials for positions requiring varying skills and abilities, responsibilities, conditions under which the job is performed, and the resulting physical and mental fatigue (internal consistency).

The recommended methodology for establishing fair and equitable pay rates for any one of the three employee levels is outlined below:

1) Perform a job analysis to obtain an up-to-date job description listing major duties, responsibilities, and goals of the position.

2) Complete a job evaluation to determine the relative value (worth) of the position. Four methods of evaluation are commonly used in the United States. These are the classification method (used by the Federal Government for United States Civil Service), point system, ranking method, and the factor comparison method. Whatever evaluation method is used, the results should position all jobs relative to each other within an employee type. Personnel/human resource departments can offer help to managers who need to implement job evaluation in the professional work environment. Also several competent outside consulting firms specialize in job evaluation and wage and salary administration.

3) Structure wage-salary classification scales for each group (level) of employees.

In summary, two important aspects of wage and salary administration are internal and external consistency. *Internal consistency* refers to the level of pay associated with the various jobs within the organization. Pay rates are considered to be internally consistent when those jobs in the organization with greater perceived value pay higher rates than jobs of lesser perceived value. During recent years, because of high demand for specific professional skills several organizations have created internal consistency problems by hiring recent college graduates with these critical professional skills at salaries greater than existing employees with similar skills. This has resulted because starting salaries for certain specialties have increased more rapidly than salary progression of individuals with simiiar or identical specialities hired a few years earlier. Lack of internal consistency leads to wage inequities which upset the employee motivation process and complicate managerial problems (see Chapter 8).

In addition to the job analysis and job evaluation approach discussed above, there are other approaches used to help a manager attain internal consistent relationships among wage rates. Since the application of these approaches is usually quite involved, the manager often needs outside help in using them. In organizations with a good personnel/human resources department, the director is an appropriate and useful source of advice and help; otherwise a consultant may be necessary. Sometimes it takes years to correct widespread internal wage or salary inequities. Since employees are very resistant to any managerial action that lower their pay rates, many of these problems are only corrected through employee transfer and attrition.

External consistency refers to the comparison of wages paid within the organization to wage rates paid outside the organization for similar jobs. When these rates are comparable to each other, a given firm's wage rates are considered to be externally consistent. External consistency is a desirable condition because it enables the manager to attract quality workers and reduces turnover among more capable employees. Good personnel departments usually have wage survey data available that indicate when wage rates need adjusting to meet the competitive market. Some managers feel they are "saving money" when they maintain a condition of paying lower than average wage and salary levels. This is almost always incorrect logic and leads to a condition where many of the better people will obtain employment with another organization with more competitive pay rates.

VIII. CONTROL SYSTEMS

The control process can be represented by either open loop or closed loop forms as shown in Figure 4.2. An open loop control system is one that either needs no further control or cannot be further controlled once it is activated. The system is guided by a predetermined set of fixed instructions or laws that are not affected by any comparison between actual and planned conditions. Once the system is activated it will run its course regardless of what is happening. A dishwasher is a physical example of an open loop system. The dishwasher does not decide to turn on just because the dishes are dirty; it must be instructed what to do. The washing is done over a predetermined time, so it stops whether the dishes are clean or not. Unfortunately, open loop control conditions are also found in management situations among professionals. An undesirable example would be a manager continuing the development of a new product without any reference or regard to the pre-planned budget.

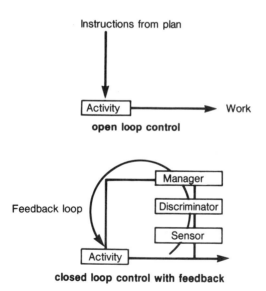

Figure 4.2   The control process

The closed loop control system provides for both the continuous comparison of actual conditions to a predetermined standard and the ability to make corrective action when deemed necessary. Attached to the system being controlled is a feedback loop. A simple physical example of feedback control is a thermostat controlling the temperature of a building. The element of control begins when the temperature of the building drops below a desired temperature, say 65 ° F. The furnace turns on until this desired temperature is reached and then turns off. There is a sensing device located in the thermostat that measures the temperature and sends impulses to the furnace whenever more heat is required. While the furnace is operating, the sensing device is constantly checking the temperature until the predetermined temperature is reached. Control with feedback is obviously desired in most management situations.

In a pure, ideal system, open loop control provides no feedback mechanism or corrective action and closed loop control implies continuous monitoring and correction. In actual practice all management systems eventually have a feedback loop, even though a system may appear to be an open loop process. Using the previously cited example of the manager working on new product developments, how long could one proceed without any reference or regard to a preplanned budget?

Feedback is the heart of any major control system where information is reported. In situations involving professional employees, feedback is effective communication. The principal objective of feedback is to identify the sources of undesirable performance and make timely corrections.

IX. SYSTEM AND INDIVIDUAL PERFORMANCE

Overall performance measurement requires information about the system variables that the manager chooses to monitor and control. The system under the direction of a manager usually consists of many subsystems. The system and subsystems almost always have multiple objectives. Each objective is usually influenced by several variables within the organization. Consequently, multiple measures of performance are usually required for effective control.[8]

While a person's motivation is an extraordinarily important factor in his or her subsequent performance, it is not the only factor. The employee must also have the ability to do what he or she has the motivation to do. Performance depends on the ability possessed. For example, motivation in Air Force students has varied experimentally by telling one group that their performance in a complex task would be an important factor in their future assignment (conditions of high motivation) and giving another group of the same size the same task but without the information (conditions of no explicit motivation). As expected, the group operating under the conditions of high motivation had a higher level of performance than the other group. Each group had within it students who had demonstrated high ability in previous exercises and others who had demonstrated lower ability. In comparing the groups, the high ability students increased their performance significantly more than the lower ability students under the same conditions of high motivation. This suggests that the relationship between ability and motivation is multiplicative and can be expressed as follows:

Performance $= f$ [(ability) (motivation)]

In most cases, performance is not equally influenced by ability and motivation. Certain individuals will obtain good performance with average ability and very high motivation. The authors have also observed the reverse situation. Ideally, the manager wants employees with outstanding ability that are highly motivated. The complexities of motivating professionals will be examined in detail in Chapter 8.

X. BUDGETS

Prior to the beginning of any major project or planning activity, a budget should be constructed. In addition to its value in the control process, a budget is frequently used to communicate plans to various parts of the organization. Budgets should be related logically and quantitatively to the business activities necessary to achieve planning objectives. Some organizations have budgetary systems encompassing each phase of planning and control of operations, while other organizations have partial budget systems concerned with particular aspects of the planning process.

There are many types of budgets. The long-range and operations planning budget forecasts relationships between revenues and cost. For example, the budgeting process in manufacturing organizations usually starts with the preparation of a sales forecast which, after approval, makes it possible to prepare sales, marketing, engineering, production, and other necessary budgets. For example, the materials budget lists the types and amounts of raw materials, parts, and supplies required for the production of the finished product listed in the production budget. There should also be budgets that detail the cost of operating departments and labor budgets that detail the cost of labor for production of the finished product.[9]

The life or time cycle of a budget is influenced by such factors as the time necessary to complete merchandise turnover, the duration of the production cycle, the timing of purchase operations, and the pattern of seasonal variations. Some organizations budget ahead for a period of one year, (operations plan), with quarterly and monthly breakdowns at the time the budget is prepared. Quarterly revisions should be made in the budgets if the original forecasts and estimates are not in accord with the actual course of events. Monthly revisions are made occasionally due to forecasting and/or planning difficulties. An annual, semiannual, and quarterly budget may be maintained by adding another month after each monthly revision of budget estimates. Some special purpose and project budgets have a life span of only a few weeks or months.

The flexible budgeting concept is also useful in cost control. It can be used to set expense allowances for stated levels of output. If properly established the budget can also be used to help predict what costs should be at an achieved level of output. When output fluctuates, a flexible budget can predict how costs will change.

Many times a study of expenses can be made by constructing a simple scatter diagram of dollars spent versus actual output or direct labor effort. A number of curve-fitting techniques can be used to fit the best curve through the data points (Chapter 2). For example, if direct labor hours are plotted versus labor dollars expended

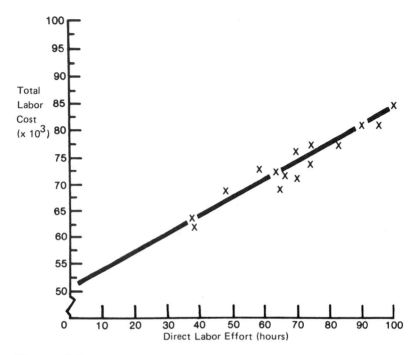

Figure 4.3   Scatter diagram analysis of total labor cost versus direct labor hours

for several jobs, the resulting graph would indicate average indirect labor costs, as shown in Figure 4.3.

The budget control procedure requires an explanation of any significant variance in the data. The budget can be separated into expense items controllable by the manager and those that are not under his or her control. Correction is usually directed toward the controllable items. The budget should be continually examined, and any variations should be explainable.

XI. MANAGEMENT INFORMATION SYSTEMS

The direction and control of an organization is enhanced by a computerized management information system (MIS). The MIS may be defined as an automated system which presents information, both internal and external to the business, that aids in making a specific set of routine decisions. Two aspects of this definition should be clarified. First, the purpose of the MIS is to aid decision making and not to automate the decision-making process itself. As a result, the decision maker should have the dominant role, *not* the MIS. This means that any attempt to design a system without the support of management is pointless. The second aspect is that the MIS should focus on routine decisions only.

Experience has uncovered several incorrect assumptions which help account for the failure of countless MIS projects. The first is that managers commonly suffer from a lack of relevant information. Although there is some truth to this, it seems more realistic to say that they suffer more from too much irrelevant information. Therefore, the MIS should do away with this type of information rather than just focusing on supplying relevant information. The second assumption is that MIS systems should be based on the kinds of information that managers need. Since many managers do not understand the structure displayed in some decision or control situations, they will likely ask for more information than is needed. This way they play it safe. The point is that any analysis should start with the decision or control process, and the MIS should be a subsystem of that process. Thirdly, if a manager has all the information needed, the decision or control function will improve. This can be proved incorrect by a simple example. Consider a traveling salesman who has calls to make in twenty-five different cities. The best (least travel time) path should be determined. If the driving time between each pair of cities is known, it is unlikely that a manager could *quickly* decide the best travel path. A more appropriate approach would be to either provide the traveler with a decision rule or by using a model, compute the travel path with minimum travel time. This example shows that whenever information is given to a manager, it is necessary to consider how the data should be used. The last erroneous assumption is that a manager does not have to understand how the information system works to use it. If the person making decisions or active in the control process *does not understand* how the information system works, he or she will probably lack confidence in the system and it will therefore be of little real value to them.

There are a few fundamental management considerations necessary for MIS design and development. First, the best systems design approach is one that encompasses a problem solving method that specifies only the final results. This permits people working together to design and implement a system to achieve the desired results. The second consideration is to identify the most vital information and data for the organization. Another consideration is to determine how often the system should be reviewed and modified. Finally the MIS system should be cost effective.

The success of an information system depends on the availability of competent MIS managers and technicians who are well informed in the organization's policies, and appropriate computer technology to support the total system. The future of information systems and computer applications is discussed in Chapter 13.

XII. CRITICAL PATH SCHEDULING

A major part of controlling and directing a project is the scheduling of the *critical path*. The critical path is defined as the most time-consuming series of tasks in a project from start to completion. Figure 4.4, for example, depicts three paths for a project. The program evaluation and review technique (PERT) is a useful scheduling tool to assist in project control. It provides management with the ability to plan the best possible use of resources and to achieve a given goal within overall time and cost limitations. PERT enables managers to control unique programs, and handle the uncertainties involved in programs where little or no standard time data are available.

The development of PERT came about when programs arose that could not be managed with simple Gantt activity/time bar charting. It was first used by the Department of the Navy in 1958 and is now used on most national defense development programs. Additionally, PERT is used in the construction industry, in large manufacturing programs, and in developmental engineering projects.

Three basic requirements have been established for the use of PERT. The first requirement is that necessary tasks must be visualized

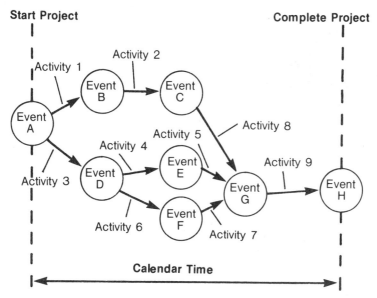

Figure 4.4 A simplified PERT network

in a clear enough manner to be included in a network comprised of events and activities as depicted in Figure 4.4. An event is defined as a specific accomplishment at a particular instant in time. An activity is defined as the time and/or resources necessary to progress from one event to the next. For example, Activity 1 represents the work and time to progress from event A (start of project) to event B. The network requires sufficient precision so that there is no difficulty in monitoring actual accomplishment as the program proceeds.

The second requirement is that events and activities must be sequential in the network under a logical set of ground rules which allow the determination of critical and subcritical paths. One of the ground rules is that no looping can take place. An example would be that no successor event can have an activity dependence which leads back to a predecessor event.

The third requirement makes use of three (judgement based) time estimates for activities: optimistic, most likely, and pessimistic.

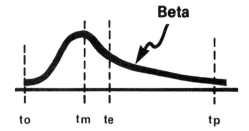

Figure 4.5 Distribution of PERT time estimates

The optimistic estimate assumes the minimum time an activity will take if all project activities are completed without difficulty. The most likely estimate assumes normal or average difficulties and represents the time that would be required if the activity could be repeated several times. The pessimistic estimate assumes the maximum time an activity should require given some initial project failure and above average difficulty.

The PERT time estimate for an activity conforms to the beta distribution as shown in Figure 4.5. Consequently, the mean time can be calculated using the following equation:

$$T_e = \frac{(t_o + 4t_m + t_p)}{6}$$

where

T_e = mean of beta distribution = the mean estimate for an activity

t_o = optimistic time estimate

t_m = most likely time estimate

t_p = pessimistic time estimate

and for the standard deviation,

$$\sigma = \left(\frac{t_p - t_o}{6}\right)^2$$

The use of PERT requires constant updating for effective project control. In most projects at least a biweekly reevaluation is useful.

Sometimes valid means of shortening lead times along the critical path must be determined by applying new human resources and additional funds. It is also necessary on occasion to change the scope of the work on the critical path to meet a required schedule.

There are many benefits gained by the use of PERT. The network development forces thinking about all project components, and the critical path analysis may reveal problems not obvious by conventional planning methods. In addition, the PERT time estimating methodology tends to improve accuracy. Perhaps the most important benefit of PERT is that it allows a large amount of planning data to be presented in a format ideal for project control.

The path times for a PERT network may be estimated by calculating times for each activity and summing for a given path. Using the network shown in Figure 4.4 to illustrate, assume that time estimates and their standard deviations are as follows:

Activity	Time estimate (T_e)	Standard deviation (σ)
1	6.0	1.2
2	8.5	1.4
3	2.0	0.1
4	10.0	1.6
5	7.5	2.1
6	4.3	0.9
7	12.1	2.7
8	1.4	1.0
9	3.6	0.8

Path times are summed as follows:

Path	Time estimates $(\Sigma\,T_e)$	Total time
ABCGH	6.0 + 8.5 + 1.4 + 3.6 =	19.5
ADEGH	2.0 + 10.0 + 7.5 + 3.6 =	23.1
ADFGH	2.0 + 4.3 + 12.1 + 3.6 =	22.0

For this network the critical path ADEGH has a total time of 23.1 and total standard deviation of 4.6 (obtained by summing 0.1 + 1.6 + 2.1 + 0.8). From basic statistics, one standard deviation implies there is a 68 percent probability that the actual time required for the project will be 23.1 ± 4.6 or lie between 18.5 and 27.7 time units. There would be a 95 percent probability (plus or minus 2σ) of completing the project in 23.1 ± 9.2 or between 13.9 and 32.3 time units.

XIII. SUMMARY

Directing and controlling are two essential aspects of management that impact on the functions of responsibility, authority, and delegation. Responsibility is the obligation to execute functions or work that is divided among available personnel. Authority is the power to decide, to command, and to perform. The traditional origin of authority implies that it is obtained from high levels of management within the formal organization and transmitted on to lower levels. Today, informal authority also exists within the organization and generates upward instead of downward. It may or may not follow the formal structure of the organization. Acceptance theory states that authority exists only when subordinates accept commands as authoritative, thus recognizing the importance of individual perception regarding power within the organization. The power of authority can be derived from office (formal boss), knowledge (the expert) and character (earned respect). The bases of power are developed in more detail in Chapter 9. Delegation is the distribution of responsibility and authority within an organization, or the decentralization of decision making. Management effectiveness requires that authority be delegated from superior to subordinate. Not to delegate should be considered a management failure.

A number of other management concerns have been discussed in this chapter. The importance of proper wage and salary administration, and incentives and performance measurement to the success of the organization was considered. The concepts of open loop and closed loop control as applied to management were discussed. The budget process and a supportive computer based management information system are requisites for proper direction and control. Critical path scheduling may be used to define the most time-consuming series of tasks in a project from start to completion. The Program Evaluation and Review Technique (PERT) is a widely utilized and proven critical path scheduling and follow-up methodology.

REFERENCES

1. W. Warren Haynes and Joseph L. Massie, *Management: Analysis, Concepts, and Cases,* 2nd ed., Prentice-Hall, N.J., 1969, pp. 161-162.

2. J.J. Gabarro and J.P. Kotter, "Managing Your Boss," *Harvard Business Review,* Jan.-Feb. 1980, pp. 92-100.

3. Richard L. Shell, ed., *Work Measurement Principles and Practice,* Industrial Engineering and Management Press, 1986.

4. Mitchell Fein, *Improshare: An Alternative to Traditional Managing,* Industrial Engineering and Management Press, 1981.

5. James F. Lincoln, *Lincoln's Incentive System,* McGraw-Hill, 1946, pp. 171-172.

6. For additional reading and examples of time-off incentive programs see Richard L. Shell and Dean S. Shupe, *Wage Incentives for Solid Waste Collection Personnel,* Environmental Protection Technology Series, EPA-600/2-77-019, U.S. Environmental Protection Agency, April 1977; and Richard L. Shell and Dean S. Shupe, "Improving Productivity of Solid Waste Collection Through Wage Incentives," *Proceedings, 27th Annual Institute Conference, American Institute of Industrial Engineers,* 1976.

7. Richard L. Shell and Dean S. Shupe, "Productivity: Hope for City Woes," *Industrial Engineering,* Vol. 8, No. 12, December 1976.

8. Richard L. Shell and Eric M. Malstrom, "Measurement and Enhancement of Workforce Productivity in Service Organizations," *Proceedings, Twenty-Fifth Annual Joint Engineering Management Conference,* 1977.

9. Jacob Paperman and Richard L. Shell, "The Accounting Approach for Performance Measurement," *Journal of Purchasing and Materials Management,* Summer 1977.

5

Decision Making and Time Management

I. THE MANAGERIAL ROLE IN DECISION MAKING

It is often said that managers are paid to make decisions and their subordinates are paid to implement them. While this statement is an oversimplification in the professional work environment, it is, at least, partially true. Professionals may make valuable inputs into the decision making process and/or they may actually determine particular choices but the ultimate responsibility for decision outcomes rests with their managers. In fact, the number of high quality timely managerial decisions in many instances determines promotional opportunities and ultimate career level for the manager.

Professionals holding line management positions need to be aware of their responsibility for decision making and make sure they have the personal qualities to feel good about making decisions. Although professional subordinates can and do offer valuable input, the line manager still has final accountability for decision outcomes. The participative management concepts that are developed in later chapters of this book always need to be considered within this context. Since professional involvement in decision making tends to increase commitment to implementation, participation often is the key to successful decision making among professionals.

Many professionals hold staff positions in line organizations, and have advisory rather than command authority in decision making (Chapter 3). Usually the staff professional must "sell" the line organization on the merits of a given decision or program before it will be implemented. Thus many of the suggestions offered for building sound staff-line relationships contained in Chapter 3 are particularly applicable to decision making among professional staff. Staff specialists should make decisions with due consideration to line managers' reaction to them. In most staff assignments it is helpful to pay specific attention to the needs and concerns of the line organization. Professionals need to manage line relationships well, because the line managers usually determine whether or not their important decisions are properly implemented. The section devoted to successful boundary spanning in Chapter 3 is designed to help professional staff in getting their decisions implemented.

Managers' value systems and propensity for risk affect their approach to decision making. Professionals need a perspective of the total organization to make quality decisions. Large amounts of specialized skill training among specific professionals often impedes their visualization of the broader organizational environment. As a consequence they may have a high propensity to take risks in areas that promote their specialty within the organization. A cornerstone of effectively managing professionals is the leader's ability to take a balanced view of the decision making process and to integrate specialty interests with total organizational needs. This integration requires the application of strong human relations skills if dysfunctional conflict is to be avoided. Although specific examples and illustrations used in the ensuing discussion of decision making may appear to relate primarily to the corporate (profit making) environment, they are equally applicable to other professional work settings including social and health services, sponsored research firms, and governmental agencies.

II. THE DECISION-MAKING PROCESS

A decision is the selection of the preferred course of action from two or more alternatives. The decision-making process may be the result of hunch or "gut feelings," or may be based on a scientific approach. This latter approach considers a clear understanding of goals, comparative alternatives, and consistent priorities.

The decision-making environment has two extremes: decision making under known conditions, and decision making under uncertain conditions. The amount of risk associated with the decision depends on the amount of uncertainty, namely, risk increases with uncertainty. Many decisions are made with inherent conflict concerning goals. For example, marketing would like extensive product features and diversity to enhance sales, while manufacturing desires product standardization to minimize production costs. Another example of goal conflict would be team marketing and manufacturing against financial management. Both may desire large inventories to provide rapid response to customer needs with minimum production delays; counter to the financial goals of the organization. A major concern of top management is to make decisions that resolve these types of conflicts and realize the best outcome for overall corporate objectives.

Some decisions are simple, while others are more complex. Several decades ago Simon classified decisions as *programmed* and *unprogrammed.* [1] Programmed decisions are those associated with routine and well-structured problems. Examples include decisions for production scheduling, payroll, and product pricing. Nonprogrammed decisions are associated with nonroutine and poorly structured problems. Examples include facility design considerations, new product development, and policy establishment. Most programmed decisions can be computerized for essentially automatic handling. Nonprogrammed decisions may only be partially solved or assisted with computerization.

Many decisions require an acceptable solution to a problem. As with the selection of the "best" alternative, there is usually more than one acceptable solution to any given problem. The initial approach to problem solving is usually undertaken within the framework of one's own experience. Other approaches include the experience of others, analytical techniques, or a combination of two or more of these approaches. In any case, it is useful to remember that *creativity* is important in many decisions. One should not attempt to reinvent the wheel when a standard wheel will suffice, but a large percentage of nonprogrammed decisions can be improved with creative input from management. The input may be based on experience or science, or just serendipity (recognizing valuable things not specifically sought).

An important point concerning the decision-making process is that judgement appears to improve with experience. While most researchers and practicing managers agree with this, it should be remembered that innate ability is also required. Good managers should profit from their mistakes and from their successes.

III. SYSTEMS ANALYSIS AIDS DECISION MAKING

The systems analysis approach structures a methodology for decision making that analyzes problems to find the most effective and efficient solution within certain constraints. Understanding this concept will improve one's decision making ability. The approach discussed in the sections that follow is taken from the classic article by Shell and Stelzer.[2]

A. Basic Steps in Systems Analysis

The systems analysis methodology for decision making is composed of the following basic steps:

 Define the problem
 Define the objectives
 Define the alternatives
 Make assumptions concerning the system
 Define the constraints
 Define the criteria
 Collect the data
 Build the model
 Evaluate the alternatives

Defining the problem may appear to be a needless step since this is the basic reason the analysis is being undertaken, but it is probably the most important step in the procedure. In the definition of the problem there must be an accurate description of the present situation showing some sort of disparity that must be eliminated. The process of determining exactly *what is wrong* can be the most consuming part of the entire analysis and the most critical, for the most perfect solution to the wrong problem does nothing to solve the real problem.

Objectives must be defined to provide a structural framework and overall goals for the systems analysis. Clearly stated objectives are also useful for establishing limits and guidelines for the remaining basic steps.

The definition of alternatives should be exhaustive, even though some alternatives are obviously inferior. The reasoning behind this is that some new constraints might arise, making the superior alternatives impossible to implement. These alternatives represent the competing "systems" for accomplishing the objectives. They represent opposing strategies, policies, or specific actions, including the required fiscal and physical resources.

Assumptions must be made about the larger system within which the alternatives will work. This system should include anything that affects the problem situation or the alternatives. Of course, facts are much more desirable than assumptions, but it is not always possible to know or predict precisely how things will be in the future. The statistical sensitivity of these assumptions will have to be tested when the model is built. This can be accomplished by modifying different assumptions and observing the effect on the desired output.

It is difficult to identify all constraints. However, more information about problem restrictions will improve the presentation of analysis and will prevent inappropriate evaluations. The first and most obvious constraint in most cases is money; after this, the list becomes hazy. Constraints do not have to be physical or even measurable, but they do have to be recognized.

One constraint that must be considered early in the analysis is top management's philosophy toward scientific management. The perfect solution to an important problem could be arrived at through systems analysis, and yet never be implemented because of top management's distrust (or fear) of scientific management. Other constraints are psychological, sociological, technical, traditional, administrative, political, and, of course, physical (personnel and equipment).

The definition of criteria is important to the analyst, for these are the rules or standards by which he or she ranks the alternatives in order of desirability. They must be relevant to the problem area, include consideration of all major effects relative to the objectives, and, ideally, be adaptable to meaningful quantification. It is important to remember that, in some cases, the mere mention that analysis is being undertaken or action is under consideration may be enough impetus to significantly alter the problem situation.

The collection of data is somewhat mundane and even boring, but it is obviously as important as any other part of the analysis. It is mandatory that all pertinent data relating to each alternative be collected in a usable format, and by a method that will not bias the solution.

Building a model is not always necessary in every analysis, but in complex problems for which a vast amount of data exists for each, a model is generally needed because experimenting with the real system is either impossible, economically infeasible, or quite dangerous, as in some defense projects. A model can also serve as an aid to thought and communication, a tool for production, and an aid for control purposes and for training and instruction.

The evaluation of the alternatives is the "putting everything together" step. This can be done through many analytical tools, using the predetermined criterion as a measuring stick. Two of the most commonly used evaluation methods are cost-benefit analysis and cost-effectiveness analysis. In cost-benefit analysis, the cost of implementing each alternative is compared with the dollar value of the benefits accrued from implementation. Cost-effectiveness analysis compares the cost of implementation of each alternative with its real benefit.

B. The Decision-Making Steps

Following the basic steps of systems analysis, the decision maker should perform a final check to answer the following kinds of questions: *Were the objectives of the problem stated correctly? Has the data changed? Are there any new assumptions or constraints?* It is possible to expend considerable time performing this final check or review, but in practical management situations the decision maker has to come up with a timely solution for implementation. The constraints defined, specifically time and money, normally will not allow the decision maker to follow the well-known theoretical problem-solving model to the perfect solution with no uncertainty (see Figure 5.1).

After the analyst has evaluated the alternatives, the decision maker must identify the best solution by considering facts, assumptions, and uncertainties for the problem. In certain situations, the systems analyst and the decision maker are the same person, but

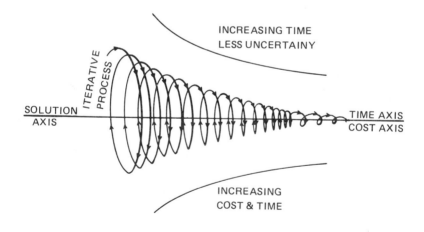

Figure 5.1 The spiral model of problem solving

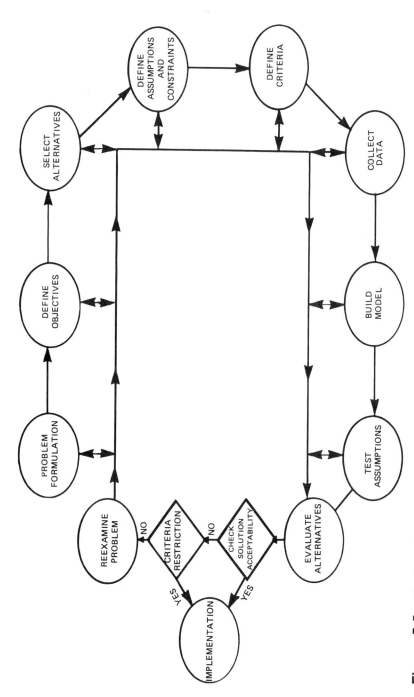

Figure 5.2 The iterative cycle

usually the analysis is performed by someone on the staff of the decision maker.

If the alternative identified is considered acceptable by the decision maker, the plan is implemented; if it is not acceptable, the decision maker must evaluate the constraints in order to determine if time and/or money is available to continue in the iterative model, as shown in Figure 5.2. In many cases, the decision maker may be forced to implement a less than optimal plan. As implied earlier, the constraints placed on the analyst are frequently so restrictive that the solution may be nothing better than an "intelligent guess." Consequently, the superior manager will work to eliminate unimportant constraints. Communication to the analyst that facilitates problem understanding is critical in the process of obtaining quality decisions.

Something should be said about what systems analysis is *not*. It is not a panacea for every decision maker. It does not tell the decision maker which alternative to choose. It is a method of investigating, not solving, problems. All of the various components of the analysis are defined by humans and often based on many untested assumptions. A correct decision cannot be assured even if the analysis is carried out to perfection. There is still a need for *experienced judgement*.

C. Importance of Quality Decision Making

The constraints imposed upon the decision maker are often subtle and troublesome. Although there were many constraints imposed upon the decision makers of the early 1900s, they are not comparable with those that have been added during recent years.

As labor unions grew in strength, management found that it could no longer assume that its employees were just another resource to be utilized in the production process. Any decision involving the labor force has to be scrutinized to ensure that a contract has not been broken. There have been many examples in which an entire factory has been closed down by a strike called because one worker was fired. Government legislation such as the Occupational Safety and Health Act, which requires an employer to assure that employees have safe and healthy work environments, requires improved decision making. The cost of labor in itself is enough to warrant the careful analysis of all alternatives.

"Consumerism" has come to light in the past several years, obliging industry to recognize its responsibility to its customers. Regulatory agencies have found new strength and courage in the public outcry for better and safer products. Most states have product liability laws that strongly favor the consumer.

Since the end of World War II and the introduction of television, the vastness of the federal government has become more and more evident to the general public. The Department of Defense can no longer give out lavish contracts to researchers for the investigation of meaningless ideas. An agency, bureau, or even the President can no longer hide major mistakes from the public. It is known in governmental circles that the public will view an area of government more critically if it discovers a major mistake within it.

The increasing public concern and environmental laws have promoted most manufacturing industries to add pollution control equipment. However, much of the public wants environmental improvements *without* product price increases. Effective decision making will aid in the development of lower cost antipollution manufacturing operations.

These are some examples of constraints placed upon decision makers that underscore the need for quality decision making. Decisions should not be made without knowing their full impact on the public as well as on the various markets.

D. Increased Number of Alternatives

Another area that has changed for the decision maker and complicated the decision process is the number of alternatives available to attain a certain objective. Recently, technology has moved so rapidly that no professional could possibly remain completely up-to-date, even in his or her own field. Of course, if the best alternative is not known, the decision maker can only make an inferior decision.

The other extreme (considering too many alternatives) is demonstrated by the fact that a newer breed of professional has entered the scene—the consultant salesperson. In many cases, these people could be called "alternative creators." Without a systematic method to evaluate all of the various alternatives presented, the decision maker may choose an alternative that fulfills the consultant's objectives, but not the organization's. Things are complicated even further when a computer is a possible component of some or all of the alternatives.

It is difficult to imagine a complex decision that does not involve the services of a computer, either as part of an alternative or in the analysis of the alternatives. To a decision maker not knowledgeable in the computer field, the various design alternatives incorporating computer technology can boggle the mind. But this should not cause rejection of the computer, because it can both improve some alternatives and expedite the analysis.

The basic factor to remember is that the computer is just another tool by which the analyst or decision maker obtains the desired objectives. Also, a computer salesperson who begins to describe the various characteristics of hardware and software systems is talking about means and not ends. The computer specialist who begins the conversation by asking what output is needed or what objectives are sought is the person who is going to help.

Time is a constraint in most decisions. In a marketplace where fad products may have a life cycle of six months, or in a world where total destruction could be complete within a day, a decision maker can ill afford not to take advantage of any tool that will speed up the decision-making process without adding uncertainty.

E. Summary

Systems analysis is a technique for structuring common sense in problem evaluation. Problems confronting decision makers have become more complex by the addition of constraints such as pollution control, more stringent product liability laws, and a more observant public. Bottom line, the use of systems analysis will improve the decision maker's problem-solving capability. The following points should be remembered:

Systems analysis is (or should be) the documentation of a method for analyzing problems.

Systems analysis can be applied to most business areas outside the scientific/technological fields.

Systems analysis is not a panacea; the decision maker must ultimately add judgement, select, and implement the best alternative.

IV. DECISION-MAKING TECHNIQUES

A. Expected Value

The expected value decision-making technique is one that is used when the manager wishes to quantify the degree of uncertainty associated with each alternative problem solution. This technique is usually well accepted and executed by the professional.

Computations of expected value can take into account changes in the environment along with the subjective probability of the occurrence of each state. The expected value of an act is defined as the weighted average of all of the conditional values of the act, each conditional value being weighted by its probability, as shown in the following equation:

$$EV = \sum_{i=1}^{n} P(S_i)W_i$$

$$= P_1(S_1)W_1 + P_2(S_2)W_2 + \bullet \bullet \bullet + P_n(S_n)W_n$$

where

EV = expected value
$P(S_i)$ = probability of occurrence of state i
W_i = worth outcome of each state

A simple example of the application of the expected value technique is the establishment of production levels by means of a sales forecast. Mr. Smith, general manager of a fast-food factory located in a small midwestern town, wants to forecast sales for the next year. He believes sales are determined mostly by personal income levels in the region. In accordance with expected value terms, the various income levels are states of nature. Mr. Smith thinks that four states of nature are possible: First, that incomes will decrease by 2 percent. Second, that incomes will not change. Third, that incomes will rise by 3 percent. Fourth, that incomes will rise by 8 percent. To these states he estimates the probabilities as 0.10, 0.30, 0.50, and 0.10, respectively. Lastly, he considers that the outcomes (sales levels for the next year) for the four states of nature are $1 million, $1.3 million, $1.9 million, and $2.5 million, respectively.

The expected value may be computed as follows:

$$EV = (0.10) (\$1,000,000) + (0.30) (\$1,300,000) + (0.50) (\$1,900,000) + (0.10) (\$2,500,000) = \$1,690,000$$

The expected sales level of $1,690,000 is based on Mr. Smith's estimate of the probabilities and worth outcomes of each state of nature.

B. Utility

The utility decision-making technique is used when management wants to include personal values in the consideration of each alternative. As with expected value, the utility concept is readily acceptable to the professional. Utility is defined as the power to satisfy human wants. The utility of an outcome is the subjective preferences placed upon the outcome and is usually measured in dimensionless units. For example, consider any desirable "item." Most people prefer more rather than less, but at a decreasing rate. For a given item or outcome an individual's utility function can be constructed by plotting units of utility (personal preference) against the amount of the item the individual possesses, as shown in Figure 5.3. In situations comparing more than one alternative, the manager should select the alternative with the maximum utility.

An example of a management decision involving the utility technique is sales forecasting. The XYZ Corporation produces product A. The sales forecaster consults with the sales manager

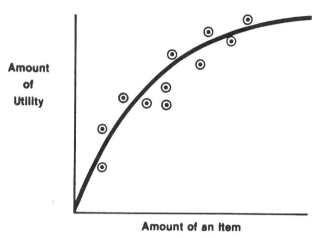

Figure 5.3 General form of a typical utility function

and they decide that the four most likely levels of sales for next year are $40 million, $35 million, $30 million, and $25 million. These four levels were developed in light of assumptions regarding the level of engineering for product design and manufacturing, consumer acceptance of the brand, actions of competitors, and retailer merchandising and promotion efforts. Furthermore, a minimum level of sales has been estimated. This is the magnitude that would be achieved if most or all of the factors determining sales-consumer desires and incomes, competitive activities, and so on operated adversely but within reason. For product A this minimum level is $10 million. Utility relationships could be developed for each projected sales level based on the manager's value of sales dollars above $10 million.

V. TIME MANAGEMENT

A major contributor to effective decision making is the availability of sufficient time to go through the needed decision making steps properly. Using one's time efficiently is a critical factor for managerial success. One of the most popular and best attended seminar topics in recent years is *How to Manage Your Time Well.* One of the reasons for the sustained popularity of this topic is the expressed feeling of many managers and professionals that they never have enough time to accomplish all of their assigned tasks or to adequately weigh alternatives in required decisions.

The increasing cost and availability of high quality executive talent is going to result in continued emphasis on effective time management. While managing time successfully is a complex process which relates to both the unique makeup and needs of individuals (Chapter 6) and the delegation process (Chapter 4), there are some basic steps that managers can take that will result in more efficient time utilization. These steps are grouped around three basic areas that compete for the professional's work time; namely, *organization and delegation, people,* and *paper work.* Although there are obvious interrelationships among these three areas, each one presents some unique demands on time.

A. Organization and Delegation

Since managers in professional work environments are responsible for a trained work force with considerable intellect, the opportunities and needs for delegation are high (Chapter 4). Competent professionals not only handle delegated assignments well, but they also *expect* managers to delegate. Remember, effective delegation releases management time (your time). However, proper delegation with regard to both choice and substance only occurs when clearly defined goals are established for the professional unit; *and* a mutual agreement with subordinates exists regarding duties and responsibilities. It is important to establish organizational priorities for these goals. A basic part of effective management is the development of an organization climate which supports large amounts of delegation with goal oriented control mechanisms (Chapter 12).

In managing time through effective delegation, the professional should guard against one of the biggest managerial time wasters— unwarranted *reverse* delegation. In their classic article, *Management Time: Who's Got the Monkey*, Oncken and Wass discuss this problem in the context of keeping monkeys off your back.[3] This is an important managerial task because monkeys require considerable care and feeding (time and energy). If you don't believe this check with your local zoo. Specifically, when others come to you with a problem it is usually theirs, i.e., the monkey is on their back. If you take the problem from them by agreeing to solve it or to get back to them after you have looked into it, for now you have their monkey (problem) in your possession. They have successfully reversed the delegation process and have delegated their problem to you! Helpful steps to protect your time from reverse delegation include the following:

1. Don't accept ownership of "others" problems.
2. Help employees work out their own solutions.
3. In most cases, don't agree to report back on solutions—otherwise employees are likely to do nothing until they hear from you.
4. Establish guidance and direction and persist with important concerns.

B. People

The biggest consumer of time facing professionals and their managers is likely to come from interpersonal relationships associated with the performance of assigned tasks. Examples of these include the telephone, meetings, drop-ins, and requests for favors. Some useful tips in handling each of these problems in order to increase time efficiency are summarized below.

1. Telephone

If secretarial help is available, have incoming calls screened. In the absence of a secretary, a phone answering machine may be used. Set aside a specified time during the day to return calls. Try to learn the nature of the call and gather the needed information prior to returning the call.

2. Meetings

Good organization, planning, and selection of personnel, minimize the need for problem solving meetings. Also, professionals can designate others to attend some meetings for them. Assigning meetings to others increases managerial time and in many instances may be perceived as a vote of confidence for the subordinate. When conducting or attending meetings press for a specified *purpose* and *agenda* as well as a *starting* and *closing time*. It is beneficial if both starting and closing times are honored.

3. Drop-Ins

People who enter your office or work area unexpectedly can consume large amoungs of valuable time. An important point to keep in mind is that eye contact promotes continued conversation. Managers who act busy and don't establish eye contact with drop-ins discourage conversation. Desks and chairs that face away from doors and corridors as well as a closed work area entrance reduces opportunities for eye contact and promotes better control over time. While informal conversation is valuable in promoting good human relations, morale, and better problem solving skills; it is advantageous to have control of this potentially large "time waster."

4. Request for Favors

It is not uncommon for employees to seek time consuming favors from managers and colleagues. While it can be desirable to honor many of these requests, they can become so burdensome time wise that personal effectiveness is substantially impeded. As an attempt to solve or prevent this problem from occurring it is useful to understand the difference between primary and secondary relationships. Primary relationships are based on emotion, i.e., family, close friends, etc. Secondary relationships can be warm and friendly but lack an emotional base. Primary relationships create a much stronger sense of obligation than secondary relationships. Thus *avoiding* primary relaitonships reduces requests for personal favors. One group of factors that contributes to developing primary relationships involves socializing after work, e.g., parties at home, organized attendance or participation in sporting events among employees. While there can be many desirable results from these activities, they do contribute to primary relationships which can interfere with both objective decision making and the professionals ability to control his/her time. Consequently, a knowledge of both the positive and negative consequences of primary relationships is desirable. Secondary relationships promote more objectivity in decision making and are likely to reduce requests for personal favors. If such requests occur it is much easier to say *no*. The desire to be liked and/or a sense of personal obligation causes managers to agree to perform time consuming tasks that should be given low priority.

C. Paper Work

Both managers and their professionals are usually confronted with large amounts of paper work each day. The ability to manage paper work is a key ingredient of personal success and good time management. In this context the requirement is to assign a priority to all incoming paper, e.g., mail, memos, other documents, so that each item is handled accordingly. Some kind of file system is needed that can separate high priority, low priority, and no priority items. High priority items should always be handled first, and low priority items should be kept out of sight until you are ready to work on them. This separation accomplishes two things. First, low priority items are not visible to constantly remind the professional of their presence which is important because a significant amount of valuable time and mental energy is expended over worrying about trivial things that are constantly brought to ones attention. Second, a good filing system helps to keep the desk uncluttered and presents the appearance of an organized, efficient person.

An important point to remember is to strive to only handle an item *one time*. Following priority assignment, when you are ready to act on an item, you should do one of the following:

delegate to support staff
perform work necessary to complete the transaction

While not previously mentioned, it is obvious that items with no priority should be discarded at the time of their first handling.

Do lists can also be very useful in managing paper work and other important task assignments. A do list should contain your personal work tasks in order of priority. The tasks listed should be attainable in specified time periods. Large assignments should be broken down into specific smaller elements that are less "threatening" and can be accomplished in reasonable time frames. Failure to sub divide large tasks will encourage long term procrastination.

VI. THE PRO-ACTIVE MANAGER AND TIME MANAGEMENT

Managerial actions and attitudes relate directly to time availability and decision effectiveness among managers. Effective managers are more likely to be pro-active than reactive. The pro-active manager takes action to prevent problems and minimizes "fire fighting" activities. Stated another way, the pro-active manager is able to "drain the swamp" in place of "killing alligators." Rather than reacting to decisions and problems created by others within the organization, pro-active managers identify potential opportunities and problems and act decisively. A pro-active management stance is also a characteristic of transformational leadership and desirable organizational change (Chapter 10). In addition to advocating pro-active decision making, this section provides several recommendations to help managers of professionals and their employees utilize time more effectively.[4]

Effective time management may be summarized as follows:

1. Establish clear-cut goals for yourself and your unit.
2. Set time priorities in accordance with these goals. It is important to focus first on doing the right things, and then attempt to do them properly. Many organizational and personal problems have surfaced because the wrong things were done. For example, some professionals fail to get promoted because although they are efficient, they are not concentrating their efforts on important high priority activities.
3. Good time management involves a willingness to delegate authority to subordinates.
4. A pro-active or planning stance is preferred to a reactive or "fire-fighting" stance. Pro-active planning gives a manager better control of potential problem situations.
5. In both setting priorities and in being pro-active, it is often necessary to refuse some specific requests for help by both superiors and subordinates. Managers who have a strong desire to be liked or build primary relationships often have difficulty saying *no* to others.

This tendency can easily result in the inefficient use of time, because a large amount of time is consumed on low priority or inappropriate activities.

6. Take steps to avoid time wasting, reverse delegation.
7. Finally, both a do list and a daily time log which accounts for where you spend your time can be helpful in solving personal time management problems. This completed log is most useful if it is matched with pre-established goals, so that the amount of time spent on low priority items can be identified. For example, low priority meetings and phone conversations will usually surface as big time wasters.

VII. SUMMARY

A decision is the selection of the preferred course of action from two or more alternatives, and is completed under known or uncertain conditions. Decisions may be classified as programmed (well structured and routine) or nonprogrammed for more complex issues. The systems analysis approach structures a methodology for decision making and is recommended for managers of professionals. Following problem definition with assumptions and constraints, data is collected and analyzed through model development to formulate various alternatives. The final decision (alternative selection) may utilize expected value and utility theory to compute the cost-benefit or cost-effectiveness for each alternative. Management judgement is still required for most complex decisions. Time management is a major contributor to effective decision making because it provides time for necessary high priority work. The manager that produces results is usually pro-active, i.e., he or she strives to prevent problems and identify potential opportunities.

REFERENCES

1. H. A. Simon, *The New Science of Management Decisions,* Harper & Row, New York, 1960.

2. Richard L. Shell, and David F. Stelzer, "Systems Analysis: Aid to De-
    cision Making," *Business Horizons,* Vol. 14, No. 6, December 1971,
    pp. 67-72.

3. W. Oncken, Jr., and D. L. Wass, "Management Time: Who's Got the
    Monkey?," *Harvard Business Review,* November-December 1974, pp.
    75-80.

4. Several of these ideas are adapted from Richard A. Moreno, "Execu-
    tive Time Management I: Organizational Support for Better Time
    Management," *Advanced Management Journal,* Winter 1978, pp.
    36-40; and B. Coulter and G. Hayo, "Executive Time Management
    II: How to Budget Your Time," *Advanced Management Journal,*
    Winter 1978, pp. 41-48.

6

Individuals and Groups: Their Needs and Behavior in Professional Work Organizations

I. UNDERSTANDING THE PROFESSIONAL

As the basis for understanding behavior of professionals and its impact on management within organizations, one must understand both employee and organizational needs. Individual needs develop from childhood and usually change slowly, while organizational needs can change quickly and unexpectedly. Since these two sets of needs develop from different bases with different characteristics, it is easy to see why conflict often develops between organizational and individual needs. Individual needs begin with early childhood and, as infants progress gradually into adulthood, their needs form a particular configuration. Variations exhibited in needs configuration can be seen in the personalities of individuals. Argyris, in his classic book, *Personality and Organization*, published in the late 1950s, discussed the development of personality from infancy to adulthood.[1] The normal adult assumes a different personality configuration from the normal child. An analysis of this development provides considerable insight with regard to adult needs in organizational life. Specifically, Argyris pointed out that adults have a need for superordination and control over their environment. Related to this need the normal adult is characterized by independence, decisiveness, and a realistic time perspective of personal and environmental events. Maturity is associated with the normal aging process, but is also affected by intelligence, education and experience. Professionals often possess higher levels of intelligence and education than do non-professionals and are likely to be more superordinate and control oriented.

A. Needs of Professionals

The categorization of needs most commonly used in organizational behavior courses, professional development seminars, and in-house company training programs is Abraham Maslow's *Hierarchy of Needs.*[2] Maslow identified five basic needs: physiological, security, social, ego, and self-actualization. As can be seen in Figure 6.1, Maslow arranged these needs in a hierarchy, with the lower needs taking on predominant importance; once satisfied, the next level of needs assumes greater importance.

Order of priority of human needs

Figure 6.1 Abraham Maslow's Hierarchy of Needs

Most organizational research tends to support the conclusion that the lower level needs are largely satisfied in organizational endeavors, and this conclusion is most appropriate for managerial and professional employees.[3] Specifically, one's needs for food, clothing, shelter, and safety are taken care of by minimum wage legislation, sustained periods of prosperity, and, of course, governmental regulations regarding health and safety. Although managers of professionals should recognize that all employees have these needs, and that they are vitally important to the well being of their subordinates, in a management sense these needs are often of minimal importance because they are largely satisfied. Also, a given employee's ability to gain friends in an organizational environment tends to be an attainable goal, and social needs are usually quite well satisfied. While Maslow's theory has been widely accepted and appears to make intuitive sense, research studies have indicated that individual need structures are more complex than this model suggests.[4] For example, needs satisfaction and importance are negatively related to physiological needs; namely as ones needs for food and shelter are satisfied they become less important as Maslow postulated. In contrast, at higher need levels (ego) when one achieves and gains additional responsibility, these needs may be emphasized even more. Also, the Maslow hierarchy is not necessarily followed in sequence once physiological needs are satisfied. An individual may move directly from physiological to ego needs, and focus little attention on social needs in the process.

As a result of research on needs, Alderfer collapsed Maslow's five need categories into three, as follows:[5]

Existence - material and physiological needs
Relatedness - needs that revolve around interpersonal relationships, including anger, hostility and friendship.
Growth - needs related to creative effort and personal development.

According to Existence-Relatedness Growth (ERG) theory the major difference in these three needs relates to their specificity, and a hierarchy is formed as one moves from existence to relatedness to growth needs. The means used to satisfy needs at each level becomes increasingly abstract. Also, as individuals satisfy their growth needs, they become *more* not less important to them. Thus, a professional recently promoted to a department manager position may now focus attention on a vice presidency which results in greater dissatisfaction than before the initial promotion occurred. Although Alderfer like Maslow suggests that individuals are likely to try to satisfy lower level needs first (physiological) and then move to more abstract needs, when frustration is experienced with attempts to attain abstract needs satisfaction, one may drop back and emphasize lower level needs. An understanding of ERG theory can help explain Maslow's model in the context of more recent research.[6]

B. Applications of Research Findings on Needs for Professionals

Many behavioral scientists believe that higher level needs should be of major concern to practicing managers. These needs revolve around the Maslow grouping that includes self-esteem and self-actualization, namely, status, esteem, and recognition; and Alderfer's growth category. Studies show that blue collar workers often attach more importance to lower level needs than do professionally oriented employees such as engineers, lawyers, physicians, scientists, and managers. Occupation seems to have more to do with individuals needs satisfaction priorities than does income or level of accomplishments.[7] These findings are particularly important in view of the significance attached to the organizational environment and an employee's desire to achieve.

Needs for certain goal realization, e.g., achievement, power, and affiliation, have emerged from a useful projection technique called the Thermatic Apperception Test (TAT) developed by H. A. Murray. The TAT consists of 20 pictures that are presented to a given subject who is asked to explain the events in the pictures, and often a varying configuration of needs for power, affiliation, and achievement as well as other needs clearly emerge in that explanation.

Needs for power, affiliation, and achievement have been investigated by several researchers including David McClelland who has analyzed the need for achievement. According to McClelland, a person's desire to do things better is due to a specific motivation to achieve, and this motivation is acquired rather than genetic and can be taught.[8] A relevant related point is that successful professional people tend to score high in achievement. Since achievement motivation is learned, organizational conditions are important to its development. Also, each individual has a unique needs pattern. One employee may be strong in the social affiliation configuration, but relatively weak in the power needs element. Another employee may have a high need for achievement, but much less need for affiliation with others. A knowledge of these factors is important in selecting, placing, and motivating employees in the professional work environment. While each professional is unique in his or her needs structure, there are similarities among individuals. For example, professionals tend to be high achievers who prefer challenging work and periodic feedback on their performance.[8]

Generally speaking, most organizational environments are competitive, and they often establish reward systems that provide greater opportunities for achievement, prestige, power, and social development for those who do well. This provision is one of the bases for the modern approaches to motivation that are discussed in Chapter 8. However, in order to understand basic organizational behavior, it is important to point out that these approaches are based on a common knowledge of the content of specific needs, the significance of these needs to individual employees, *and* the fact that the organization plays a major part in satisfying these needs.

II. CAUSES OF CONFLICT BETWEEN PROFESSIONAL EMPLOYEES AND ORGANIZATIONS

While an organization can have a profound impact on the development of individual needs and the realization of high levels of self-esteem, many organizations do not respond to individual needs favorably, and often create a considerable amount of needs frustration and conflict. A quick review of organizational purpose yields considerable insight as to *why such conflict often exists.* First, most organizations are rational. (If you happen to be working in a totally irrational organization you may want to consider updating your resume.) They have a specific purpose toward which they are directed which usually focuses on a profit-making or efficiency objective; consequently, organizations operate most effectively if behavior is kept on a prescribed course. As a result employees are often put into a confining situation. Their freedom must be *restricted* if the organization is to move toward goal attainment, and work assignments are not necessarily conducive to individual development or perceived by employees as supportive of their own specific needs. This situation results in conflict between individual and organizational needs that Argyris postulated several years ago.[9] As a general statement, little progress has been made in alleviating this type of conflict; namely, most organizations have not developed the kinds of jobs and promoted the freedom that will allow for individual self-expression and individual needs satisfaction, particularly for higher level needs. Two common explanations for this problem reside in the fundamental characteristics of modern organizations: First, the chain-of-command principle which places a subordinate under the control of one superior; and secondly, task specialization which had its origin in manufacturing firms, has wielded its way into most other types of enterprise. The presence of these factors tends to make employees feel inferior and frustrated.

In the professional work environment, this particular type of conflict can be severe. Since professionals are usually well educated, they are particularly concerned with ego and status needs, seek recognition for good work, and a relatively free environment in which they can set out to attain or achieve that recognition.[10] There is much evidence in the literature to support the conclusion that many environments do not provide this freedom or the much-needed recognition. Consequently, many professionals become frustrated and devote energy to activities which are designed to deal with frustration at the *expense* of organizational effectiveness. Managers of professionals must have an acute awareness of how the professional relates to the organizational environment in order to derive needs satisfaction that can lead to greater effectiveness. In view of the important impact of the organization environment on the profesional as well as the choice of appropriate management styles, it is useful to examine closely the organizational environment as it impacts on individual behavior.

III. CULTURE AND STATUS

Cultural patterns significantly influence both individual behavior and the organizational environment. Culture can be defined as *the value systems or modes of behavior to which people in a given geographical area subscribe.* Thus, by definition, country boundaries would offer the clearest example of cultural differentiation. The individual behavioral patterns and the organizational environment found in Japan are quite different than in the United States. The Japanese system, which is an outgrowth of feudalism that characterized Japan in the early part of this century, supports the welfare concept and yields a paternalistic type of management that has proven to be successful among Japanese firms. The depression of the early thirties in the United States reduced employee perceptions of identity of interests between non-managers and managers and made paternalistic management practices suspect. Additionally the competitive education system and the values traditionally taught American children by their parents for achievement and recognition have made it difficult for paternalistic patterns of management to work well in the United States. This fact is particularly true in professional work environments because the employees who staff these types of organizations are an outgrowth of systems where competitiveness, recognition and individuality have been common place.

A. Subculture

Subcultural differences within any given set of country boundaries also impact on corporate environments and individual behavior. Work patterns in unionized urban areas are quite different than those patterns demonstrated in nonunionized rural areas in the United States. For example, management practices that work well in the Chicago area may fail in small cities in the southeast. Due to the impersonal environment of the urban area with its large number

of unionized industrial workers, effectiveness is improved if pater-
nalism is minimized by supervisors. Specific channels of appeal
through union grievance procedures or the application of bureaucratic rules by supervisors is more acceptable to urban employees.
Managers are expected to be "tough but fair." Conversely, in rural
areas less characterized by a history of unionization and impersonal
work relationships, informal appeals and emphasis on company
loyalty by supervisors may work quite well. Managers with strong
success records are likely to apply different management styles in
accordance with subcultural variations.

B. Social Structure

An analysis of culture alone is insufficient to gain an understanding
of the complexity of the broader organizational environment. Each
organization is a part of the broader social structure of a given culture, such as within the United States or Japan. Its position within
that structure has a certain amount of significance attached to it
through the employees and clients who interact with the organization. Because organizations occupy a definite place in the social
structure, they are able to afford specific positions with regard to
prestige and performance to their individual members. Each position in the organization carries with it certain expectations with
regard to performance, status, and privileges that accrue to the in-
cumbent. A set of expectations identifies a defined role for the in-
cumbent. More rigid expectations result in more specified roles.
The significance of this fact is that many employees are responding
to what they regard as the proper role for their job or the jobs of
others, rather than expressing their true feelings about performance,
supervision, or interaction with other professionals or client groups.
Professionals are likely to have higher status positions in the social
structure because of their training and skills. For example, physicians and other health care professionals have traditionally en-
joyed high ranking positions in the social structure; and in innovative manufacturing firms, scientists and engineers usually have
considerable amounts of prestige and privilege.

C. Perception

Another important variable related to roles and expectations in the organizational environment is perception. Perceptions relate not only to how professionals see the world around them (in this case, the organizational environment), but to how they see themselves. A position in a job hierarchy coupled with the place that the organization may occupy in the broader social structure has an important impact on how incumbents in a given position see themselves and their corporate environment, as well as how other organizational members see and relate to them as employees. Professionals in an organization tend to be differentiated from non-profesionals by the majority of organizational members or clients. When this situation occurs, it specifically affects the complexity of the managerial task. For example, the engineering manager supervises nonengineers or other nonprofessional support staff. Because of differing perceptions, there may be communication problems among the subordinates precipitated by feelings of favoritism or a lack of understanding of each other's jobs that substantially reduces effectiveness within the organizational unit. Engineers may be perceived as occupying a very rigidly defined role which results in narrow applications of technology to job tasks, and communication may not be as open with other groups. Managers who supervise both professionals and other groups must try to break down these narrow perceptions by realistically reflecting the expanding role of today's professional. This will help to dispel charges or perceptions of "favorable" treatment and increase the general level of cooperation among all subordinates. Management is a more complex task when engineers, scientists and other professional subordinates include support groups that are more generalists than technicians such as human relations types. Managers in these situations should be aware that nonengineering professionals have the same needs for self-expression, independence, and recognition as engineers. If engineers and scientists are perceived to be getting greater opportunities for freedom and advancement because of favoritism, managerial problems will likely be intensified.

Some organizations have addressed this problem by separating scientific, research and development, and specialized engineering groups from the rest of the corporate staff. Often there is a different geographical location, or if this is impractical, a separate building may be allocated to these special groups at the corporate site. Since both of these solutions may be too costly for many organizations and impractical in small ones, strong interpersonal skills are particularly useful to managers in these latter situations.

D. Status

Status, one of the strongest influences on professional behavior in the organizational environment, may be defined as a *hierarchical ranking or ordering of people in* a *given society.* Barnard identified three conditions that determine one's status in an organizational environment as follows: First, the differences in the *abilities* of the individuals; second, the differences in the *difficulties of doing* various kinds of work; and third, the differences in the *importance of various kinds of work.*[11] All three of these conditions are involved in determining status. Since the work that is done must be perceived by others as being important, the presence of superior ability or doing a job of extreme difficulty does not necessarily provide one with high status.

In looking at these variables, note that status is something *given to an individual by others.* Since status is given or earned and outside the control of the individual, it cannot be demanded successfully. In the U.S. culture, status is highly valued by individuals, and is usually associated with the nature of employee jobs and positions. Since it is so highly valued by employees, it is an important determinant of behavior and is vigorously protected. For example, changes in the organizational environment that threaten the status of an individual employee (Chapter 10), and communications from managers or others that are perceived to be threatening to the status of an individual employee will be resisted (Chapter 7).

Professionals attempt to protect their status position by exhibiting behavior purposely designed to influence others to perceive their work as being difficult and important, and they resist all kinds of communication that downgrade the importance of their work or the abilities they possess. Managers need to understand that status and recognition are vitally important to professional employee groups. Studies indicate that status is an important motivator among lower level scientists.[12] Also pay and status should be commensurate with achievement and managers should give careful attention to the impact of specific rewards on individual status. One study showed that scientists who lack recognition by the organization relative to perceived achievement by colleagues are more likely to leave their jobs.[12]

Professionals will *resist activities by management* that downgrade the importance of their work or reflect adversely on their abilities as individual contributors to the organizational effort. Also, they will tend to resist actions by management that tend to suggest that nonprofessionally oriented employees that work around them are of equal status or importance to the organization in the jobs that they do. It is usually true that managers can support the status systems of professional personnel and build a more effective team by differentiating these groups from others and reinforcing their status positions. Differentiating the professional is often accepted by nonprofessionally oriented employees because of the varying sets of expectations that determine the roles for their respective occupations. Nonprofessional employees have a different set of expectations with regard to themselves and the employees around them. They often do not perceive themselves as being as high in status as a professionally oriented employee, and will accept differential treatment that supports this perception. On the other hand, professionally oriented employees, such as engineers or medical specialists do not have this perception, and they become very resistant to attempts to put them on an equal status basis with a nonprofessional employee.

E. Status Congruency

Status congruency exists when the perceptions that two or more employees have toward each other are mutually supportive. Examples of status congruency are as follows: Individual A perceives individual B as a peer; B also perceives A as a peer—or as a second example, A perceives B as a superior, and B perceives A as a subordinate. In each of these two examples the individuals are on the same wavelength in their relative status perceptions of each other. When people of perceived lower status are given symbols and insignia to indicate higher status by management, this decreased status congruence in the organization promotes ineffectiveness.

Whyte's classic study of *the restaurant* indicates a very interesting aspect of status relationships and organizational life, which has direct applicability to professionals. Whyte found that people behave toward others in a direct relationship to their status perceptions with regard to themselves versus others.[13] People of perceived higher status will resist orders from peers and people of perceived lower status; consequently, organizational efficiency is decreased to the extent that status relationships are not congruent with the decision-making process in the organizational environment. Additional early research concerning status relationships supports their relevance to the level of effectiveness of the organizations studied.[14]

There are many symbols that are indicative of one's status in an organization, such as size and location of the employee's office, number of support personnel, administrative or occupational titles, rate of pay, and even the number of telephone lines. Status symbols can be used to support existing relationships, namely, to promote status congruence within the organization. Moreover, this process requires an understanding of the perceived status relationships that exist within an organization, and a reinforcement of those relationships that promote organizational effectiveness.

F. Summary

Culture, social structure, expectations and role, and status work hand in hand to weave the complex environment of the professional work organization. Managerial effectiveness is enhanced when these factors coupled with the very complex and unique sets of needs associated with professional employees are understood. There is a continuous interaction between individual needs and the organizational environment which, in fact, determines the effectiveness and the efficiency of that management system. Of course, all professionals are not alike and will exhibit both differing strengths or desires for various needs and reactions to need frustration within the organization. One refinement in professional definition draws a distinction between professionals that are self-employed and those that work for others. Examples of professionals that are commonly self-employed include physicians and attorneys who also maintain strict loyalty to a professional code of ethics. Other professionals that are usually not self-employed include engineers, accountants, and human resource managers who are considered to be more dependent on and more interested in the organization. Analysis of individual needs suggests that self-employed professionals are very interested in autonomy and support to perform their work, whereas professionals working for others are most desirous of power and participation in organizational affairs.[16]

IV. EMERGENCE AND SIGNIFICANCE OF INFORMAL GROUPS

Intense conflict between individuals and the organization can often be minimized if employees become an integral part of a collegial group of fellow workers. There is a natural tendency for employees who see each other regularly or have common friends or associates who see each other quite frequently to develop a bonded relationship which is defined as an informal group. Groups are an outgrowth of common employee needs. Needs for understanding, identification with one's self and others, support, friendship, and security are the more prevalent needs that stimulate group development.[16] Groups usually are spontaneous because they are an outgrowth of these needs.

When an employee is frustrated because of an environment that is impeding personal needs satisfaction, and that environment is fostered by an upper level management which this particular employee cannot influence, it is natural to engage in some kind of adaptive mechanism. Research shows that conflicting expectations between professionals and their organizations lead many of these employees to focus on outside interests such as family, community affairs, or professional associations. Professionals who adapt in this way adjust to the organization reasonably well, i.e., they become less concerned about advancement, high earnings or other signs of organizational power.[17] Professionals who successfully make this adaptation tend to be more passive in their professional role, but their adaptive behaviors are associated with lower productivity levels. Professionals who make their work a central life interest, are more likely to leave the organization in conflict laden situations, or to use adaptation mechanisms associated with their internal work environment. One common adaptive response is to strengthen informal group ties with professional colleagues.

Proper interaction with informal groups is an important aspect of management, and the understanding of group behavior can contribute directly to the effectiveness of the organization. Conversely, the manager who does not understand or ignores group behavior will have difficulties. Groups of professionals constitute *greater* threats to management efficiency and effectiveness than do individuals. They can either upset *or* enhance cooperation with the organization because they can facilitate *or* reduce motivation among their members.

Informal groups can take three stances with regard to management. First, a positive stance, which supports management activity. Second, a negative stance, which involves working against management activity and goals. And third, a neutral stance, namely, not really impacting positively or negatively on organizational goals. The stance posture is best seen as part of a continuum as shown in Figure 6.2, with group behavior occurring at any given point on the continuum depending on the time and situation. The ideal managerial situation is to have informal groups support management's activities and goals by increasing the level of cooperation.

During recent years, much has been stated about the advantages of certain professionals "working at home" via telecommunications. While computer based technology permits the conduct of certain work away from the central location, the lack of group interaction and the resulting benefits will likely reduce the overall

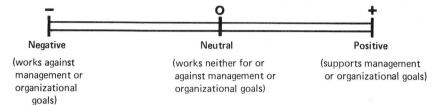

Figure 6.2 Continuum showing possible informal professional group positions with regard to the formal organization

effectiveness of the professional. This assumes, of course, that the group has been managed so it has adopted a positive stance.

A. Nature of Informal Group Control

Groups play a very important facilitative role in enforcing a given stance simply because they have control over the relative level of need satisfaction for certain important needs of their membership. In general, employees of the organization are particularly concerned with protection, understanding, warmth, support, friendship, and security, but professionals are often preoccupied with autonomy and recognition for their productive contribution. In this context, professionals are likely to have group norms which support the comparative importance of their skill contributions to those of other employee groups. Also, intergroup communication flow may be purposely restricted by professionals (Chapter 7). When information flow is reduced, the group is using a negative stance tactic which works against organizational goal attainment (Figure 6.2). Since group pressures can dramatically impact on others (managers and employees) within the organization, group behavior can substantially enhance or reduce each professional's level of need satisfaction.

Denial of group membership, privileges, or support can be very influential in lowering the sense of security, belonging, or identification for individual professionals. Ostracism and denial of group privileges is an important factor in the control of individual behavior which is under the influence of the group. A review of the relevant literature on groups indicates that norms are primarily enforced for behaviors that are viewed as important by most group members. Those behaviors that ensure group survival, facilitate task accomplishment, improve morale or express the groups central values are likely to be brought under normative control.[18]

B. Importance of Group Cohesion

The group's ability to impose sanctions, such as ostracism, is partially dependent upon the cohesiveness of the membership of the group. Cohesiveness is *the strength of the bonds among the membership* or the relative tightness of the bonds within the group. Cohesiveness is the function of four basic factors: First, the characteristics of the work environment. Second, the prestige of the group. Third, the availability of membership in other groups in the same general environment. Fourth, the strength of the informal leadership within the group. Informal or emergent leadership is usually assumed by a member of the group that most clearly identifies with the norms and values of the group as a whole, and as a result, is supportive of what the group wants to do.

If the group has high status relative to other adjacent groups, or if none exist to bid for its membership, and the group has an emergent leader with strong leadership qualities who embodies the values that the group membership supports as a whole, the ingredients are present for a cohesive group which can be very powerful in enforcing its codes of behavior. Membership in that group will be desired, and the leadership function will be sufficiently strong to enable the group members to carry out their objectives and maintain a liaison with each other. This type of group can be a pivotal force in determining the effectiveness of the management. If the group has these characteristics but assumes a negative stance, management can have endless problems in trying to sustain cooperation and motivate its employees. Conversely, management will have one of its strongest allies if the group is cohesive and strong, and members are convinced that managerial and group goals are similar and mutually desirable. In this case the manager has a valuable tool to increase motivation, cooperation, reduce conflict, and raise the overall level of effectiveness of the particular unit. This is a major element of sound management practice in professional work organizations.

Characteristics of the work environment determine the particular stance that groups of professionals will take toward management. Groups with a negative or neutral stance can often be converted to a positive stance, and this conversion is part of the task of management. Converting groups that are neutral or negative to a positive position will significantly increase the effectiveness of the organization. Several management practices are useful in accomplishing this task.

Specifically, the manager needs to be able to identify and work with the informal leadership of the group in question. Most every group has some leadership function, and sometimes this is complicated by the fact that it is performed by more than one individual. Usually leadership changes from one individual to another when a situation changes, but often these situations can be categorized. For example, one particular group member may be a leader in dealing with complaints and conflicts with management, and a different individual may be the leader in imposing sanctions and control on the group's behavioral patterns. A third individual may emerge as group leader when crises situations arise where immediate behavioral change is necessary. Managers of professionals need to understand this complex leadership process and be able to identify particular leaders in given situations, so they can meet with them when consultation would be both beneficial and desirable. Negative stances are strengthened in direct proportion to the inability of management to identify and solve problems of individual employees. As indicated earlier in this chapter, when professionals are frustrated with management's failure to respond to their needs, the seeds of a strong group which will probably assume a negative stance have been sown by the management. Thus, if managers can work directly with individuals to release employee frustration, they have made significant progress in minimizing their problems with groups. These desirable ends are often attained by designing jobs that will be stimulating and rewarding, and providing a monetary and need-satisfying reward system that recognizes good performance. Since a major issue with many professionals is a high degree of autonomy in the work environment the extent that management is able to take active steps to provide these rewards and protect or increase existing levels of autonomy, will relate directly to their ability to build a more effective results-oriented team.

In relating with groups it is important to understand that management cannot eliminate the group as long as a liaison is taking place among employees. Sometimes managers make the mistake of trying to shut off communication among group members, isolate group members, or engage in other similar activities hoping to eliminate group presence. This course of action is generally unwise because it will only serve to reinforce the membership's belief that management is not supportive, but exploitative. The impact of this perception will be to strengthen the group bonds among members and in some instances force group activities to go "underground." Underground activities are simply destructive group behavioral patterns, such as sabotage, which are purposely done in a secretive manner. Such activities are difficult to discern, therefore, pinpointing responsibility for negative consequences is difficult, so corrective action is delayed. When group bonds are strengthened from a negative action by management, the end result usually will be a *negative impact* upon the goals and effectiveness of the organization.

C. Groups in Professional Work Organizations

Studies show that groups in professionally oriented organizations are as prevalent as in manufacturing or other types of organizations.[19] Similarities in the presence of groups among organizational types is explained by their nature. As previously mentioned groups usually are formed because of spontaneity of contacts, a common need which results in a common bond, and some kind of shared interest in particular organizational outcomes. These conditions are shared by individuals who work for the same manager or perform a common task. Thus, the nature of the supervision and/or nature of the task have major influences on the composition, size, and cohesiveness of the group. Professionals are commonly bound together by similar tasks, and they will group with each other accordingly. Most professional environments have concentrated supervision which has a direct impact on the needs of individual employees. Common supervision provides the catalyst for group development and tends to set definite boundaries on the size and membership of the group itself.

Sometimes professional personnel will purposely limit their scope of behavior and develop what is commonly called a conservative type of work group in dealing with their managers. This is particularly true when these professionals possess unique skills which, because of their education, training, and experience with a given firm, cannot be replaced easily from the outside. If these skills are vital to the overall objectives of the management, these groups are potentially strong. Most professionals are quick to realize that they maintain considerable power as a group, and although one of them might easily be replaced, the entire group simply cannot be replaced in short-run situations. These types of groups often have highly centralized leadership, but they have restrained pressure tactics which are used for the attainment of specific objectives. They are difficult for management to interact with because management realizes that failure to cooperate with them can be extremely costly to the organization. In fact, management must respond to the specific demands of the group because of the high costs associated with losing group cooperation.

Health professions often foster widespread development of conservative groups. Physicians may use a conservative group tactic to change hospital policy, and nursing personnel may confront hospital administrators with specific demands as a group. If these demands are not at least partially satisfied, physicians may take their patients to competing hospitals and nurses may reduce their levels of productive service. Any group of professionals that offers an important specialized skill to the organization that is in short supply has considerable power through the application of informal group influence. Consequently, it is essential that managers of professional groups attempt to identify potential problem areas before they surface into major conflicts, and try to smooth the path to needs satisfaction and goal attainment for group members. The manager who fails at this effort will likely be managing a group that assumes a definitive negative stance against the organization. Periodic group meetings with subordinates where differences can be aired and acted upon by management are helpful for sustaining group support. However, these meetings should not be held too frequently and work best when they are conducted for a known purpose or in response to specific employee requests. An agenda for each meeting will help to generate results that are meaningful to the employees.

As will be discussed extensively in Chapter 12, management by objectives (MBO) is a useful tool available to bring groups together for a common objective, namely, the cooperation and attainment of goals for the organization. MBO permits group involvement, and according to Likert enables the manager "to develop management by group objectives."[20] This is an essential element of the *Likert System IV* process of management, which is heavily oriented toward getting the group to become an integral part of the formulation, development, and attainment process with regard to organizational objectives. It is important to note that the attainment process is a critical element in group behavior because groups will often determine the number of objectives that are achieved. MBO enables a manager to automatically integrate the formulation and attainment aspects of management into the group structure, which will certainly enhance the probability that the attainment of important objectives will be an end result.

V. GROUP DECISION MAKING AMONG PROFESSIONALS

Since the 1970s there has been more emphasis on using groups in the decision making process. Groups tend to make better decisions on complex problems than individuals, and there are definite increases in creativity and commitment. Figure 6.3 highlights many of the reasons why management may prefer to use groups in problem analysis and decision making. These benefits are not automatic and it takes skillful management of group processes if they are to be fully realized. When groups work together well, favorable results are likely, but when groups experience high levels of conflict the

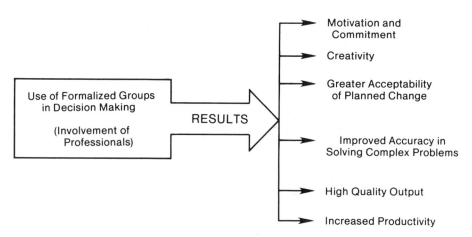

Figure 6.3   Benefits from group process decision making among professionals

probability of improved individual performance diminishes. Groups function well if both task and maintenance functions are provided within the work environment. The task environment for the group should contain clearly stated measurable objectives in order of priority. Also the task environment should foster the development of group leadership. As alluded to earlier in this chapter, leadership is important to cohesion, and also makes positive contributions to group performance.

Leadership in formalized professional groups is most effective if it is not imposed but emerges from inside the group. Since leadership needs are determined by the nature and tasks of the group as well as the perceptions of group participants, management often can influence the choice of group leaders by defining the group problem. Once chosen, a group leader plays the role of diagnostician and becomes very sensitive to the needs of the group. When the membership composition of the group is highly professional, it is important that the leaders credentials and values are congruent with the group as a whole. This congruence is especially important in specialized scientific environments, i.e., research and development, engineering, health professions, and academia.

Effective leaders see that the group maintenance functions are performed, namely, that the interpersonal interaction follows a constructive rather than a destructive pattern. The status and self esteem of each group member must be sustained, i.e., the value of each professionals' skill must be supported to encourage balanced constructive communications. Group members who either tend to dominate the group or put up obstacles to consensus need to be "dealt with" by the leader. Thus, effective group leaders play multiple roles which include boss, coordinator and motivator. Fig. 6.4 indicates group conditions which call for each of these three roles.

The boss role is most effectively performed when the use of *direct authority* is minimized. Peer pressures from other group

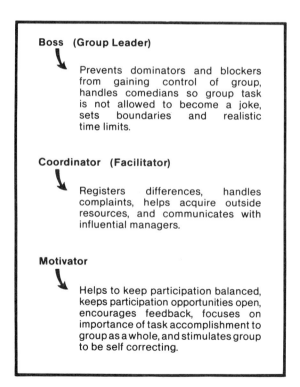

Figure 6.4   Functions of leaders in formalized decision making groups

members are the best way to control destructive communications among professionals. While this is a difficult and complex task for the leader, many leaders are able to accomplish it. These individuals help to develop consensus around productive group norms which encourage supportive behavior and discourage deviants. Also when coordination, facilitation and motivation roles clearly emerge, the *need* to exercise direct authority is minimized.

Each leadership role may be handled by a different person within the group. The most effective groups often have multiple leaders. When these functions are handled well the outcome is likely to have very high payoffs for both the manager and the organization. For example, representative committees and task forces among professionals are particularly helpful in providing creative inputs and innovative problem solving in the professional work environment.

VI. SUMMARY

While the importance of individual needs in determining behavior is firmly established, increasing attention is being given to the impact of the social environment on individual behavior (Chapters 8 and 12). A major component of this broader environment includes both formal and informal groups. Among professionals peer attitudes and evaluations are major determinants of individual behavior. Managers of professionals need a clear understanding of these phenomena in order to be successful. A major purpose of this chapter has been to provide valuable insight into the complex relationship among individual needs, group development, and behavioral outcomes.

REFERENCES

1. Chris Argyris, *Personality and Organization,* Harper & Brothers, New York, 1957, p. 50.

2. Abraham H. Maslow, "A Theory of Human Motivation," *Psychological Review,* Vol. 50, 1943, pp. 370-396.

3. Mason Haire, Edwin E. Ghiselli, and Lynam Porter, "Cultural Patterns in the Role of the Manager," *Industrial Relations,* February 1963, p. 113.

4. For a more detailed discussion of this issue, see R.J. Aldag and A.P. Brief, *Managing Organizational Behavior,* St. Paul, West Publishing Company, 1981, pp. 71-97.

5. C.P. Alderfer, "An Empirical Test of a New Theory of Human Needs," *Organizational Behavior and Human Performance,* Vol. 4, 1969, pp. 142-175.

6. For a detailed discussion of Alderfer's theory, see C.P. Alderfer, *Existence, Relatedness and Growth,* New York, Free Press, 1972.

7. William E. Rief, "Intrinsic Versus Extrinsic Rewards: Resolving the Controversy," *Human Resource Management,* Summer 1975, pp. 2-10.

8. D.C. McClelland, "That Urge to Achieve," *Think,* Vol. 32, No. 6, November-December 1966, pp. 19-23.

9. Chris Argyris, *Personality and Organization: The Conflict Between System and the Individual,* Garland, N.Y., 1987.

10. Donald C. Pelz and Frank M. Andrews, *Scientists in Organizations,* University of Michigan Institute for School Research, Ann Arbor, Michigan, 1976, p. 8.

11. Chester I. Barnard, "Functions of Status Systems in Formal Organizations," in W.F. Whyte (ed.), *Industry and Society,* McGraw-Hill, New York, 1946, pp. 46-70.

12. Donald K. Pelz and Frank M. Andrews, *Scientists in Organizations: Productive Climates for Research and Development,* Wiley, N.Y., 1976, p. 111.

13. William F. Whyte, "The Social Structure of the Restaurant," *American Journal of Sociology,* Vol. 54, January 1949, pp. 302-308.

14. R. L. Stogdill, E. L. Scott, and W. E. Jaynes, "Leadership and Role Expectations, Research Monograph," No. 86, The Ohio State University Bureau of Business and Economic Research, Columbus, Ohio, 1956.

15. J.A. Raelin, "An Examination of Deviant/Adaptive Behaviors in the Organizational Careers of Professionals," *Academy of Management Review,* Vol. 9, No. 3, July 1984, pp. 413-427.

16. Leonard R. Sayles and George Strauss, *Human Behavior in Organizations,* Prentice-Hall, Englewood Cliffs, N.J., 1966, p. 83.

17. L. Bailyn, "Involvement and Accommodation in Technical Careers: An Inquiry into the Relation to Work at Mid-Career," in J. Van Maanen (ed.), *Organizational Careers: Some New Perspectives,* London: Wiley 1977, pp. 109-132.

18. Daniel C. Feldman, "The Development and Enforcement of Group Norms," *Academy of Management Review,* Vol. 9, No. 1, January 1984, pp. 47-53.

19. Mark Abrahamson, "Informal Groups in the Research Laboratory," *Research/Development,* April 1965, pp. 29-32.

20. Rensis Likert, "Human Resource Accounting: Building and Assessing Productive Organizations," *Personnel,* May-June 1973, pp. 8-24.

7

Building Effective Communication

I. WHAT'S NEEDED FOR PROFESSIONALS

Many of the surveys done in recent years asking managers to establish priorities on the problems that confront them report that achieving good communications ranks number one. A study of executives asked which college courses best prepare an individual for leadership; oral and written business communication was selected as "very important" more often than any of the other thirteen courses surveyed.[1] These findings are not surprising because communication makes the organization work. It determines the direction the organization will take and impacts on both the motivational level of employees and the understanding that employees have of organizational purpose and goals. Communication, in essence, is the major determinant of the supervisory-subordinate relationship, and is a fundamental management task. Organizations that list responsibilities for their managers often list "communicating effectively" among the top five. Unfortunately, communication is so pervasive that it is often perceived as everybody's responsibility, and this fact dilutes the ability of management to pinpoint particular

149

communication problems or deficiencies. The achievement of good communication is a complex and difficult managerial task. This chapter will offer analysis, concepts, and insight designed to help managers communicate effectively.

A. Formal and Informal Communication

There are two major types of communication within organizations, namely, formal and informal. Formal communications tend to be *written* or are subject to specific procedural design within the organization. Informal communications are usually *oral*, and they do not necessarily follow any procedural design or pattern of flow. Studies of communication pertinent to the professional work environment have revealed that oral communication is likely to be more current, efficient, and important than formal written communication.[2] Communications that flow from superior to subordinate are likely to be formal and are often transmitted in written form. Information that moves from subordinate to superior is often informal and usually oral rather than written. One study comparing the importance of communication skills for executive success in 1970 and later in 1983 found that top managers of 58 California companies attributed communication skills as a major factor in their advancement to a top level executive position. While 66 percent of the respondents in 1970 said communication skills had a major effect on upward mobility, over 84 percent responded this way in 1983.[3]

A number of studies have addressed the question as to what are the most important elements or skills needed for effective communication. The most important skills that emerge are clarity, conciseness, organization, grammar, and spelling for written communications.[4] Also, business school graduates working in professional work environments write letters, memoranda and short reports more often than any other type of written communication.[5]

A comprehensive study regarding the perceptions of 71 presidents, personnel and training directors, and other corporate officers in 45 corporations regarding communications practices and listening behavior found that sending messages was regarded as more important than receiving them. However, receptive skills such as listening was considered more important than reading or speaking and expressive skills such as clarity and conciseness were more important in the written mode.[6]

B. Dimensions of Communication

The three major dimensions of the communication process are *downward, upward,* and *horizontal.* While upward and horizontal communication are usually informal, downward communication is most frequently formal in nature. Good formal and informal communication are both critically important for the organization to function effectively. Historically, the downward dimension has been given the most attention by researchers and practicing managers who have studied communication problems. Downward communication flows from superior to subordinate within the organization. As a practical matter, downward messages are given much attention by managers because without them the organization would cease to function.

The other side of downward communication is, of course, feedback or upward communication, namely, information flowing from subordinate to superior. Over the last 30 years communications authorities have indicated that upward communication is essential for downward communication to be effective, because the vital element of feedback is necessary for downward communication to be understood. Also, several studies show that feedback is necessary for effective communication among professionals.[7]

Unfortunately, even though much has been written about it, upward communication often gets little consideration from management. There are four principal reasons for this neglect:

1. Upward communication involves considerable time and energy on the part of management. For example, listening is very time consuming, and managers often feel too pressed to devote this extra time to listening to what employees have to say.
2. Upward communication may be perceived as threatening to managers, particularly if things are not going

very well. As a result of this threat, managers often turn off to what is being said, and try to get employees to avoid talking about important work issues. Since individuals' normal tolerance for criticism is often low, they do not listen to what subordinates have to say when they feel that those messages may contain personal criticism.

3. Professionals promoted into managerial positions are more likely to focus on task accomplishment than information flow because of their technical training. Subordinates often realize that managers resent criticism, and that they usually have some control over the well being of subordinates, such as promotions and pay raises. Subordinates are therefore often reluctant to talk to superiors about specific problems that might be interpreted as criticism because they realize that these things may be used against them by their managers.

4. The organization tends to design its information flow devices to support the managers' downward movement of communication, but the upward flow does not have equal support in terms of devices, e.g., secretarial assistance, staff support, or proximity of contact, so it is much more difficult for subordinates to get their messages across to higher level managers.

C. One-way Versus Two-way Communication

While the preceding points help explain why upward communication and feedback are neglected, research evidence continues to suggest that managers of professionals should make an extra effort to counteract these problems and assure that feedback flows freely. The authors have conducted experiments which illustrate this point using a popular diagramed exercise at several management seminars attended by professionals throughout the United States. In this exercise, participating managers are asked to draw interconnected rectangles on the basis of explanations made by a group leader who stands in front of the group.

Two specific methods are used to explain two different sets of rectangles. In the first method, the communicator stands behind a movable blackboard or other barrier and describes the relationships among the rectangles without the aid of direct visual contact with the group. The group is *not* allowed to ask any questions of the leader or to make any verbal gestures that indicate either understanding or lack of understanding of the explanations being made. In the second method, the leader comes out from behind the barrier and stands in front of the group to explain another set of specific rectangles. In this particular situation, the leader can invite questions from the group and the group can ask the leader questions at any point in the explanation. The first method is an example of communication *without* feedback, and the second method exemplifies communication *with* feedback.

Six basic conclusions regarding effective managerial communication with professionals can be drawn from the results of this exercise:

1. Participating managers and professionals overwhelmingly prefer two-way communication with feedback to the one-way method.
2. Communication accuracy measured in terms of the number of participants who draw the rectangles correctly is much improved when feedback is present.
3. There is a general feeling of greater satisfaction with the work process when participation takes place. This satisfaction level tends to move upward with increases in the number of professionals within the participant group.
4. While a majority of leaders prefer the democratic method (feedback) to the autocratic method (without feedback), a few leaders do not.
5. The democratic method (feedback) requires more time and is often perceived as a more difficult process by the leaders than the autocratic method (without feedback).
6. The verbal skills of the communicator are an important influence.

The results of this exercise indicate several points of practical value to managers who wish to improve their communication skills. It clearly illustrates that feedback improves accuracy, morale, and general understanding of the intended message. However, it also shows that this understanding and accuracy is gained at some cost, namely, more time is involved. Thus, for very simple messages or messages where accuracy is not a critical problem, it may be desirable to use one-way methods of communication because they are more efficient time wise. Since a bigger percentage of communicators than receivers prefer the one-way method, there is an apparent tendency for many managers to use communication methods without feedback. Although the ability to understand communications is less without feedback, nonfeedback methods are quicker and easier. Also, in the absence of specific evidence, some managers incorrectly believe that communication without feedback is the most effective type.

While there are some situations that clearly call for communication without feedback, most managerial situations involving professionals require communication feedback. This is particularly true when the nature of the information is complex, accuracy is important, and commitment by the subordinates is necessary or desirable. Very simple or trivial day-to-day communications are examples that do not warrant the extra time needed to include feedback or participation, but these situations are more commonly found in non-professional work settings.

D. Communicating with the Professional

While the basic principles of good communication contained in this chapter relate to all employee groups, effectively managing professionals requires firm application of many of these principles. Since professionals usually have a large investment in their education, they are sensitive to interpersonal relationships that do not permit their involvement. Consequently, communications that limit feedback are often ineffective.

It is useful for each manager who is faced with problems of motivation, understanding, and morale of professionals to ask the following two questions. First, *what is it that I really want to ac-*

complish in communicating with my subordinates or other staff experts? Usually the answer to this question is, I want to correct deficiencies and move to keep the department, laboratory or over-all organization on a prescribed course toward the attainment of specific goals. Additionally, I want to maintain or establish a colle-gial atmosphere among my staff. The second question then be-comes, *what alternative is likely to yield this result most frequently*? The answer to this question is the approach that will breed the lesser amount of defensiveness on the part of the receiver. Defensiveness is defined as the process of defending one's self when threatened by a communication from others. Common examples of messages that cause defensiveness are those that are perceived to downgrade one's status or self-esteem.

Both the communicator's and the receiver's ability to hear and understand are directly affected by the level of defensiveness that is present in the communications process. Several years ago Gibb de-veloped a sound approach to reduce the potential amount of de-fensiveness.[8] Gibb indicates that once an individual feels threatened either personally or as a group member by a communication, he or she will become defensive, and then all subsequent communication is directed at defending one's self and the true substance of the message is lost. He also points out the types of communication that breed defensiveness, and proposes solutions to counteracting that defensiveness. Specifically, communication that is directed at evaluating or controlling others tends to breed defensiveness. Most professionals become defensive when they feel they are being con-trolled or evaluated on a *personal* basis. Gibb maintains that these kinds of communication problems can, at least, partially be alle-viated by more supportive techniques in communication.

Rather than communicating personal evaluation or control in problem situations, the manager should be descriptive and attempt to identify the problem with the receiver. If done properly, this ap-proach will develop an effective rapport and minimize the personal nature of any negative feedback or criticism that may be provided. For example, if a technical manager goes to a subordinate and says, "Bob, you are doing a lousy job and you're getting our lab-oratory way behind in its scheduled development. I insist that you correct your problems immediately and move on a constructive course of action," it is apparent that the substance of this communication contains personal evaluation and contains a control element directed at the subordinate. It is also clear that the subordinate will probably become defensive in his or her response to this particular type of communication. An alternative approach is as follows: "Bob, I notice we're a little behind on this precribed schedule, and I have been reminded by the front office of our commitment to meet that schedule for the laboratory. Are there any particular reasons that explain our problems that I don't understand, and are there any things that I could help you with to move us back on a prescribed course?" This latter communication is objective, describes the problem, and does *not* assume the superior-controlling tone of the first approach. The probability of positive results with professionals of this latter approach is considerably higher, and overall effectiveness should increase.

Professions characterized by considerable amounts of graduate education such as medicine and law may view other organizational participants as "second class citizens" which often impedes intergroup information flow. Communications are improved with these groups when they are non-directive and the benefits to their profession of positive action are made clear. Almost any perceived infringement by managers on the freedoms of M.D.'s, university faculty, engineers, scientists, and established lawyers in utilizing their skills on the job will likely meet strong resistance. This resistance will reduce both managerial and organizational effectiveness. A major mistake many managers make in communicating with these groups is to become defensive when encountering resistance. This defensiveness is most likely to occur when several status positions are involved. Namely, M.D.'s, faculty, or lawyers may see the status associated with performing their professional duties as clearly *superior* to the status associated with management and administration. If managers avoid becoming defensive over this perceived superiority by other professionals, effectiveness will likely be sustained.

As developed in Chapter 6, status is an important determinant of behavior among all employee groups. When direct or implied action downgrades any group (professionals, managers, etc.) both defensiveness and conflict are likely to increase. As with so many management problems, understanding the negative consequences of likely responses in interpersonal relationships is a most important part of solving the problem.

There is strong research evidence that supports using these kinds of communication approaches when interfacing with professionals. It is clear that defensiveness impedes understanding and it is important to avoid a defensive mode when communicating with professionals.

In discussing the communication problems of scientists in business and industry, McLeod argues that these employee groups feel that originality, imagination, and freedom of expression are often discouraged in the corporate community.[9] These qualities are valued by scientists, but they are too frequently found only in university-oriented research teams. In fact, many scientists believe that status is only achieved by moving into managerial positions. Unfortunately, limited communication may actually tend to increase status as long as one remains a scientist, thus scientists may not communicate freely about their work. Whenever possible the scientific manager helps his subordinates blend their interests in pure research into the applied research needs of the company. In order to achieve this desirable goal, communication concerning pure or fundamental research should be supported and valued because these interests must be understood before effective integration with organizational needs can be attempted.

II. THE GRAPEVINE

The grapevine is an important part of informal communication and understanding the nature and function of the grapevine is useful in developing effective communication skills. The grapevine is defined as the *rumor mill* or word-of-mouth information that is transmitted informally and at frequent intervals throughout the organization. The grapevine operates very rapidly and is effective in spreading news through the organization. It exists whenever employees get together, such as in lunch or snack areas, or during the contact that results from the regular performance of duties. Studies have shown that employees often expect to hear important managerial or organizational news by the grapevine rather than by *any other method*.[11] Official memoranda (one-way communication) from the supervisor are usually ranked second or third. One study indicated that more grapevine sources were outside the employees' chain of command than within it, which indicates that the information passing through the grapevine came around management rather than through management.[11] It is also true that a considerable portion of communication among people within a given chain of command is of the informal grapevine type.

A. Making Constructive Use of the Grapevine

Managers cannot eliminate the grapevine, and since it is an important source of information to employees, *it should be used effectively*. The following points are particularly useful:

1. Managers should not withhold information that is important to subordinates for long periods of time based on the belief that they will not get this information until management decides to let them know about it, because the grapevine will probably get it to them quickly. Information transmitted in this way will have a negative impact on management credibility, particularly if managers deny the truthfulness of the information until a later date.

2. Information passing through the grapevine is likely to be more acceptable to subordinates and other staff specialists than information going directly through the chain of command. Thus, if a problem exists in getting a certain communication accepted, it may be useful to move it through the grapevine first, rather than by official announcement or memorandum.

3. Information received informally through grapevine channels should be assumed to be quite credible until proven otherwise. If this information needs managerial action, it should be investigated quickly based

on the assumption that it is truthful so action can be taken before major problems develop.

4. The grapevine should not be regarded as a liability, but an asset which can be constructively used to enhance the level of understanding within the organization.

III. HORIZONTAL COMMUNICATION

Horizontal communication is usually informal and by definition takes place at peer levels, and is one of the major ways that important problems are solved within the organization. The horizontal flow of communication is particularly important in professional staff and engineering operations because it enables specialists to pool their knowledge in a professional group and improve problem-solving ability. Although given little attention in the literature, horizontal communication is often very useful in professionally oriented groups to enhance problem-solving and skills development.

An environment that promotes feedback also encourages horizontal communication. Since managerial action that fosters the growth of both the upward and horizontal communication dimensions is desirable, managers who engage in such activity can easily realize a double payoff.

IV. NONVERBAL COMMUNICATION

While the content methods of communication are highly important, many studies indicate that nonverbal elements determine at least one-half of what is understood or heard in the communication process.[12] Among the most important elements of non-verbal communication are culture, context, hidden messages, voice cues and body language.

Culture as developed in Chapter 6 refers to the value systems of the communications environment. Professionals tend to be associated with high performance cultures. Communications that down play individual contributions in terms of quality, quantity, or importance are likely to cause defensiveness. Each professional group may develop a sub culture that is characterized by greater relative importance to the rest of the organization. Any communication in this climate that reduces the relative importance of the professional group is less effective.

Context refers to physical surroundings or other environmental factors apparent to communicating parties. An individual who walks in on a work group during their break and observes many employees standing around chatting and being non-productive may interpret this behavior as a normal work pattern and conclude the group lacks motivation. Conversely, an observation made of this same professional work group during a crisis situation when everyone is very busy can lead to the conclusion that the group is highly motivated and works extremely hard. In reality, both conclusions can be wrong, but the major point is that general perceptions were determined from brief observations. The communications that follow will be a product of these perceptions. If a high ranking manager from the central office is the observer in the case, and he or she is otherwise unfamiliar with the group, damaging communications may follow. Effective managers of professionals use context to support group norms whenever possible. Namely, if the group is productive, arrange visits from other influential managers when the context supports the message.

Quantity and quality of furnishings and physical arrangements of the work setting impact directly on communications. Seating arrangements and physical barriers in the communication setting have an important nonverbal effect on what is understood. When people sit across from each other with a table between them, they more often see the climate as competitive rather than cooperative. Once this barrier is removed and they sit adjacent to each other, e.g., at a round table, the environment is more likely to be seen as cooperative. Rapport is more easily established and upward communication flows more freely when physical barriers such as desks and tables do not exist between communicating parties.

It is desirable for managers to have two types of seating arrangements in the office: one that contains a barrier, such as a desk, and one in which physical barriers do not exist. There are a few situations such as layoffs or transfers where it may be desirable

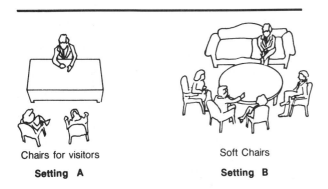

Chairs for visitors   Soft Chairs

Setting A   **Setting B**

Figure 7.1   Two contrasting types of communication settings

to minimize feedback, and sitting behind a desk is useful. Conversely, in many instances feedback and rapport are essential, and in these cases being able to sit and talk more informally without physical barriers between the communicating parties is desirable. Figure 7.1 illustrates both types of communication settings. In setting A, the desk acts as a definite barrier which reduces feedback and rapport. In setting B, the sofa, low cocktail table, and soft chairs promote feedback and rapport. Thus, a knowledge of the impact of these factors on nonverbal communication can be directly applied to improve the level of understanding in the professional environment.

Hidden messages are often contained in specific verbal communications. For example, the *way* something is said may determine what is heard. A simple "great job!" comment from the manager, upon successful completion of a difficult task is likely to be motivational. However, the same "great job!" following a marginal performance may be heard as a criticism and damage morale. Sometimes the perceived "hidden messages" do not accurately reflect the substance of the intended communication. Good communicators are aware of the context of the communication and avoid potentially damaging "hidden messages."

Voice cues are another important part of this complex process. Nonverbal communication requires "body expression" such as *tone of voice, posture, facial expression,* and *eye contact* while communicating messages in a verbal fashion to others. Tone of voice, eye contact, and posture have an impact on the ability of a communicator to get attention, establish credibility, and elicit feedback from subordinates. It is important to look at who you are speaking to, and to assume a posture that indicates attentiveness and value attached to what is being said. It is important to assume a tone of voice that emphasizes those elements of your communication that are regarded as essential. In any kind of communication, tone of voice should be purposely varied to emphasize those elements that are more important and deemphasize the elements that are less important. The time of day, minor work problems, or personal appearance should ot be given the same emphasis as a primary work deficiency. Supportive facial expressions such as smiling, and "open body stances," e.g., when the arms and legs are not held closely to the body in a tense manner, promote dialogue and discussion. Appropriate choice of body language, coupled with the use of other good oral communications techniques alluded to earlier in this chapter, increases levels of rapport, understanding, and managerial effectiveness.

V. MAKING EFFECTIVE PRESENTATIONS

One of the keys to being an effective manager of professionals is to possess the skills needed to make effective presentations. Managers spend considerable time presenting proposals for organizational changes, and most of these changes are likely to require cooperative effort by subordinates if they are to be implemented. Good presentations motivate employees to cooperate in the change process.

A good presentation is organized to control the listener's train of thought. All of us have sat through presentations wondering such things as *When is the communicator going to get to the point?*, or *How much cost and time is involved in implementation?* The steps that are involved in making this process work include:

   1. *Subject.* Write down the subject of the communication in one sentence. Read it back to yourself as if you

were the listener. Very often you will discover that the terminology is important to the communicator but not to the listener. If that's the case, re-do it so that the subject is stated from the viewpoint, words and interest of the listener. Good presentations integrate listener needs with the subject of the presentation.

2. *Need.* Write down in one sentence the need as it relates to the listener. Again, read it back as if you were the listener to make sure the need is a real one and that it is a priority for the listener. Most management proposals that involve employees can be shown to be important to them. When employees have a personal stake in the subject they are more likely to pay attention and want to become involved.

3. *Idea.* Describe your idea which must represent a solution to the need. This description should be understandable to the listener and is hopefully perceived as a solution to his or her needs.

4. *Benefit.* Indicate in order of importance each of the benefits the listener will receive when the idea is accepted. Individual motivation is based on need satisfaction (see Chapter 8) so in discussing benefits with employees don't overlook potential problems with implementation. In fact, it is usually helpful to identify important problems for professional employees as accurately as possible.

5. *Evidence.* A common reason for breakdowns in persuasive communication with professionals is that the communicator is communicating from a narrow perspective. Each profession tends to fall into an evidence trap, e.g., bankers use figures, lawyers use case histories, salespeople use dollars and cents and personal experience, engineers use experts and statistics, etc. Each professional group is likely to have a favorite form of evidence and the communication to persuade usually follows that type of evidence. There are several forms of evidence, and a well organized report,

recommendation or presentation can utilize many different tools. Among the more useful forms of evidence are experience and example, analogy, statistics and experts. The presenter's personal experience is usually a strong form of evidence because it adds to the communicators credibility. Credibility is particularly important to professionals, and often must be established in order to gain their attention and cooperation. Analogy is probably the least used form of evidence but it is potentially the most powerful tool to increase understanding of an idea or concept quickly and clearly. Analogies drawn from the profession are effective because the professional relates well to them. Analogous subjects are usually effective to the extent that they relate to the listener's interests. Statistics are a frequently used form of evidence, but there are many examples where figures lie and liars figure. Thus, it is important to attribute the source (experts) of your statistics.

It is helpful to illustrate statistics with visual aids and provide additional facts. Maintain eye contact with your audience when using visual aids. Facts are basic truths that can relate to company principles or stated company direction. When facts are combined with statistics and the expert opinion of outsiders, the credibility of your presentation is enhanced. Also, many times, examples can be used to demonstrate the feasibility of the proposal.

In planning a presentation it is important to look at various forms of evidence and to select those that are most congruent with your proposal and audience (professional employees). Each listener reacts uniquely to different situations. Technically trained people often relate well to statistics and facts. While others with more general backgrounds respond to expert opinion, and examples. If the right tools of evidence are selected the probability of persuading professionals substantially improves.

Effective managerial presentations usually conclude by stating a recommended action. This action should specify what individual employees need to do and establish a time frame for accomplishment.

VI. APPROACHES TO IMPROVING
MANAGERIAL COMMUNICATIONS

Improving communications among professionals involves recognizing the complexities of both the dimensions and types of communication. Managers should also take responsibility for the general
level of communication within their respective organizational units.
This requires meeting with subordinates to discuss the problems of
communication flow and finding mutual solutions to these problems. The number and type of meetings held should be carefully
planned by the manager, because poorly planned meetings can do
more harm than good. As Drucker points out, an excess of meetings may indicate that jobs have not been properly defined or structured.[13] Many times the presence of a strong need to meet to solve
problems suggests that the manager has failed to help plan, organize, and communicate job tasks effectively. Also, meetings conducted on short notice to solve crisis problems may be resented by
subordinates.

The ability to communicate and to widen one's range of problem-solving potential is based in part on the willingness of the communicator to share knowledge, attitudes, and feelings with others.
In fact, the extent to which pertinent information about ourselves
is kept from others, or they keep information from us, reduces the
level of two-way understanding. One widely used communications
model identifies four major areas or situations involving interpersonal communication.[14] These four situations are the *arena, blind
spot, facade,* and *unknown.* The arena is defined as the area where
important facts about the communicator are known by both parties namely, the communicator and receiver. The blind spot is where
important elements relating to the communicator are known by
the receiver, but kept from the communicator. The facade is where
some of these aspects are known by the communicator, but they
are kept from the receiver. The unknown is where important information relating to the communicator is unknown by both parties.
In order to be most effective, communication must take place where
important elements are known by both parties involved, consequently effective communicators enlarge the arena whenever possible. The arena can be enlarged by reducing the blind spot, facade,

or unknown areas. The facade is reduced by giving information about yourself, the blind spot is reduced by asking questions and getting information, and the unknown becomes known by exploring with the receiver the elements of the communication that are not understood.

Professionals are likely to maintain facades in communication situations which threaten the value of their special skills to the organization. A valuable aid to managers of these groups in both getting and receiving information is to be very supportive of professional employees in order to increase their level of self disclosure. For example, if an employee offers personal or critical information about himself or herself which is not supported by the responses of the manager, it will be difficult for the manager to gain further information. When managers protect the professional's self worth and reinforce his or her skill value to the department and organization, the size of the arena increases and meaningful communication flow is enhanced. It is important to support professionals when they offer personal information, and at the same time educate professionals on the importance of supporting others in order to establish rapport and build effective communication. Good communication takes time and managers should be willing to devote the time necessary to make communication more effective.

As pointed out in Chapter 6, studies show that status factors have a particularly strong impact on information flow in the professional work environment. Professionals tend to be more status conscious than non-professionals. Status consciousness creates high levels of sensitivity to "hidden messages," and to clearly delineated status hierarchies within the work group. Experiments by social psychologists have shown that, in organizations characterized by status hierarchies, high and low status employees have difficulties communicating with each other. For example, it is common among specialists to find that those with high skills and/or education (professionals) form a tightly knit group characterized by effective internal communication, but seldom discuss technical matters with the less skilled (non-professionals). This type of clique behavior can disrupt organizational performance because communication and idea flow suffer. To solve this problem the manager should work to build a cooperative team that involves the entire network. For example, one researcher suggested that strong ties among a small number of professionals can impede the diffusion of information throughout the total network.[15] Strong ties represent mutual sociometric choices among a small number of people, whereas a weak tie has a one-way or indirect sociometric choice connection. It is argued weak ties increase information flow across groups, while strong ties breed local cohesion and a fragmentation of the total network.[15] Among professionals, weak ties are necessary for the integration of the entire network into the organizations' task.

One effective way to increase information flow and to build teamwork is for the manager to develop goals that draw both high skill and low skill employees together. Specifically, it is important to make highly skilled professionals see that information from the non-professionals may be very useful in attaining the basic goals of the organization. Attainment of these goals must result in rewards to both groups. This type of goal approach is valuable to both professional and non-professional groups, but it is not useful to focus it on the professional groups because usually the non-professional groups want to communicate with the higher status professionals. It is clear that successful management of the communication process can be difficult for the manager who supervises personnel with diverse educational backgrounds. Many of the points stressed throughout this chapter are useful to help resolve some of the group conflicts that can emerge. Successful development of team effort does not just happen; it requires strong and purposeful problem-solving action by managers. This action can have high payoffs because studies clearly show that improved internal communications among professionals will make a direct contribution to organizational effectiveness. For example, a series of studies conducted at the Sloan School of Management at the Massachusetts Institute of Technology, concluded that few ideas flow into the laboratory directly from the scientific and technological literature. In one study, for example, only fifteen percent of the idea generating messages could be attributed to the literature.[16] Outside or extraorganizational channels consistently performed more poorly than internal information channels in the provision of technical information. Lack of technical capability within the laboratory was often responsible for the decision to use outside sources. When information must be obtained for projects, it is often more useful to seek the capabilities within the organization than outside the organization. Among professionals several sources rather than one single source often contribute to the discovery and formulation of a particular idea.

VII. NOISE AND COMMUNICATION

For many years it has been known that noise control is critical for effective communications particularly for groups. The main problem is *speech interference*, however, higher levels of noise can even produce detrimental health effects.[17] In addition, most mental tasks performed by professionals that demand a high level of perceptual capacity or information-handling usually suffer a performance degradation.[18] Yet countless managers continue to ignore this important aspect of communication.

Noise from a practical viewpoint may be defined as *any unwanted sound*. Sound waves originate from the vibration of an object, which in turn creates a succession of waves of compression and expansion through a transporting medium. For oral communication the medium is air (sound waves in air travel at a velocity of about 1,100 feet or 340 meters per second). Sound may be defined in terms of frequencies which determine its tone and quality, and amplitudes which determine its intensity. The human ear can distinguish frequencies from about 20 to 20,000 Hertz (cycles per second). The greater the sound wave amplitude, the greater the sound pressure which may be measured on the A-weighted decibel scale represented as dB(A). This scale is used because it accommodates the very large variation of sound intensities encountered in the physical environment, and it matches the hearing range of humans. The dB(A) scale is logarithmic and consequently an increase of 10 dB(A) implies a *doubling* of the perceived sound (noise) intensity.

Whenever a continuous source of sound is present in a room, two sound fields are produced. One is the direct sound field emitting from the source, the other is the reverberant sound field reflecting from the surface of walls, ceiling, floor, or other objects. In general, for locations very close to the continuous sound source, adding sound absorbing material in the room will have little effect on sound levels. Conversely, at greater distances the sound level will be reduced by about 3 dB(A) for each doubling of the total sound absorption. A sound level of approximately 55 dB(A) is satisfactory for conferences in normal voice at a 1.0 to 1.5 meter table. A raised voice is required to project distances of 4.0 meters.[19] Relatively small increases in sound levels will cause difficulty in communication. For example, sound levels of 63 dB(A) are unsatisfactory for conferences of more than 2 or 3 people; 65 dB(A) represents a "very noisy" office environment and is unsatisfactory for effective communication.[19] Figure 7.2 depicts typical levels for sounds commonly heard in the environment. Note that 90 dB(A) is the maximum permissible noise exposure as specified by the U.S. Occupational Safety and Health Act (OSHA).

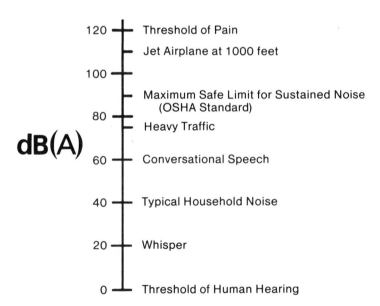

Figure 7.2 Typical sound levels in decibels (A Scale)

A. The Cocktail Party Effect

When two people are alone in a room and relatively close together, the acoustical characteristics of the room have negligible influence on their ability to carry on a conversation. However, if several people are talking in the room, the reverberant sound (pressure) level will increase by 10 log N (where N is the number of people talking), and make conversation difficult unless the room has substantial sound absorption qualities. This explains the common difficulty of effectively communicating when several people are talking at the same time. If all talkers in the room were to reduce their individual acoustic outputs, the background level of reverberant sound would be reduced without altering the relative pressure level of the direct sound field. Unfortunately, when a large number of talkers are present in a room the so-called "cocktail party effect" comes into existence as each talker raises his or her individual acoustic output in order to be heard. On the average this does not increase the intelligibility of communication, but merely serves to increase the background sound level to an unproductive high value.[20]

The cocktail party effect can be controlled by ensuring that important group meetings are held in facilities that have good sound absorption/control characteristics. In addition, it is necessary to organize the meeting so that simultaneous communications are minimized.

VIII. SUMMARY AND CONCLUSIONS

This chapter has analyzed the complexities of the communications process. The focus has been on solving communications problems and improving information flow in professional work settings. Figure 7.3 shows the interaction among the variables that impact on message content, flow, and probable outcomes. An important aspect of communication is the perceived impact of message content on the self image of the receiver. Messages that contribute to greater self esteem generally produce more desirable results. Studies clearly show that professionals characterized by high self esteem, and central positions in communications networks account for much of the information flow and innovation within an organization.[21] Effective

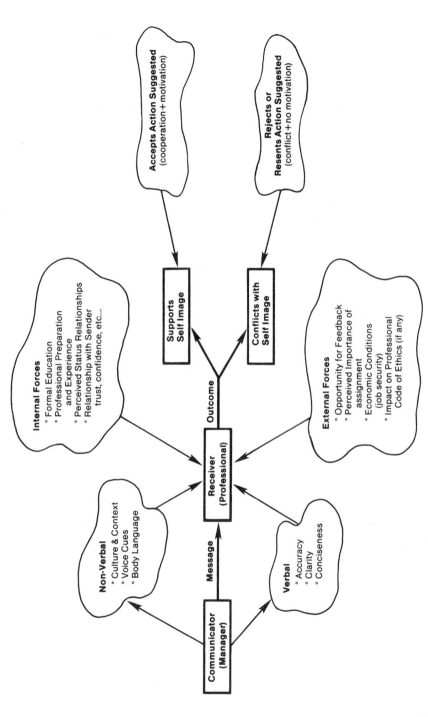

Figure 7.3. Variables that affect message outcomes

171

communication requires control of excessive noise, particularly for group meetings.

Several other points that will help information flow among professionals are summarized below:

1. All communication is much more effective if it is not simply a blanket communication. For instance, a communication such as, "Sue, I want you to do this," is much more effective than a general announcement at a meeting that a certain task must be accomplished by the group or some individual within the group. In the former instance, the communication is directed toward both a person and a purpose, but in the latter instance it is not.

2. It is important to understand that subordinates may not tell management how they really feel, which is commonly referred to as filtering. Subordinates filter because they believe that bad or realistic news may be used against them later on by the management. Negative information used against cooperative employees reduces effectiveness.

3. Emphasizing to professional employees that their information is vitally important and will be considered very carefully may alter their feedback. For example, stressing the importance of messages is often perceived by subordinates to mean that what they say is likely to be used against them if it is negative or critical, and they will filter their information carefully.

4. Every communication deserves a response; when a question is asked, a specific statement is made that is indicative of an appropriate response, and a reply should be given, even if that reply is "no." Professionals are often very quickly turned off when managers do not take action on their problems. Managers should pay attention to subordinates and make them feel that they are a significant part of the organization by both responding to and hopefully taking action on reasonable requests.

5. Abrupt interruption or change of subject during a conversation makes a subordinate feel insignificant. Good communicators bring action or closure on initiated messages from subordinates before other matters are discussed or interruptions become too distracting. Since a manager is judged by his or her subordinates through action more than words, the effectiveness of communication is reduced when managerial promises are not fulfilled. Every manager should be careful about making "empty promises" to temporarily alleviate employee conflict.

6. It is recognized that due to advanced training, professional personnel may use complex and technical language in communicating their ideas and problems to managers and others. This fact may result in communication breakdowns between professionals and other less technical employee groups, which can impede managerial effectiveness. Encouraging professionals to use more common and understandable words in communicating with others can be an effective means of alleviating this problem.

7. It is useful to avoid talking about things or history when responding verbally to others. Remember, it is the present or future and not the past that is perceived as being most important, and often the relationship between past and present is not understood or appreciated.

8. Good communicators avoid saying "yes but" when they mean "no," because wrong interpretations can lead to much greater problems later on. Often a manager's desire to be liked leads to a "yes but" when "no" is meant; however, the end result may be less respect and friendship from subordinates than an honest "no" will provide.

9. Managers should minimize the number of levels through which a message passes because more levels increase distortion, which is a frequent cause of communication

breakdown. Drucker argues that the multiplication of the number of management levels is the most common and serious symptom of malorganization.[22] Strive to minimize the number of management levels for the shortest possible chain of command.

10. It is important not to overload a message with more information than can be comprehended by the receiver. This typically leads to communication breakdown.

11. Studies show that a combination of oral and written communication is most effective.[23] Thus, vitally important information to subordinates or staff specialists should be communicated both orally and in writing.

12. Managers of professionals should focus more on the purpose and direction of communication and tailor it to specific work needs rather than focus on the volume of information flow. A study involving professionals concludes that the direction and amount of communication to other organizational units is more important than the overall amount of communication.[24] Results of this same study suggest that more successful project managers tailor their communication patterns to fit their specific work needs.

13. Make communication a dialogue whenever possible. Open questions such as, What?, When?, Where?, or How? promote dialogue. Closed questions such as, Will you?, Can you?, Do you? which can be answered with a simple yes or no, discourage dialogue. Also encourage feedback with frequent specific praise and empathy.

14. Support words with action. In the final analysis managers are judged more by what they do than by what they say. It is important to avoid oral commitments that are difficult to keep.

15. Avoid the overuse of "buzz words" and cliches, as they often are not associated with action by the receiver.

This chapter has contained a concise analysis of the realities and complexities involved in attaining effective communication in the professional work environment. Given the primary importance of communication, much attention has been given to specific action that managers can take to improve their communication skills. The development of good organizational communication is the cornerstone of building a results-oriented team of professionals. Managers who maintain effective communication and develop teamwork among their subordinates will have taken the basic steps that are necessary to prove their capabilities to top management.

REFERENCES

1. H.W. Hildebrant, et al., "An Executive Appraisal of Courses Which Best Prepare One for General Management," *The Journal of Business Communication,* Winter 1982, pp. 5-15.

2. J. Czepiel, "Patterns of Inter-Organizational Communication and the Diffusion of a Major Technological Innovation," *Academy of Management Journal,* Vol. 18, No. 1, 1975, pp. 6-14.

3. J.C. Bennett and R.J. Olney, "Executive Priorities for Effective Communication in an Information Society," *Journal of Business Communication,* Spring 1983, pp. 13-22.

4. D. Stine and D. Skorzenski, "Priorities for the Business Communication Classroom: A Survey of Business and Academy," *The Journal of Business Communication,* Spring 1979, pp. 15-30.

5. C.G. Storms, "What Business School Graduates Say About the Writing They Do at Work: Implications for the Business Communications Course," *The ABLA Bulletin,* December 1983, pp. 13-18.

6. Gerald Carstens, "Perceptions of C.E.O.'s, Personnel Managers, and Training Directors of Communication Practices and Listening Behavior in Large Scale Organizations," paper presented at the Annual Meeting of the Speech Communication Association, Louisville, Kentucky, November 1982.

7. P. Diehl and J.R. Howell, "Improving Communication Within the R & D Team," *Research Management,* Vol. XIX, No. 1, January 1976, pp. 23-27.

8. Jack R. Gibb, "Defensive Communication," *Journal of Communication,* Vol. XI, No. 3, September 1961, pp. 141-148.

9. Marian B. McLeod, "The Communication Problems of Scientists in Business and Industry," *Journal of Business Communications,* Vol. 15, No. 3, Spring 1978, pp. 27-35.

10. Keith Davis, "The Care and Cultivation of the Corporate Grapevine," *Dun's Review,* July 1973, pp. 44-47.

11. Keith Davis, "Grapevine Communication Among Lower and Middle Managers," *Personnel Journal,* April 1969, pp. 269-272.

12. Merwyn A. Hayes, "Nonverbal Communication Without Words," in *Readings in Interpersonal and Organizational Communication* (Huseman, Logue, and Freshley, eds.), Holbrook Press, Boston, 1977, pp. 55-68.

13. Peter F. Drucker, *Management: Tasks Responsibilities,* Harper & Row, New York, 1973, p. 548.

14. Joseph Luft, *Group Processes: An Introduction to Group Dynamics,* National Press, Palo Alto, Calif., 1963.

15. M.S. Granovetter, "The Strength of Weak Ties," *American Journal of Sociology,* Vol. 79, 1973, pp. 1360-1380.

16. Thomas J. Allen, "Communications in the Research and Development Laboratory," *Technology Review,* Vol. 70, No. 1, October-November 1967, pp. 31-37.

17. K. Kryter, *The Effects of Noise on Man,* New York: Academic Press, 1970; and G. Jansen, "Relation Between Temporary Threshold Shift and Peripheral Circulatory Effects of Sound," *Physiological Effects of Noise,* Welch and Welch eds., New York: Plenum Press, 1970.

18. Mark S. Sanders and Ernest J. McCormick, *Human Factors in Engineering and Design,* 6th ed., McGraw-Hill, 1987, pp. 456-485.

19. Stephen Konz, *Work Design: Industrial Ergonomics,* 2nd edition, Columbus, OH: Grid Publishing, 1983, pp. 399-401.

20. For additional reading and theoretical development reference Lawrence E. Kinsler and Austin R. Frey, *Fundamentals of Acoustics,* 2nd Edition, Wiley, 1962, pp. 436-438; and J. MacLean, *Acoustical Society of America,* Vol. 31, No. 79, 1959.

21. R.T. Keller and W.E. Holland, "Communicators and Innovators in Research and Development Organizations," *Academy of Management Journal,* Vol. 26, No. 4, December 1983, pp. 742-749.

22. Peter F. Drucker, *Management*: *Tasks Responsibilities,* Harper & Row, New York, 1973, p. 548.

23. D.A. Level, "Communication Effectiveness: Method and Situation," *Journal of Business Communication,* Fall 1972, pp. 19-25.

24. Michael L. Tushman, "Technical Communication in R & D Laboratories: The Impact of Project Work Characteristics," *Academy of Management Journal,* Vol. 21, No. 4, December 1978, pp. 624-645.

8
Motivating Today's Professional

I. OVERVIEW AND TRENDS

Since a manager is responsible for the performance of others, motivation is a critically important component of the manager's job. The dominant management philosophy prior to the 1930s in the United States was that employee motivation at all organizational levels was a function of two basic factors—wages and working conditions. Managers commonly believed that regular increments in wages and improvements in work conditions would result in corresponding increases in productivity. The results of the Hawthorne studies conducted at the Western Electric plant near Chicago in the 1920s and early 1930s did not support this widely held view. In contrast these classic studies suggested that the social system was a key determinant of worker performance.[1] Moreover, the Hawthorne studies revealed that employee motivation was a complex process, and provided impetus for much ensuing research. Motivational research following the Hawthorne studies focused on the employee needs structure, social environment, supervision, assigned tasks, and performance appraisal. Employee needs theory provides a more in-depth understanding of worker behavior, and is applicable to the professional work environment.

When needs theory is used to explain motivation, the emphasis is on individual employee need deficiencies. This approach suggests that employees work to satisfy frustrated needs, and this activity largely determines their level of motivation. In fact, many of today's most popular and widely understood theories of motivation are a product of the 1940s and 50s. While managers of professionals often have the advantage of highly self-disciplined subordinates, they may still experience motivational problems because of the complex needs of these employees.[2] Responding to a 1960 research investigation, engineers and scientists indicated that, as a group, over fifty percent believed their needs are different from those of other workers.[3] Also, two-thirds of the scientific personnel in the sample had common personality traits significantly different from the normal population.[3] The typical professional employee is high in both achievement and self esteem, and attaches great importance to the satisfaction of these two related needs. The substance of various needs theories and models is similar, and there is considerable applicability to the professional work environment which will be developed throughout this chapter.

In more recent years (since the mid 1960s) there has been a shift away from needs based theories to newer approaches that place greater emphasis on the social environment, goal setting, and methods of performance evaluation. Among professionals it is clear that peer opinion and evaluation has a distinct effect on behavior. Increases in professional training are often accompanied with a narrower view of other individuals who are competent to judge one's work. Specialists in the health professions, law, and academia tend to feel their productive contributions can not be properly evaluated by others that have lesser credentials in their respective profession. Thus a potentially effective motivational tool available to managers of professionals is peer evaluation. Also as their training and credentials increase, individuals are likely to take a more internal view of their assigned work. A major characteristic of professionals who are *internally oriented* is the tendency to take personal credit for job success and responsibility for future job performance.

Professionals with internal orientations exhibit a strong relationship between motivation and overall job satisfaction, i.e., satisfaction with pay, promotion, supervision, etc.[4] Consequently, managers need to pay attention to these variables as they impact on performance among professionals with strong internal orientations as compared with other subordinates that are more externally oriented.

Research on goal setting consistently shows that professional employees are more highly motivated in work environments where goals are present. One study of professional engineers which examined the motivational impact of goal setting and performance found goal setting was clearly superior to non-goal setting, and that frequent feedback had a favorable impact on performance.[5] Another study suggested that organizational processes that encourage high levels of employee commitment in the goal setting procedure are likely to have a positive payoff.[6] Also, supervisors rate employees significantly higher in performance, ability, effort, and goal commitment when high participation exists in the goal setting process.[7] Participation has a positive effect on both the superior and subordinate in professional work environments. Supervisory participation supports skill values of professional subordinates, and subordinate inputs regarding goals builds on these skills and raises commitment. Managerial involvement in goal setting should establish high expectations because supervisory expectation levels have a definite impact on performance.[8]

Beginning in the 1970s, considerable attention was given to the impact of perceived equity among employees on their levels of motivation.[9] Equity approaches argue that employees are motivated by a desire for fairness. Specifically, professionals who believe they are treated unfairly will follow behavior patterns designed to restore their sense of equity. Perception of being underrewarded has a much greater effect on behavior than overreward. Professionals who feel underrewarded and have little influence over the reward process are likely to openly express dissatisfaction, work less, and be absent more frequently than when perceived equity exists.[10] The better, more mobile professionals are likely to seek work elsewhere and leave the organization. A professional work environment that is perceived by employees to equitably distribute rewards is a cornerstone of sustaining high performance, and successful managers attach a high priority on developing it.

Shell, Souder, and Damachi, in their assessment of technical (professional) workers, found that a manager's power and authority influences his or her ability to motivate. They concluded a technical worker's performance can be enhanced by integrating the following principles into the organizational environment:[11]

> The manager's responsibility should include utilizing and controlling the influence process.
>
> Both power and authority should be present in the management structure (Chapter 9).
>
> The legitimate, reward and expert power bases are the most useful in a technical work environment (Chapter 9).
>
> An effective leader utilizes a democratic style modified by the situation (Chapter 9).
>
> An effective leader motivates the technical work force by removing barriers; focusing on problems, not people; providing aids to enhance the opportunity to do a good job; and utilizing a flexible reward system.
>
> People are best motivated using positive factors; e.g., achievement, recognition/advancement, interesting work assignments and the identification of growth possibilities.

It is clear from this introductory overview of motivation that an understanding of the rich body of literature from applied behavioral science can be very helpful to managers of professionals who want to raise performance levels within their organizational units, but it is also important to adapt this knowledge specifically to the professional work environment. Also there is a close relationship between effective leadership skills, as developed in Chapter 9, and motivation. In discussing the supervisor's role in motivating professional subordinates, some researchers suggest that these managers should be strongly encouraged to learn about human relations and motivation because ignorance of this aspect of the managerial role is an invitation to failure.[12] One study of research and development managers which supports these conclusions found that managers who received the highest performance ratings considered their role as a motivator more important than did those managers in lower performance categories.[13] In essence, the manager's concern for motivation among subordinates impacts positively on job performance.

Managers of professionals need to confront the issue of employee motivation directly, and be well versed in the tools and techniques that can provide substantial help in making that confrontation successful. In spite of what many management practitioners believe, there is considerable agreement among leading behavioral scientists on what it takes to motivate today's professional employee. As developed in Chapter 6, employees exhibit clear-cut needs that emerge over a long period of development from infancy to adulthood. Behavioral research has been able to demonstrate clearly that employees are motivated directly by management's ability to link job performance to the satisfaction of these emergent needs. At the outset, two problems often face the manager in accomplishing this task. First, as previously pointed out, these needs are often both different and more complex for professionals than for most other occupational groups. Second, managerial restrictions and controls from outside organizations, such as Civil Service and labor unions, or simply the inability of the manager to focus on the complex needs of professionals can lower motivation in many situations.

A. Basic Managerial Steps in Motivating Professionals

The preceding overview of trends in the study of motivation suggests several steps that managers can take to improve performance levels within their units. Needless to say, successful application of each of these steps will not solve all difficult and complex motivational problems, but a working knowledge of them will be extremely helpful to today's manager. Although these steps apply to many organizational settings, each step will be specifically analyzed in the context of the professional work environment. The primary emphasis will be on practical application rather than theoretical development. Several research studies will be mentioned to document many of the significant conclusions, and provide references for those individuals interested in more in-depth reading. Simply stated, the six steps to successful employee motivation are as follows:

> Proper understanding of the managerial function
> Attaining mutual agreement on job expectations with subordinates and mutual goal setting
> Understanding the relationship between employee selection and motivation
> Developing the ability to apply popular and useful motivation models
> Realizing the complex impact of money on motivation
> Learning how to deal with ineffective performers

These six steps including important support issues are discussed in the sections below.

II. UNDERSTANDING THE MANAGERIAL FUNCTION

The first step needed to motivate any employee is to understand the managerial function. Specifically, it is the function of the manager to manage the work for the employee and *not* to actually do the employee's job. The managerial function is essentially *facilitative* which involves planning, organizing, and providing the support needed so that subordinates can carry out assigned tasks effectively and efficiently. As developed in Chapter 4, all too many managers fail to delegate, or if they do delegate, they continue to try to perform the work for the subordinate. This kind of activity consumes managerial time and energy that should be spent more productively. Energy that should be used to strengthen the planning, organization, and facilitative functions that are so important to sound management practice instead is ultimately interfering with the ability of the subordinates to do the job. Because of their innovative and self-disciplined nature, professionals are very likely to respond negatively to managerial interference. Professionals are often promoted into management from the technical functions that they now supervise. While technical knowledge is useful and necessary, particularly at the lower echelons of management, these managers must learn when and where *not* to apply it. There is a natural tendency for those managers, whose educational training and experience is similar to their subordinates, to be highly reluctant to delegate important job tasks and to continue to perform those duties as managers. A strong conscious effort to learn when and how to delegate is particularly important among professionals, because failure to delegate is often regarded as managerial interference by subordinates (see Chapter 4). In other words, job duties important to subordinate development and satisfaction are being interfered with and largely performed by supervisors. Managerial action of this type is a major factor that reduces the sense of responsibility associated with job performance. In a survey of 282 employees of Texas Instruments, Inc., which included many professionals, Myers found that lack of responsibility was the most detrimental long-term factor that created dissatisfaction.[14]

Since there are only so many hours devoted to work activities in any given time period, managers who perform subordinate tasks are taking critical time away from their planning and organizational activities. Inadequate attention devoted to planning, organizational, and facilitative functions can substantially reduce potential levels of employee motivation.

When supervising professionals it is important to understand the full impact of the managerial function on the development and motivation of subordinates. While more insight into this matter is contained in Chapter 9, four important points are summarized below:

1. All developmental activities that are within the province of the professional's work should be delegated.
2. Avoid performing tasks as a manager that reduce subordinate responsibility.
3. Before performing tasks that are clearly nonmanagerial, be sure to determine if subordinates could perform these same tasks satisfactorily. If they can, managerial time can probably be spent more valuably on other duties, namely, planning, organizing, and facilitating.

4. Be sensitive to cues from subordinates that suggest unwarranted interference with their work.

III. ATTAINMENT OF MUTUAL AGREEMENT ON JOB EXPECTATIONS AND GOAL SETTING

The second step in motivation involves managerial discussion with the subordinate that is designed to reach agreement over job expectations for a given period of time. Reaching agreement with subordinates on duties and responsibilities minimizes interpersonal conflict on sensitive areas between superiors and subordinates, and increases commitment to task through personal interaction. Several studies emphasize the importance of feedback to both good communication and motivation in the professional environment.[15]

Agreement on job duties also helps to keep the subordinates focused on the more important objectives for the departmental unit; without it, subordinates may concentrate on work activities that have been assigned a lower priority by their manager. A well defined agreement on job expectations is a necessary prerequisite to mutual goal setting which is an important part of the useful management tool, management by objectives which is discussed in detail in Chapter 12. As previously suggested, goal setting increases performance levels when done properly and managers need to gain an understanding of what can be accomplished by their individual employees during a given time period. When true give and take occurs in this process employee commitment to task accomplishment tends to increase.

A. Importance of the Facilitative Managerial Role

Once agreement has been reached on an expected level of accomplishment for the subordinate, discussion can then turn to the type of managerial support needed to attain specific objectives. For example, sometimes a manager can make special transportation available for sales calls to clients, provide secretarial help, maintenance, or other types of assistance. All of these things help the manager to be perceived as supportive, which is given very high marks by professionals. It is particularly important that the supervisor be willing to go to bat for employees and to take an interest in their problems. Professionals should feel that it is useful to sit down and talk with superiors about their problems. Research conducted at the University of Michigan shows that these kinds of supervisory practices often determine whether employee and work group attitudes will be favorable or unfavorable.[16]

The preceding analysis suggests it is important for each manager to answer the following question: *Am I managing properly*? Specifically:

> Am I planning work activities so that it is easier for my subordinates to accomplish their assigned tasks?
>
> Have I helped them organize their work?
>
> Have I organized their relationships in the office, laboratory, or production floor so that they have easy access to people or equipment that can help them?
>
> Can they understand how their work relates to the total end product or result desired?
>
> Do I have adequate control mechanisms set up that enable me to determine when their progress is straying off course, so that I can assist them to recover before serious damage occurs, which may result in reprimanding or other negative communication?
>
> Am I taking an interest in my subordinates as people and not simply treating them as instruments of production?
>
> Does the decision making process support their self image and reflect the value of their professional training?

The more these questions are given an affirmative answer, the greater the probability exists that the professional work group will have favorable work attitudes that are likely to result in high levels of sustained motivation. A negative response to any of these questions suggests areas where changes in supervisory practices and behavior should lead to increased effectiveness.

IV. RELATIONSHIP BETWEEN EMPLOYEE SELECTION AND MOTIVATION

The third important step involved in motivating professionals is to clearly understand the role of selection and placement in the motivational process. Many behavioral scientists recognize the fact that the quality of the employee often determines his or her level of motivation. There is considerable evidence that employees with high growth needs (professionals) are motivated by interesting and challenging jobs, but employees with low growth needs are extremely difficult to motivate.[17] As discussed in Chapter 6, an employee who has high intelligence and an extremely mature personality is not going to respond well to a job that is very immature and has little challenge or intrinsic satisfaction associated with its performance. On the other hand, an employee who has immature needs development, which relates to lower intelligence and less education, may respond satisfactorily to a simple job and regard it as challenging. Unfortunately, some employees are not motivated by any job assignment. Managers need to analyze the relative maturity and intrinsic satisfaction contained in the jobs that they are managing, because this is a necessary step in matching the intrinsic nature of these jobs with appropriate individuals whose level of maturity indicates that the job will be satisfying to their own personality needs.

A. Job Enrichment

A strong argument has been made for taking the simple jobs and making them more satisfying and challenging to mature employees because these workers are more flexible and will contribute better quality performance to the organization. This process is commonly referred to as job enrichment. Job enrichment can increase the motivational level of mature employees.[17] When current practices seem to be resulting in increased time pressure, reduced autonomy, and little performance feedback, modifications in managerial practices should be considered. Job redesign (enrichment) is useful when there is little challenge or intrinsic satisfaction associated with the specific task assignments, and when employees are permitted little control over work methods.[18]

While job enrichment is at least a partial answer to dealing with the rising educational level of today's professional, enrichment programs often involve significant dollar costs to the organization. Alber obtained information from 189 companies and six government agencies that indicates five major costs are commonly associated with job enrichment.[19] These costs include pressure for increased wages and salaries by "enriched" workers with new modified job duties. When jobs are modified and made more complex, more floor area or storage space is needed in several instances. This additional space can be translated into increased cost of facilities. Also, inventory costs may rise because larger parts inventories are needed to accommodate differing processes.[19] Training and implementation costs can rise as special or new training is needed for the existing supervisory or trained staff, and some firms report that outside consultants were hired to assist with new training needs.[19]

The nature of many professional job assignments makes them conducive to job enrichment without excessive facility changes; consequently, many of these enrichment costs will be lower in professional work units. Nevertheless, each manager should be aware of possible increased costs and approach job enrichment decisions with adequate time and caution. The decision-making process outlined in Chapter 5 can be useful in organizing these kinds of decisions. Since many firms in the Alber study experienced several benefits from their job enrichment efforts, this decision can be difficult. In fact, increased production and improved quality and greater job satisfaction were related to job enrichment in a large number of the firms.[19] Some of these firms also experienced a reduction in employee turnover and absenteeism. Thus, as is the case with most complex decisions, managers must weigh the potential costs of enriching jobs against probable benefits in order to determine the impact of a job enrichment program on organizational effectiveness.

The work of Hackman, Oldham, Janson, Purdy, and others provide five specific characteristics of enriched jobs, i.e., jobs which give the worker a sense of meaningfulness and responsibility in performing the work.[20] Janson has put these dimensions in a pragmatic framework useful to professionals.[21] Individuals who perform jobs with the following characteristics are more likely to experience higher degrees of job satisfaction and internal motivation. Job assignments that contain a high degree of *skill variety* are viewed as being more meaningful. Professionals need work that requires different skills, and managers can accomplish this by putting together separate tasks for each work assignment. Their assignments should provide *task identity*, namely, the job requires completion of a "whole" piece of work that has a clearly identifiable outcome. Managers need to look for natural units of work to assign to professionals. It is important that professionals feel that their work is *significant*. Significance is increased when work is perceived to have a substantial impact on the work of others. In fact, if client relationships are established, task significance increases. Fortunately the nature of many task assignments to professionals contains a "built in" client relationship. For example, client relationships are a basic characteristic of professional positions in both health and academic professionals. Finally, professionals need *autonomy* and *frequent feedback* in performing their work. Effective managers need to practice involvement management (see Chapter 12) and design performance appraisal systems based on performance standards that provide regular information to both the professional employee and manager when jobs are done well. The facilitative managerial role discussed earlier in this chapter raises levels of both autonomy and feedback for the employee.

While the five job characteristics discussed above apply to most employees, they are particularly congruent with the individual needs structure of professionals. In fact, their managers need to be, in part, miniature personnel managers who understand managerial functions and the problem of selecting employees whose needs match the job for which they are responsible. When this match does not occur, managers need to modify the job or change the employee. Ideally changes should always move toward more enriched jobs that will satisfy mature professionals.

V. POPULAR AND USEFUL MOTIVATION MODELS

As a fourth step in the motivation process, it is desirable to be able to apply the most useful elements of the most practical motivation models. Several behavioral scientists have made substantial contributions toward understanding human motivation since the 1950s. Among the most useful motivation models that have current widespread applicability to professionals are Maslow and Alderfer's Needs Theories, McGregor's Theory X and Theory Y, Herzberg's Motivational Hygiene Theory, and Vroom's Expectancy Theory of Motivation.[22] A study of 300 practicing personnel managers in the United States indicates that the content of McGregor's approach is familiar to approximately 9 out of 10 of the managers surveyed.[23] Herzberg's Motivation Hygiene Theory ranks a close second in this same survey, and Maslow's Hierarchy of Needs ranks a respectable third. Eighty-seven percent of the managers surveyed are familiar with Herzberg's work, and eighty-three percent are familiar with the work of Maslow. Thus, three of the four motivation models are very widely known, and the Vroom model is becoming increasingly familiar to practicing managers.

A. Needs Theory: Maslow and Alderfer

Since the Maslow model is a good categorization of the specific needs of individuals and Alderfer's work contributes to a greater understanding of the complexity of employee needs structures, both models were developed in the section of Chapter 6 that presented individual needs development. These same models also provide an excellent beginning to the understanding of human performance because they introduce an assumption about motivation that is agreed to by most behavioral scientists. This assumption simply stated is that "all behavior is a function of needs satisfaction," namely, employees are motivated to the extent they perceive that performance of a given act will relate to the satisfaction of a specific need. Moreover, Maslow indicates that satisfied needs do not motivate. Basic physiological and safety needs which make up the lower part of the Maslow hierarchy are the strongest potential motivators. Since almost all current professional work environments satisfy these needs, the upper level needs which include ego, self-esteem, and status offer the greatest motivational potential.

Several elements of the Maslow Hierarchy of Needs model have been subjected to empirical testing with mixed results. While some components relate to increased effectiveness under given sets of conditions, other elements have been suspect. Nevertheless, Maslow's approach does show that the upper level needs are motivators for the majority of professionals, and managers who take steps to satisfy these needs by initiating both environmental change and altering management style can improve performance. Alderfer's Existence, Relatedness, Growth (ERG) Theory agrees with the satisfaction-progression process of Maslow, but suggests that a frustration-regression process is also at work. A person who is frustrated with attempts to satisfy growth needs will redirect activities to increase satisfaction of lower level needs. Increased satisfaction of these lower needs can then compensate for frustration of higher needs and motivation levels can be sustained. However, the comparative high level of importance attached to growth needs by professionals may make this regression less likely or attractive than it is for non-professionals.

B. McGregor's Theory X and Theory Y

An understanding of Douglas M. McGregor's Theory X and Theory Y is helpful in providing direction to the proper modification of management style and organizational environment. This approach places considerable emphasis on the organizational environment as a primary factor in determining levels of motivation.[24] McGregor's argument is that practicing managers have traditionally been very reluctant to allow workers any amount of freedom in performing their jobs because they believe that workers are inherently lazy and will take advantage of management by doing little work unless they are closely supervised or policed while on the job. McGregor identifies this conventional approach to management as Theory X. He maintains that Theory X management stifles creativity, and instead of increasing output and motivation, it actually reduces effectiveness because it is human nature to resist this type of control.

The application of Theory X insults the worker's intelligence, which McGregor believes is greater than managers are willing to accept. In contrast, McGregor proposes that management create a freer environment that enables workers to fully utilize their intrinsic abilities. This new environment trusts the worker's willingness to work, thereby minimizing the need for close supervision, and creates jobs that are more challenging and interesting because it introduces greater amounts of worker responsibility.

While McGregor's conclusions can be questioned in some or-ganizational situations, they seem to have particular applicability to professionals. Several studies have already been cited which in-dicate that professionals prefer large amounts of autonomy and work best in an environment that is conducive to responsibility, growth, and recognition which is precisely the type of environment that McGregor proposes for Theory Y.

C. The Great Jackass Fallacy

Harry Levinson concludes that in spite of all that has been written about motivation managers continue to rely heavily on two primary means to motivate employees, namely, the carrot and stick.[25] The carrot provides the reward, but if this fails, the stick is used to punish individuals that exhibit uncooperative behavior. This approach is similar to what has been traditionally applied to motivate a "jack-ass," and the employee is, consequently, being managed in much the same fashion. While the "jackass" is often resistant and does not respond to these techniques, human beings are likely to present an even greater problem.

Since employees are (usually) more intelligent than jackasses, they not only fail to respond to these two motivational techniques, but often *outsmart* the management. As Levinson points out, they devise ways to get the carrot and avoid the stick. Since the carrot is primarily measured in dollars, management continues to pay more money for less performance. For example, common job security pro-visions in collective bargaining agreements and Civil Service regula-tions make it extremely difficult for employers to discharge poorly motivated employees or even to use milder forms of disciplinary action. On the other hand, these same bargaining agreements historically have provided substantial wage and fringe benefit packages that apply to all employees covered in the contract.

Due to competitive pressure, precedent, and because it often breeds less conflict, managers are likely to distribute rewards on an even basis among subordinates. These same pressures, coupled with a strong sense of professionalism, may make managers reluctant to punish problem performers. The end result is that those employees who do less are often protected from the stick, but are still able to get their average share of the carrot. Consequently, there is a logical argument that strongly suggests the carrot and stick approaches to motivation are often not effective, particularly among professionals. The two motivational techniques of the jackass fallacy are important elements of conventional management as described in McGregor's Theory X.

Levinson argues that a better approach to motivation focuses on employee needs and stresses the fact that effective managers should attempt to understand the needs structure of their employees. The organizational environment should be supportive of those needs for motivation to take place.

D. McClelland's Learned Needs Theory

McClelland has developed an approach to motivation based on learned needs that is particularly applicable to professional work environments. Three of the needs most commonly associated with McClelland's work are needs for *achievement* (n ach), *affiliation* (n aff), and *power* (n pow)![26] The strengths of each of these needs varies from individual to individual, and are acquired from one's cultural background. Professionals tend to be high in n ach and respond to challenging goals, and engage in activities that utilize their abilities and acquired skills. One study designed to raise achievement levels of businessmen including many with professional characteristics yielded long term positive motivational results.[27] Another relevant aspect of McClelland's work concludes that increasing amounts of n pow are needed to make successful managerial decisions.[28] As stated earlier in this chapter, power relates positively to motivation, and professionals who make the transition into management need to shift their needs orientation more in the direction of power rather than achievement. This shift is not that difficult for many who may already have experienced power (which may have attracted them to management activities), but for others who are promoted into management solely because of outstanding achievements as professional employees the needed shift may be more difficult to accomplish.

E. Motivation Hygiene Theory

Frederick Herzberg developed his Motivation Hygiene Theory in the mid 1950s, and this approach has gained a considerable following and some empirical testing over the years. Herzberg maintained that the work environment could be divided into two sets of factors as follows: First, factors that lead to employee growth and development; namely, recognition, advancement, achievement, and the job itself, which he defined as motivators. Second, according to Herzberg, the environment also contains hygiene factors such as wages, working conditions, company policy and supervision, which essentially maintain the work place for the employee.[29] One of the basic elements in the Herzberg approach is that hygiene factors affect job dissatisfaction and improving hygiene reduces dissatisfaction for a given employee. In contrast, motivators affect job satisfaction, and employee motivation is a function of the level of job satisfaction. Herzberg maintains that job satisfaction and job dissatisfaction are two mutually exclusive factors in the organizational environment.[29] A central point in his theory is that motivation is not increased by manipulating the hygiene factors, but can only be improved through the application and development of motivational factors. This process, as indicated earlier in this chapter, is known as job enrichment, which has been shown to impact favorably on motivation. From 1954 to 1958, Herzberg and his associates at the Psychological Service of Pittsburgh interviewed approximately 200 professionals, (engineers and accountants) employed in industrial firms in the Pittsburgh area in order to gain insight into the relationship between job attitudes and performance. Each respondent was asked to discuss a time when he or she felt exceptionally good or exceptionally bad about his or her job, and to identify the factor(s) most responsible for those feelings. The five most commonly mentioned causes of dissatisfaction (bad feelings) were company policy, technical supervision, salary, supervisory relationships, and working conditions. The five satisfiers (good feelings) mentioned most frequently were achievement, recognition, the work itself, responsibility, and advancement.[30] Since the differences between engineers and accountants were negligible with regard to dissatisfiers and only moderately significant among the satisfiers, these findings are useful to managers of professionals.[30] They specifically support the fact that Herzberg's factors that contribute to motivation and dissatisfaction are applicable to the professional work environment.

Davis conducted a similar study of 36 professionals in a Phoenix electronics firm.[31] Each professional was asked through a questionnaire to report in detail a situation resulting in unfavorable feelings about the job. These data generally support Herzberg's findings. The same factors show up as motivators (satisfiers) and hygiene (dissatisfiers) as in previous studies, including Herzberg's. Also, salary was neutral, which is consistent with other research data. For example, a dozen studies involving 1685 employees in a variety of occupations found salary to rank only slightly higher as a hygiene factor than as a motivator.[32] Apparently, wages can be either a motivator or hygiene factor which places them in a unique category. The role of remuneration in motivation will be given special attention later in this chapter.

Achievement was the most frequently identified motivator, which is consistent with Myers' survey of a group of professionals at Texas Instruments, Inc.[33] Myers also found that recognition is a relatively stronger motivator for scientists than for engineers at Texas Instruments, but advancement provided stronger incentive for engineers than scientists.

Since empirical evidence indicates the applicability of the Herzberg approach to professionals, knowledge of this theory of motivation is particularly important to managers of professionals. Managerial attention to providing a professional work environment in which achievement, recognition, and advancement flourish can substantially raise performance levels. Supervisors who take a special interest in the design of jobs and can provide tasks that are both challenging and rewarding should also attain high payoffs.

F. Similarities and Differences Among Motivation Theories

Some of the important similarities among McGregor's approach, Herzberg's Motivation Hygiene Theory, Maslow and Alderfer's needs theories, and McClelland's Learned Theory are depicted in Figure 8.1. These models all emphasize the growth needs of individuals and imply that a democratic or involvement style of management will be effective in raising the level of employee performance. As can be seen in Figure 8.1, an integrated relationship exists among these approaches to motivation. Alderfer and Maslow focus on the identification and development of individual needs, Herzberg puts these needs in the context of the job and supervision, McGregor stresses the importance of the total organizational environment, and McClelland identifies differences in needs strength. Each approach supports the other; McGregor's environmental factors foster the development of Herzberg's motivational factors, which in turn relate to the satisfaction of higher level needs.

There are also important differences in these three approaches. For example, while needs theory assumes that any need can be a motivator if it is relatively unsatisfied, Herzberg argues that only higher level needs serve as motivators; and that a worker can be relatively dissatisfied in both higher order and lower order needs simultaneously. Alderfer and Maslow's lower order needs are similar to Herzberg's hygiene factors.

The level of dissatisfaction can become so great that motivational factors are meaningless. For example, although wages may be considered a special case, if the average annual compensation for a specific type of professional in a given geographical location is in excess of $60,000, a professional in this area with similar training and experience that receives only $40,000 annually might not respond to motivational factors. The lower rate of pay received

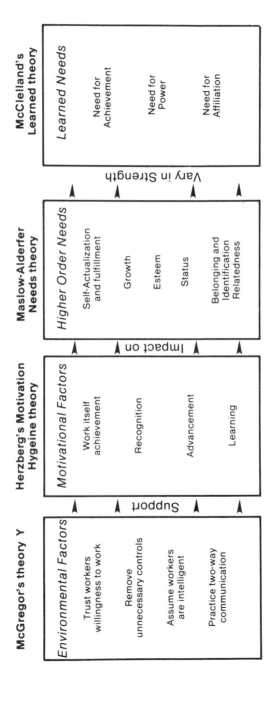

Figure 8.1   Basic similarities among McGregor's Theory Y, Herzberg's Motivation Hygiene Theory, Maslow-Alderfer Needs Theory, and McClelland's Learned Theory.

relative to other similar professionals would result in so much dissatisfaction that job enrichment activities would be useless. Similarly, company policy or working conditions may be so poor that employees do not respond to either recognition or interesting task assignments.

It must be pointed out that empirical testing of Herzberg's model does not prove its validity in many situations. As previously indicated, Herzberg clearly separates satisfiers and dissatisfiers. The satisfiers which include achievement recognition and the job itself are assumed to contribute primarily to job satisfaction. Conversely the dissatisfiers which include company policies and pay are assumed to almost exclusively influence job dissatisfaction. The traditional approach emphasizes that if the presence of a factor contributes to satisfaction and that factor is removed, job dissatisfaction will result. Graen's detailed analysis of nine employee groups supported the traditional approach which includes a unidimensional theory of job satisfaction where some variables have a more potent effect upon satisfaction than others and satisfaction-dissatisfaction are on the same continuum.[34]

Even when full consideration is given to the questionable validity of many of the assumptions upon which two-factor theory is based, it is still a very useful contribution in the understanding of employee motivation. Specifically it helps to put part of the work of Alderfer, Maslow, and McGregor in a more meaningful context. It stresses the importance of higher order needs and the environmental factors of job enrichment which are part of the McGregor's Theory Y, and focuses on the specific needs in the Maslow model that have the greatest potential for motivation. Herzberg's motivational factors are particularly important to professionals; and their managers should help provide a work environment that encourages the development and use of recognition, advancement, achievement, and growth, as well as an interesting and challenging job.

G. Application of the Herzberg Theory

Herzberg has provided clues as to how this model can be applied, and some of his most useful points follow.[35] (1) Eliminate simple and nonchallenging job responsibilities when possible; (2) communicate directly with employees, thereby minimizing levels and distortions in the communication process; (3) delegate to subordinates a considerable degree of responsibility for their work; (4) allow and encourage employees to become specialists in their fields of interest; (5) if the employee serves a client, encourage that client relationship to become personal and rewarding; (6) reward and recognize subordinates who do outstanding work. Since many of these suggestions can be applied without additional financial or administrative support, they are valuable to all supervisors who manage professionals. Herzberg's points support the enrichment of jobs done by professionals that were advocated earlier in this chapter. There is considerable research evidence that indicates that scientists who engage in a variety of work are more productive.[36] Thus, when managers encourage subordinates to be specialists in their fields of interest, they must be careful that the end result is not narrow specialization with little variety. In direct support of Herzberg, studies show that professionals have more job satisfaction when there is more challenge in their jobs.[37] A variety of interesting and challenging work assignments among subordinates will reduce the motivational problems that confront the manager in the professional organization.

H. Vroom's Expectancy Theory

The Expectancy Theory of Motivation initially developed by Vroom and refined by Lawler and Porter and others is a motivational model that is receiving increasing attention by managers.[38] The model is based on the assumption that motivation is a product of the needs one seeks to fulfill and a preception by that individual that certain acts will lead to the fulfillment of those needs. In general, expectancy is the belief that a particular act will yield a particular outcome. For example, if a human resources professional believes that hard work will result in highly rated performance, then a strong expectation exists regarding hard work and positive performance evaluation.

The Vroom model attempts to determine those outcomes that are pleasurable and those that are painful by including the concept

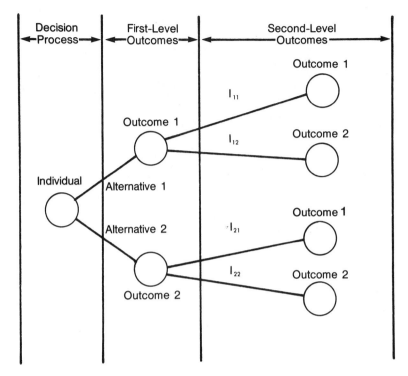

Figure 8.2   Diagram of individual choice alternatives for the Vroom model.

of second-level outcomes.[39] The second-level outcomes are events that happen based on the course of action from the first-level outcome as shown in Figure 8.2. The method of determining preferences for first-level outcomes makes use of two terms, *valence* and *instrumentality.*

Valence refers to the strength of a person's preference for one outcome versus other possible outcomes. Those outcomes that are strongly desired, such as advancement or recognition, would have very high valences, and less preferable outcomes would have lower valences. Examples of outcomes of lower preference could include a minor change in management policy or a rearrangement of office furniture. If an individual has no preference for an outcome, the valence would then be zero; or if it were preferred that an outcome did not happen, then the valence would have a negative value.

Instrumentality indicates an individual's perception of the relationship between a first- and second-level outcome. In the previous example, if hard work and good performance are perceived to likely yield a promotion, there is a high degree of instrumentality present. Thus, promotion would be the second-level outcome. Expectancy differs from instrumentality in that it relates efforts to first-level outcomes, whereas instrumentality relates first- and second-level outcomes to each other. For example, if an accountant believes that he or she has the ability to be perceived as doing a good job, then that person would possess a high degree of expectancy. If good performance is perceived by this accountant as leading to a promotion, then a high degree of instrumentality would be present. If promotion is a highly valued end result, this employee is likely to be motivated to do good work. Thus, both instrumentality and expectancy are critical factors in determining performance behavior patterns.

I. Usefulness and Application of Expectancy Theory

There have been several studies by Vroom, Galbraith, Cummings, and Hill that give credibility to the Vroom model. Specifically, research supports Vroom's contention that motivation is related to productivity in those situations where the acquisition of desired goals is related to one's individual production.[40] It is clear that reinforcement is a vital factor in Vroom's approach, and it is continuously necessary for managers to provide instrumentality by rewarding employees for good performance. Several authorities on motivation including Lawler stress the vital importance of relating rewards to employee performance.[41] Considering the work of Maslow, Argyris, and others, there are a variety of methods for satisfying higher level needs which are the desired outcomes that expectancy theory often is based on. In fact, there are more vehicles available to managers for satisfying higher level needs than lower level needs, because these needs are never completely satisfied for normal employees.[42] The typical professional never reaches a point of complete satisfaction with his or her accomplishments because as one set of job goals is attained, new goals which require different and often greater accomplishment take their place. Most professional employees are capable of being continuously motivated by managers who help them realize their goals, recognize their accomplishments, and then provide aid in setting new work-related goals that will provide even greater internal satisfaction.

Although expectancy theory has had widespread support among academic researchers, some of its assumptions have been questioned by research evidence. The original Vroom model posited that the level of motivational force acting on an employee was the product of multiplying the model's valence and expectancy variables. Namely, increases in expectancy should result in proportionate increases in motivation. However, more recent research indicates that increases in expectancy may result in disproportionately small increases in motivation.[43] Studies also indicate many individuals exhibit a significant level of motivation even when their expectancy of success is small or zero, and increases in the expectancy of success result in declining marginal increases in motivation.[44] These findings do not reduce the usefulness of expectancy theory to the manager of professionals, rather they indicate additional complexities. As Harnell and Stahl suggest, the expectancy valence model can explain the value that individuals associate with first level outcomes, but it is likely that some editing process occurs regarding alternatives and outcomes.[44] Also, expectancy theory can explain the level of motivational force acting on an individual but many individuals employ additive information processing. It is this additive information process that may result in sustained motivation when expectancy levels are very low. For example, a given professional may look at job alternatives, supervisory relationships, location, etc., in making a final decision about performance levels.

J. The Performance-Satisfaction Relationship

The work of Porter and Lawler makes an important contribution to the understanding of how performance and satisfaction interact to increase or decrease motivation levels among professionals. They start with the assumption that motivation does not equal satisfaction or performance, but is a function of several aspects of the work environment which include reward and performance.[45] Of particular importance to managers of professionals is the emphasis placed on equitable rewards and job satisfaction. Assuming employees have the ability and desire rewards (valence in expectancy theory), they will put forth the effort (motivation). Of course rewards can be both internal (job) and external (environment) when the result (given level of performance) is rewarded, leading to satisfaction or dissatisfaction. Satisfaction is not only determined by the actual rewards received but also by the perceived equity associated with these rewards. When perceived equity is high, satisfaction results. Thus, performance which is perceived to be rewarded equitably yields satisfaction. Continued employee satisfaction loops back into the system and either sustains or raises levels of motivation. In a study designed to identify important features of an engineer's or a scientist's work relating to productivity, Vincent and Mirakhor found that a statistically significant relationship existed between productivity and job satisfaction.[46]

Overall, management activities that increase job satisfaction will impact favorably on motivation. The preceding simplified explanation of the interrelationship among these variables is useful. Specifically, professionals need to perceive that rewards are distributed equitably within the organization if motivation is to be sustained. Therefore, considerable managerial attention should be directed at achieving equity. Also, employee selection should identify workers who have the potential to perform assigments successfully.

VI. DOES MONEY MOTIVATE?

The fifth step to successful employee motivation requires the manager to understand the complex issue of how money influences the individual. This is not as simple as one might initially believe. A major determinant of perceived equity involves the handling of remuneration among professionals. In fact, money is often seen as the cornerstone of perceived equity in an organizational environment.

If money is improperly handled by the manager, and its distribution is seen as unfair, then the perceived favorableness of the organizational environment by employees may be reduced to such a low level that other motivational factors simply do not work effectively. It is fallacious to assume that since professionals are self-disciplined, well-educated, and achievement oriented, money is of little importance to them. Money, in fact, measures many of their achievements, and because of their high degree of intelligence and education, they are quick to perceive any inequities that may exist in the remuneration process.

The proper use of wages and salaries substantially increases managerial effectiveness. Some helpful points about constructive management of the remuneration process are as follows:

1. Managers should retain control over some "dollar pool" for merit increases that is distributed periodically to professional employees for good performance.
2. Managers should clearly communicate to these employees the criteria that will be used in the distribution of merit increases. It is desirable to solicit input from professional employees in the development of these criteria.
3. Effective wage and salary administration is a continuous process, and attempts should constantly be made to have wage and salary equity within the employee group. Equitable wage and salary conditions usually have two fundamental characteristics: First, a direct relationship exists between perceived skill requirements, job difficulty, and pay scales; and second, both seniority and good performance are recognized with salary increments.
4. Most professionals see wage reductions as seriously threatening their self-esteem, and strongly resist any action that reduces their pay. Obviously, motivation, morale, and performance can be adversely affected. When individual employees are overpaid, it is often necessary to handle these problems through natural

attrition and the granting of smaller pay raises than those amounts given to other employees.

5. Although it may be corporate policy that individual wages and salaries are to be kept secret, this secrecy cannot be guaranteed. In fact, if significant inequities exist they will probably surface and will have to be dealt with. Consequently, wage and salary equity is vitally important in all organizations.

6. Always consider the impact of specific salary adjustments, merit increases, or bonuses on other employees. The impact of these ''money'' decisions are not isolated to the professionals who receive them, but usually spread throughout the entire employee group. An excellent example of this would be the large bonuses received by executives in the U.S. automotive industry during the mid 1980s.

7. The demand for wage increases by professionals may be symptomatic of more complex problems associated with the organizational climate. Since wages are very tangible and measurable, wage increases are often requested to compensate for other deficiencies that are less tangible and harder to verbalize. For example, subordinates may be dissatisfied with the management practices of their supervisors, but find it difficult to describe or complain about them. Thus, as an alternative, they request more money. In this case, however, granting a wage increase will not solve their basic problem. In order to be most effective, managers should try to identify the real problem(s) when money requests appear to be symptomatic of other issues.

Money is a complex element in the motivational process. Although the role of money is often de-emphasized by many behavioral scientists, it is vital to employee motivation. Money is important for several reasons. First, it provides a measure of recognition, status, advancement, and achievement. Second, it is tangible and measurable by its recipient. And third, it is the variable that often can be easily manipulated by the management of a given organization. Since it can have a positive role in reinforcing many of the motivational elements, and since in many instances it can be manipulated by the management, it may substantially raise levels of motivation among subordinates. Conversely, careless handling of remuneration issues can have a negative effect on employee performance.

VII. HANDLING THE PROBLEM PROFESSIONAL

Finally, the sixth step to successful employee motivation requires that the manager recognize and take corrective action when a professional employee is performing ineffectively. During any given period of time, individual and/or group motivation may substantially decline, creating personnel problems for the manager and the organization. While a decline in motivation can occur at any stage in one's career, it is often associated with advancing age and tenure on the job. One study of 2500 professionals in seven large organizations found a negative correlation after age 35 between age and performance rating.[47] Specifically, professionals over 35 are more likely to receive lower performance ratings by their superiors. It is not automatic that older employees will become less effective performers, because this same study found that the top third of the professionals over 50 were almost as highly valued as the top third in any group.[47] Ineffective performers can be found in any employee age group and although easy or total solutions to these problems do not usually exist, there are some managerial actions that can be helpful. An attempt should be made to categorize the causes of poor performance. Causes that are related to organizational climate or management can often be corrected.

There are several causes of employee problems among professionals. These causes may occur independently of each other or in combination. Most problems associated with professionals at work are related to skill deficiency or poor attitudes. Skill deficiencies are easier to handle because they can often be corrected by additional training or employee transfer. Attitude problems are more difficult for managers to solve because their causes are usually complex and may be hidden. Managers need to identify the cause of the problem as soon as possible after the problem has surfaced. Once the cause is determined, appropriate corrective action should be taken. Allowing problem behavior to continue while causes are being investigated makes attaining satisfactory solutions more difficult. Several steps to help managers succeed in resolving problem behavior are outlined below:

1. The manager should remain calm and confront the employee. Identify the problem explaining why it concerns you and express your desire for change. Don't allow the discussion to become "person centered," keep it problem oriented. Address the employee specifically regarding the problem and focus the discussion on finding a solution. For example, "John, your level of absenteeism is too high for you to be successful at your work. I am having trouble covering your assignments when you are away, and as a result our important production schedules are not being met. Let's explore possible solutions to this problem together."

2. Try to get the employee to explain the reasons for this behavior. Open questions are most appropriate at this stage, e.g., "John, could you tell me why you have missed so many work days recently?" Utilize listening skills developed in Chapter 7 at this stage.

3. Ask for the employee's ideas for solving the problem. Remember the basic behavioral principle stated earlier that employees are more likely to change in directions that they suggest themselves.

4. Offer your help as manager and press for agreement on an action plan. In closing the discussion suggest a time for a future meeting to discuss the employee's progress.

Throughout this entire process express support and reassurance. Maintaining the self-esteem of the employee is a basic part of changing problem behavior caused by poor attitudes. Two rules that can be applied to preserve self-esteem are not to allow the discussion to focus on personal traits as causes, and to maintain the objective of reaching agreement on potential solutions before the discussion is terminated. Kindness, firmness, and tact by the manager are helpful in attaining agreement.[48] A kind and friendly posture encourages employee loyalty and helps preserve attachment to the organization. Tact supports self worth and firmness helps to keep the discussion problem centered. Also maintain some social distance between yourself and the problem employee.

Successful counselling requires finding a proper balance between distance and intimacy in the counselling relationship. Maintain high levels of dignity throughout the discussion. Dignity relates closely to your respect for the firm, and job as well as your employees' jobs. Professionals respond most favorably to this kind of environment. Dignity helps to keep a proper gap between you and your employee, but also respects his or her territory and position within the firm.[48] Also, remain courteous; courtesy is the simple use of good manners which show respect for the other person.

Some other tips in handling the problem professional are as follows:

1. If the problem is psychologically based, determine if the employee will accept help. If so, make attempts to provide appropriate professional counselling. In some instances these skills are available within the organizational unit; however, it may be both necessary and worthwhile to go outside the company to obtain the best professional aid.

2. Recognize the importance of a dual promotional system in motivating older employees. Many professionals become dismayed when they find that they must become managers to receive continued advancement and recognition in their firm.

3. If the causes of poor performance are unrelated to or beyond the control of management, the alternatives of transfer, early retirement, or discharge should be considered. Older employees who are ineffective can

sometimes be given financial inducements to retire, which are less costly than inefficiencies resulting from retaining them. Younger employees that hold strategic positions where their poor performance disrupts the work of colleagues may be transferred or discharged. Specific reasons for transfer or discharge should be well documented by the manager.

4. Large numbers of ineffective performers often suggest poor placement policies or the need for better training and work orientation programs. If managerial analysis suggests that either of these conditions is causative, corrective action should be taken promptly.

5. Large numbers of ineffective performers may also indicate poor management of that unit. There are cases where an individual has been promoted into a management position that is totally unsuited, i.e., the employees are ok but the manager is faulty. In this situation, higher level management must take corrective action with the manager to resolve the problem.

Correcting these kinds of performance problems requires a considerable amount of managerial time, insight, and courage. However, the ability to meet the problem of ineffective performance in a direct manner is an important characteristic of an outstanding manager.

VIII. BUILDING THE PROPER MOTIVATIONAL ENVIRONMENT

Managers in professional environments can benefit from the motivation models discussed throughout this chapter. As can be seen in Fig. 8.3 managerial attention should be given to the higher level needs of these employees. Professionals have high needs for autonomy and freedom in their environment, and they seek recognition for achievement often in the form of increased status and advancement. Managerial practices have a lot to do with how well these needs are perceived as being met. Anything the manager can

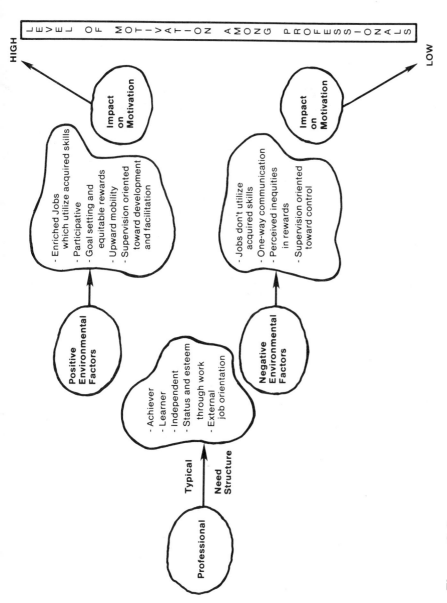

Figure 8.3 Motivational impact of alternative work environments.

do to relieve restrictions, make the work environment more autonomous, and at the same time provide some semblance of effective control over output is an essential part of being effective.

Unfortunately, there is considerable evidence that many managers of professionals are failing to accomplish these managerial tasks. A poll and in-depth interview conducted a number of years ago by the Opinion Research Corporation on job satisfaction among industrial scientists and engineers revealed that only 34 percent were well satisfied.[49] In this same study, a survey of a subsample of engineers and scientists who were considered the most valuable by company management found that only 42 percent were well satisfied with their jobs. Thus, a majority felt that they were misunderstood and had little input to management. Managers were not perceived as doing an effective job, even by their most valued professionals. Moreover, there is little evidence that these attitudes are improving as rapidly as needed. A more recent study of several hundred engineers and scientists who had left their previous jobs showed that the single most important reason for leaving was the absence of motivational factors.[50] Insufficient use of acquired skills and lack of opportunity for advancement were specific factors cited as causing turnover among these professionals. It has been emphasized throughout this chapter that these factors are motivational in nature.

Freedom and autonomy within the organizational environment permit subordinates to utilize their acquired skills, but some control is needed to move the organization toward its goals. Pelz and Andrews suggest that both freedom and coordination are compatible and desirable for professionals.[51] Generally, they support the conclusions of Likert that employees in higher producing departments believe that they exert considerable influence on decisions that affect them. The new trend toward involvement management that is developed in detail in Chapter 12 reflects the fact that organizations are actively seeking to build this kind of environment, and specific tools and knowledge needed to increase employee professional involvement are contained in this later chapter. For example, management by objectives which is an effective tool for accomplishing the difficult but important managerial task of providing an environment characterized by freedom, coordination, and control is analyzed. One survey of problems in supervising professionals revealed that two major difficulties were insufficient definition of company objectives by top management and the related inability of lower level personnel to define problems.[52] Wherever possible, mutual goal setting should take place and rewards should be related to performance based on an effective periodic review. It is not uncommon for managers to be perceived by their subordinates as being bureaucratic pencil-and-paper pushers who set up obstacles to the accomplishment of important work. Conversely, these managers see the subordinate as being a specialist who lacks concern for efficiency and is not cost conscious. Management by objectives provides a framework for effectively addressing these problems.

It is clear that a specific managerial climate is optimal for motivational purposes. Some of the most useful characteristics of that climate are high trust, open communication, mutual goal setting, and economic reward that is equitable and based in large part on goal attainment. Managers who recognize the importance of climate and take steps to develop it are working in a constructive manner to solve current or potential problems involving morale, motivation, and performance.

IX. SUMMARY

The analysis of motivation contained in this chapter, which has ranged from understanding the managerial function to applying the more useful elements of current models, clearly suggests that motivation is not simply an application of the golden rule. Also, it is not solely a function of the personality of the people involved, and therefore unrelated to specific skills that can be learned and acquired by the manager. If managers go through the steps outlined and make a sincere attempt to understand the current state-of-the-art knowledge concerning the motivational process, they can substantially improve performance within their units and make their jobs as managers much more enjoyable and rewarding. In essence, the intrinsic job satisfaction that is so important to motivation can be greatly enhanced for the manager who makes a strong effort to understand the complexity of the motivational process and to apply the useful knowledge that has been developed regarding this intricate but important problem. Finally, a careful reading of Chapter 12 can be a valuable supplement to building an understanding of the environment needed when large numbers of professional employees are involved.

REFERENCES

1. A comprehensive account of the Hawthorne Studies is found in F.J. Roethlisberger and W.J. Dickson, *Management and the Worker,* Harvard University Press, Cambridge, Mass., 1939.

2. Donald C. Pelz and Frank M. Andrews, *Scientists in Organizations,* University of Michigan Institute for Social Research, Ann Arbor, MI, 1976, p. 7.

3. Lee E. Danielson, *Characteristics of Engineers and Scientists Significant for Their Motivation,* University of Michigan Press, Ann Arbor, MI, 1960.

4. D.R. Norris and R.E. Niebuhr, "Attributional Influences on the Job Performance—Job Satisfaction Relationship," *Academy of Management Journal,* Vol. 27, No. 2, June 1984, pp. 424-431.

5. J.M. Ivancevich and J.T. McMahon, "The Effects of Goal Setting, and Self Generated Feedback on Outcome Variables: A Field Experiment," *Academy of Management Journal,* Vol. 25, No. 2, June 1982, pp. 359-372.

6. Jay S. Kim, "Effect of Behavior Plus Outcome Goal Setting and Feedback on Employee Satisfaction and Performance," *Academy of Management Journal,* Vol. 27, No. 1, March 1984, pp. 139-149.

7. D.L. Dossett and C.I. Greenburg, "Goal Setting and Performance Evaluation: An Attributional Analysis," *Academy of Management Journal,* Vol. 24, No. 4, December 1981, pp. 767-779.

8. For discussion of this issue see D. Eden, "Self Fulfilling Prophecy as a Management Tool! Harnessing Pygmalion," *Academy of Management Review,* Vol. 9, No. 1, January 1984, pp. 64-73.

9. For a discussion of equity theory see M.R. Carrell and J.E. Dittrich, "Equity Theory The Recent Literature, Methodological Considerations and New Directions," *Academy of Management Review,* No. 3, 1978, pp. 202-210.

10. T.R. Mitchell, "Motivation: New Directions for Theory Research and Practice," *Academy of Management Review,* Vol. 7, No. 1, January 1982.

11. Richard L. Shell, H. Ray Souder, and Nicholas A. Damachi, "Using Behavioral and Influence Factors to Motivate the Technical Worker," *Industrial Engineering,* Vol. 15, No. 8, August 1983.

12. G.C. Bucher and R.C. Gray, "Principles of Motivation and How to Apply Them," *Research Management,* Vol. XIV, No. 3, May 1971, pp. 15-22.

13. Joseph A. Steger, G. Manners, A.J. Bernstein, and R. May, "The Three Dimensions of the R. & D. Managers Job," *Research Management,* Vol. XVIII, No. 3, May 1975, pp. 32-37.

14. M. Scott Myers, "Who Are Your Motivated Workers?," *Harvard Business Review,* January-February 1964, pp. 73-88.

15. P. Diehl and J.R. Howell, "Improving Communication Within the Research and Development Team," *Research Management,* Vol. XIX, No. 1, January 1976, pp. 23-27.

16. Rensis Likert, *New Patterns of Management,* McGraw-Hill, New York, 1961, p. 17.

17. J. Richard Hackman, Greg Oldham, Robert Janson, and Kenneth Purdy, "A New Strategy for Job Enrichment," *California Management Review,* Vol. XVII, No. 4, 1975.

18. For additional support of the job enrichment concept, see W.J. Paul, Jr., K.B. Robertson, and F. Herzberg, "Job Enrichment Pays Off," *Harvard Business Review,* 1969, pp. 61-78.

19. A.F. Alber, "The Real Cost of Job Enrichment," *Business Horizons,* Vol. 22, No. 1, February 1979, pp. 60-72.

20. J.R. Hackman, R.G. Oldham, R. Janson, and K. Purdy, "A New Strategy For Job Enrichment," *California Management Review,* Summer 1975, pp. 55-71.

21. Robert Janson, "Job Design For Quality," *The Personnel Administrator,* October 1974, pp. 14-18.

22. For a theoretical discussion of these models, see J.L. Gibson, J.M. Ivancevich, and J.H. Donnelly, *Organizations Behavior Structure Processes,* Plano, Tex., Business Publications Inc., 1985, pp. 97-180.

23. Desmond Martin and William Kearney, "The Behavioral Sciences in Management Development Programs," *Journal of Business,* Seton Hall University, Vol. 16, No. 2, May 1978, pp. 26-32.

24. Douglas M. McGregor, *The Human Side of Enterprise,* McGraw-Hill, New York, 1960.

25. For a discussion of Levinson's Analysis of the Motivation Problem, see H. Levinson, *The Great Jackass Fallacy,* Harvard University Press, Cambridge, Mass., 1973.

26. D.C. McClelland, "Business Drive and National Achievement," *Harvard Business Review,* July-August 1962, pp. 99-112.

27. D.C. McClelland, "Managing Motivation to Expand Human Freedom," *American Psychologist,* March 1978, pp. 201-210.

28. D.C. McClelland and D. Burnham, "Power is the Great Motivator," *Harvard Business Review,* March-April 1976, pp. 100-111.

29. For a concise discussion of the Motivation Hygiene Theory, see Frederick Herzberg, *Work and the Nature of Man,* World Publishing Co., Cleveland, 1966, Chapter 6.

30. For a discussion of this research, see F. Herzberg, B. Mausner, and B.B. Snyderman, *The Motivation to Work,* John Wiley & Sons, New York, 1959. For a more current discussion of the implications of this research, see also F. Herzberg, *The Managerial Choice: To be Efficient and To be Human,* Irwin, Homewood, IL, 1974.

31. Keith Davis, "How Do You Motivate Your Engineers and Scientists?," *Arizona Business Bulletin,* February 1969, pp. 27-32.

32. Frederick Herzberg, "One More Time: How Do You Motivate Your Employees?," *Harvard Business Review,* January-February 1968, pp. 53-62.

33. Myers, "Who Are Your Motivated Workers?"

34. G.B. Graen, " 'Addendum to' An Empirical Test of the Herzberg Two-Factor Theory," *Journal of Applied Psychology,* Vol. 50, No. 6, 1966, pp. 551-555.

35. Frederick Herzberg, "The Wise Old Turk," *Harvard Business Review,* September-October 1974, pp. 70-80.

36. F.A. Andrews, "Scientific Performance as Related to Time Spent on Technical Work, Teaching, or Administration," *Administrative Science Quarterly,* September 1964, pp. 182-193.

37. D.T. Hall and E.E. Lawler III, "Job Characteristics and Pressures and the Organizational Integration of Professionals," *Administrative Science Quarterly,* September 1970, pp. 271-281.

38. E.E. Lawler and L.W. Porter, "Antecedent Attitudes of Effective Managerial Performance," *Organizational Behavior and Human Performance,* Vol. 2, 1967, pp. 122-142.

39. For a detailed discussion of Expectancy Theory see Victor H. Vroom, *Work and Motivation,* John Wiley & Sons, New York, 1964.

40. J.G. Hunt and J.W. Hill, "The New Look in Motivation Theory for Organizational Research," *Human Organization,* Vol. 28, No. 2, 1969.

41. Edward Lawler, *Motivation in Work Organizations,* Brooks/Cole Publishing, Monterey, CA 1973, p. 145.

42. Chris Argyris, "Personal Versus Organizational Goals," *Yale Scientific,* February 1960, pp. 40-50.

43. S. Rynes and J. Lawler, "A Policy-Capturing Investigation of the Role of Expectancies in Decisions to Pursue Job Alternatives," *Journal of Applied Psychology,* Vol. 68, 1983, pp. 620-631.

44. A. Harnell and M. Stahl, "Additive Information Processing and the Relationship Between Expectancy of Success and Motivational Force," *Academy of Management Journal,* Vol., 29, No. 2, June 1986, pp. 424-433.

45. For a detailed discussion of the Porter-Lawler model see, L.W. Porter and E.E. Lawler, III, *Managerial Attitudes and Performance,* Homewood, IL, Richard D. Irwin, Inc., 1968.

46. H.F. Vincent and Abbas Mirakhor, "Relationship Between Productivity Satisfaction, Ability, Age and Salary in a Military R. & D. Organization," *IEEE Transactions on Engineering Management,* EM19-45, May 1972, pp. 45-53.

47. G.W. Dalton, P.H. Thompson, and R.L. Price, "The Four Stages of Professional Careers: A New Look at Performance by Professionals," *Organizational Dynamics,* Summer 1977, pp. 19-42.

48. W.M. Morgenroth and R.L. Morgenroth, "Memo to Managers: Handling the Difficult Employee," *Business and Economic Review,* April-June 1986, pp. 12-16.

49. R.D. Best, "The Scientist Versus the Management Mind," *Industrial Research,* October 1963, pp. 50-52.

50. Arthur Gerstenfeld and Gabriel Rosica, "Why Engineers Transfer," *Business Horizons,* April 1970, pp. 43-48.

51. Pelz and Andrews, Scientists in Organizations, p. 32.

52. Lauren B. Hitchcock, "Problems of First Line Supervisors," *Research Management,* Vol. X, November 1967, pp. 385-397.

9

Leading Professionals

I. IMPORTANCE OF LEADERSHIP STYLE

One of the best ways that managers can increase the level of motivation among subordinates is to be effective leaders. Leadership can be defined as a *process of influence in which the leader is able to get the follower to stay on a prescribed path toward the attainment of specific goals* that are desired by the leader. Thus, by definition the art of leadership is an important part of effective management. In their experience the authors have observed some individuals that could adequately perform most of the management functions, but lacked leadership qualities. This suggests that the art of leadership may be inherent within the individual. If leadership can be acquired through education and training, it may be the most difficult quality to "learn."

Managers in the professional environment are likely to have specialized training and are often preoccupied with the technical or scientific aspects of subordinate jobs. Consequently, they may pay little attention to the development and application of leadership skills. This situation is particularly characteristic of technical supervisors at lower management levels. For example, studies have shown that this technical orientation decreases as professionals trained as engineers advance in the management hierarchy.[1] An understanding of leadership including the selection of style and attendant managerial relationships with subordinates is important at all levels of management.

Much has been written about leadership in the last thirty years, and some authors have developed ten or more possible leadership styles that can be used in managing employees. There is considerable controversy over the nature and extent of influence that leadership style has on employee performance.

This controversy is illustrated in the results of several leadership studies which have applicability to professionals. Lieberson and O'Connor compared the impact of leadership effects to environmental and organizational influences in 167 corporations. They concluded from their longitudinal analysis that more variance in organizational performance is attributed to environmental factors than to the personal leadership skills of managers.[2] However, in a re-analysis of these same data, as well as additional examination of 193 manufacturing organizations over a nineteen year period, Weiner and Mahoney found that leadership did account for more variance in organizational performance than did many environmental or organizational factors.[3] Another study by Smith, Carson, and Alexander, which occurred in a professional work environment, found that a group of superior performers demonstrated their impact not only within their own organizational unit but also across many organizational units.[4]

When overall organizational success is related to leadership qualities, it is clear that effective leadership can and does make a difference. For example, when high ranking managers are asked to identify key factors that they attribute to their success in rising to top levels in their respective organizations, they often attribute their success to specific leadership qualities.[5] Leadership qualities assume great importance in the professional work environment, because professionals are highly sensitive to how they are managed.

In analyzing leadership, four basic styles are delineated in this chapter. These styles are autocratic, bureaucratic, laissez-faire, and democratic. While this categorization of leadership style is older and more traditional, newer classifications are really modifications or extensions of these four basic styles. The major differences among these styles can be determined by looking at the way the power source is perceived and used by the leader.

II. AUTOCRATIC LEADERSHIP

The autocratic leader perceives himself or herself as the source of power, and makes all the decisions in an organization in terms of being the absolute center of authority and control. A major advantage of working for the strict autocratic leader is that the subordinate always knows where he or she stands with the leader, namely, the leader will both make decisions and take responsibility for them. This fact simplifies work relationships for the subordinate because all this employee subordinate has to do is cooperate and carry out assignments. The obvious disadvantage is that creativity is stifled and individual development is neglected. Creative people such as scientists in the health professions or in corporate research and development usually have great difficulty with a strict autocrat because they are highly self-disciplined and tend to be frustrated by control-oriented leaders. University faculty represent another work group that usually resists autocratic leadership.

A modification of strict autocratic is *benevolent autocratic.* This individual makes all the decisions, but tends to constantly communicate to employees that decisions are being made in their "best" interest. This style is, in part, an outgrowth of the "identity of interests" concept of management, which was prevalent in the United States prior to 1930. According to this concept, owners, managers, and employees of a business automatically have the same interest, which is the growth and success of the firm. Consequently, the manager's choice and actions in leadership and decision-making situations will always be in the interest of the subordinates because managers are paid to run the business in the best and most efficient possible manner.

There are some difficulties with this approach to management. One problem is that its success is predicated on the assumption that subordinates will accept the fact that the managers *know* what is in their best interest and have the wisdom and judgement to make those kinds of supportive decisions. Professional people at times can be critical of the managerial function. Since they are highly trained and skill oriented, they are not predisposed to accept the judgement of their leaders as being necessarily in the interest of their own goals or those of the organization.

The benevolent autocrat must continually rely on *rewards* to gain the support and cooperation of subordinates. If the organization experiences economic hardship and these rewards become less available or nonexistent, a crisis ensues. The impact of this state of affairs is likely to cause the subordinates to view with disfavor the actions and leadership control functions performed by their boss. Although benevolent autocracy, accompanied by rewards, has been shown to work quite well for short periods of time with nonprofessionals, situations where this style works best are not common in the professional environment.

Some managers tend to practice the autocratic style simply because they are basically *insecure* in their jobs. Insecurity can cause managers to tighten control because there is a subconscious feeling that greater competency is needed if more people are allowed to become involved in the decision-making process. When insecurity or fear of incompetence causes a manager to tighten control and retain most of the decision-making authority, this leader is commonly referred to as an *incompetent autocrat*. This style of leadership is ineffective because most employees perceive that incompetence does exist, and lose respect for the manager. This fact is true even if the decision outcomes are correct from the standpoint of the organization and the employees themselves.

While there is a substantial amount of research that suggests that autocratic management can be effective in increasing productivity, this research generally is associated with short-run time periods or situations characterized by a poor organizational climate.[6] Usually, important human relations factors such as morale, loyalty, feeling of warmth and support, and identification are not as positive under autocratic leadership. Thus, while short-run productivity may rise, there is a price being paid for this improvement by the human factors within the organization. The value of human assets usually decrease as they are exploited by autocratic leaders.

Exploitation of human assets is recognized by Likert, who developed the idea that human resources valuation should be measured on the balance sheet along with other "tangible" assets. He concludes that certain leadership styles and management practices that are increasing the output of the organization in the short run, are actually reducing the value of its human resources in the long run; and this condition should show up in the value of the total assets of the organization. Likert calls his system for evaluating human assets *human resources accounting.*[7] Although several articles have appeared on human resources accounting in the last 15 years and there has been some interest in it among practicing managers, it has had little application.[8] The human resources accounting concept could be used in professional organizations to show that when autocratic leadership is practiced, the value of the professional staff may in fact be decreasing. Human resource accounting has also been linked with Management by Objectives (Chapter 12) as a combination that offers significant potential to increase managerial effectives.[9] However this linkage has not yet been put into practice and is still in a very early stage of development. The important point is that successfully combining these tools would tend to prevent exploitative leadership practices.

III. BUREAUCRATIC LEADERSHIP

The bureaucratic style of leadership is an approach that is used in many large organizations. Bureaucratic styles of management are taken from the term bureaucracy, which is *a system of management that utilizes formal rules and regulations as the power base.* The bureaucratic leader sees rules and regulations as the power source for making decisions within the organization. When practicing this style, the leader goes by the book and does not get personally involved in the decision-making process. In a few limited instances, this can be an advantageous approach because there are times when it is desirable for the manager to be personally removed from an unpopular decision. Successful application of bureaucratic management in these kinds of situations involves convincing the subordinates that the application of rules cannot be avoided. The ability of managers of professionals to convince employees that nothing can be done about applying the rules is a function of several factors which include the subordinates' perception of the strengths and weaknesses of the manager, their training and professionalism, and their perception of the specific situation.

It is more difficult to convince professionals that formal regulations must be followed than it is to convince paraprofessionals who may have been taught to follow the rules from their induction into the organization. Also, if professionals believe that there is nothing their managers can do about the rules, managerial strength may be altered, and the ability to motivate and gain the cooperation of these employees is reduced. Much of the research tends to show that American employees prefer managers who are strong and have upward influence with their superiors in the organization.[10] The more these managers rely on rules and convince subordinates they can do nothing about these rules, the less they are perceived to have upward influence in the organizational hierarchy. Thus, the factors needed to sell bureaucracy as a style of management and to increase the managerial effectiveness are often working at cross-purposes with each other.

A. Bureaupathic Behavior

Thompson has pointed out some additional negative effects of bureaucratic leadership. Specifically, continued application of bureaucratic leadership can cause leaders to assume certain common characteristics which are described as *bureaupathic behavior.* "Bureaupathic" refers to an organizational environment with four basic characteristics: Petty insistence on the rights of office; ritualistic attachment to routines and procedures; excessive aloofness; and resistance to change.[11] These conditions result from the manager's attempt to adjust to rules and regulations which must be constantly applied. As a means of adjusting and retaining individuality in this environment, the rules and regulations become ends in themselves, and self-expression is realized through the application and protection of rights of office. Managers tend to be excessively aloof because it is desirable to be insulated from the complaints and frustrations of subordinates. Change is resisted because the existing system becomes the most important factor in the managerial environment, and it is protected by individual managers against modification. Changing the system would involve managerial effort and readjustment, but change is usually not viewed as being constructive. Bureaupathic leadership impedes organizational effectiveness because it stifles creativity and increases employee frustration. Bureaupathic behavior is a tremendous liability to the professional environment which thrives on creativity, new thought processes, innovation, and initiative.

In conclusion, although an argument can be made that it may be desirable for managers to remove themselves personally from a decision-making situation by applying rules, the evidence suggests that these situations are relatively few and that the liabilities of using bureaucratic leadership extensively in managing professionals are great. Consequently, the usefulness of this particular leadership style is limited.

IV. LAISSEZ-FAIRE LEADERSHIP

The laissez-faire manager can be distinguished from other managers by the fact that a power source is not perceived or used, and this leader does *not* function as an effective personal force in managing subordinates. In spite of this apparent weakness, there are some advantages to laissez-faire management, particularly in creative professional environments. Since professionals are usually highly self-disciplined, they tend to do their best work with a minimum of interference, particularly if they maintain a lively interest in a variety of research problems.[12] This is precisely what laissez-faire management provides. Since there is no interference by the manager and the subordinate is completely free, a very autonomous environment exists. However, laissez-faire leaders are only effective when problem-solving skills and knowledge necessary to the job are self-contained within the subordinate group, because little or no help will come from the manager. Additionally, if extensive cooperation is needed among several professionals to accomplish the task, little goal setting or facilitative activity will come from the manager. Finally, these managers do a poor job of relating the productive efforts of the subordinate group to the greater organization. When a product is completed or a job is well done, this may not be communicated effectively to the rest of the organization, so little appreciation is gained from the greater organization to the subunit for completing their task. Similarly, recognition from the laissez-faire manager to subordinates for a job well done is often nonexistent. Earlier chapters on needs and motivation stressed that this kind of recognition is vital for professionals.

The conditions in which laissez-faire management can work are those where the job knowledge is self-contained within the subordinate unit; there is little intragroup dependency or cooperation needed to perform the task among unit members; and the subordinates are highly educated self-initiators, with high levels of self-discipline. Also, laissez-faire management can be combined with certain types of communication feedback such as monthly reports by subordinates delineating that month's accomplishments, which is then passed on to the appropriate levels of upper management. In these kinds of conditions, laissez-faire management may actually work better than any other leadership style, and the level of motivation that results from its use may be high. Conversely, in situations where the job knowledge is not self-contained, a considerable amount of intragroup dependency is present, managerial recognition is needed to support specific accomplishments, and the relationship of subunit tasks to the greater organizational purpose is not clear, laissez-faire management will be ineffective.

V. DEMOCRATIC LEADERSHIP

The democratic manager believes that *power is derived from the subordinate group.* This style gained impetus from the acceptance theory of authority as developed by Barnard in the late 1930s that was mentioned in Chapter 4. In his book, *The Functions of the Executive*, Barnard maintained that any manager's authority over a subordinate group was limited by the willingness of that group to accept the authority of the manager.[13] For example, if a boss tells a subordinate to do something, but the subordinate refuses, a serious management problem exists. It is doubtful that threats or physical force will change this behavior on any long-term basis, and acceptance of the manager's authority is necessary for long-term change. Many practicing managers have accepted this reasoning over the years, which has laid the groundwork for a strong belief in democratic management.

The work of Lewin in the late 1930s and early 40s involving small boys in experimental leadership groups built a good case for democratic management. Lewin found that democratically managed boys who engaged in productive tasks exhibited more cooperation, less frustration, greater satisfaction with task, and better overall performance than similar groups managed by laissez-faire or autocratic leaders.[14] Leadership style was shown to be *more* important than the personality of the leader in determining the behavioral patterns of the subordinates. However, much like Likert, in short-run situations, Lewin found productivity could be equally high or even greater among autocratic as opposed to democratically managed groups.

This analysis of style thus far could easily lead to the conclusion that democratic leadership is usually the most useful. However, such a conclusion is far too simple and not necessarily supported by research data. While democratic leadership has been widely discussed and advocated by many management authorities since the mid 1950s, what the implementation of democratic management actually entails is still widely misunderstood. In order to help alleviate this confusion, it is important to point out several elements that are *not* characteristic of the democratic style.

It is *not* giving up control and total decision-making power to the subordinates.

It is *not* necessarily making decisions by majority vote among subordinates.

It is *not* allowing subordinates to become involved in decision making only when the outcome of these decisions is unimportant to the leader.

It is *not* a style of management that is designed to eliminate most conflict.

When stated affirmatively, the above points are often erroneously associated with the democratic style. In looking more positively at the characteristic elements of good democratic management, the following statements are associated with sound democratic management:

1. There is true "mutual" involvement in the decision-making process, e.g., the manager and subordinates both make significant input into important decisions (see Chapter 12).

2. It is both appropriate and often necessary for the manager to be sure that the goals are set and understood by subordinates with regard to his or her organizational unit. These goals serve as both guides and boundaries which help to keep behavior on a prescribed course. The goal-setting process for management by objectives as described in detail in Chapter 12 is congruent with sound democratic principles. It is usually desirable but not always possible to solicit input from subordinates during the goal-setting process.

3. Applying democratic management requires the continuous development of subordinates. The democratic manager should help to provide a work climate that fosters the development of objectives, stimulates a capacity and desire by employees to become involved, and includes employees with varying levels of technical knowledge. This point is particularly applicable to professionals.

4. There are many situations where lack of knowledge or time constraints make democratic principles inappropriate, and in these cases they should not be used.

Democratic management involves a climate of mutual trust, shared knowledge, and clear-cut goals when used properly; and managers should fully understand that attaining managerial effectiveness through applying democratic management techniques is a complex process.

More recent leadership styles focus on the interactive processes that may occur in meaningful decision procedures. Among the more useful of the categorizations, is the one developed by Scandura, Graen, and Novak which includes five types as follows:[15]

1. Autocratic Decision - When the leader follows the strict autocratic style described above and makes the decision without asking for opinions or suggestions of subordinates.
2. Minimal Decision Involvement - This approach is still very autocratic. Although the leader solicits opinions from subordinates, he or she still makes the final decision with limited influence.
3. Consultation - This approach moves slightly to the democratic side of the continuum. The leader meets with subordinates and his or her final decision reflects as much of their respective input as possible.
4. Collaboration - The collaborative leader closely matches the democratic style described above. The leader works with the subordinate to analyze the problem and the amount of subordinate input into the final decision often approaches that of the leader.
5. Delegation - Here the leader moves a little beyond democracy toward the laissez-faire style described above. The subordinates are allowed to make the decision after receiving maximum or minimum input from the leader. In minimum input situations, laissez-faire leadership is present.

VI. CHOOSING AN APPROPRIATE LEADERSHIP STYLE

It is increasingly apparent that the *situation* should often dictate the appropriate choice of a particular leadership style as there are advantages to each. The major advantage of the autocratic approaches is that they are quick, simple, and assume that the manager's job is simply to manage and make decisions. In many organizational activities, the right of the manager to manage goes without question, and autocratic leadership is most effective. Specific examples of situations that can be effectively handled autocratically are as follows: secretarial relationships, where it is usually the manager's job to set priorities and tell the secretary precisely what to do in terms of certain work activities; and maintenance supervision, where there is a breakdown in laboratory equipment and the job is to repair it quickly. Also, in time of crisis where both time and direction are important, autocracy usually works best, and these conditions support its acceptance. These latter situations commonly occur in the health professions.

Specific situations can also favor either bureaucratic or laissez-faire approaches. Bureaucratic leadership can work in instances where disciplinary action must be invoked by rules or cases that are touchy from the standpoint of personalities, which make the application of rules and regulations desirable. Laissez-faire management can work best in laboratories or hospitals where highly skilled MDs, PhDs, and other professionals are brought in for their unique expertise to research a problem or perform clinical judgement. Once the problem is defined and the assignment made, these skilled professionals may work more effectively when left completely alone. However, in situations where the acceptance and quality of decisions are critical, and the growth and development of subordinates are a desired goal, the democratic style is more likely to be successful.

Thus, the real answer to the question of choosing the appropriate leadership style is a complex one, which is related to several environmental factors, including the power and personality of the decision maker or leader, the characteristics of the situation, and both the time involved and characteristics of the task. Leaders may change their management style hourly, depending on the specific decision-making situation. Autocratic or democratic management should be depicted as a matter of degree rather than being absolute.

Thamhain and Wilemon, analyzed the impact of leader-centered (autocratic) and team-centered (democratic) styles on managerial effectiveness among project managers. A measure of this effectiveness was obtained through a rating of the superiors of 68 project managers. The overall quality of the work environment coupled with the application of an appropriate leadership style has the greatest impact on managerial effectiveness according to the results of this research.[16] In an organizational climate characterized by good communication, work continuity, and career growth, democratic, team-oriented approaches are most effective. Where a poor climate exists, the more autocratic, leader-centered approaches work best.[16] Two basic explanations of these results are offered. In a poor organizational climate, leader-centered direction provides order to the work and may reduce employee anxieties (you have heard the expression "bring order to chaos"). In good organizational climates where communication flows freely and anxieties are low, employees are more responsive to team-building efforts. While overall conclusions from this study suggest that a good organizational climate conducive to team-centered leadership (democratic) is preferable to a poor climate, it recognizes that managers need to be flexible in their approach to leadership. Flexibility is needed because the factors that determine organizational climate are beyond the control of the manager in many instances, and rapid change is not unusual in the work environment.

Since organizational climate is so important to managerial effectiveness, Thamhain and Wilemon offer some specific suggestions on managerial action to improve it in a particular type of professional work environment (project management) which can apply to other professional employee groups:[16]

1. An organizational audit should take place aimed at determining the causes of poor climate.
2. A program should be undertaken to correct poor climate conditions that can be changed.
3. Specific attention should be given to long-range and project planning which can help reduce employee anxiety.
4. In project management, a system for phasing projects effectively is needed. Personnel transfer policies

as well as interproject training programs will be a useful part of this system.

5. As was stressed in Chapter 7, free-flowing two-way communication is one of the major factors that influences the quality of the organizational climate.

Vroom and Yetton have developed a decision-process flow chart, which offers help to managers of professionals in determining the proper points on the autocratic-democratic continuum given the nature of the decision.[17] While a detailed analysis will not be made of the Vroom and Yetton approach, it is useful to indicate some pertinent questions which when answered help determine the extent of democracy needed in the decision-making process. Among these more important questions are as follows:

Do I have enough information to make a high-quality decision? Obviously, the more managers depend on others for information, the more consultative or democratic they need to be.

Is acceptance of a decision by subordinates critical to effective implementation? If the answer to this question is yes, it is more important to be democratic than if the answer is no.

If I were to make the decision by myself, is it reasonably certain that it would be accepted by my subordinates? If the answer is yes, then it is less important to be on the democratic side of the continuum.

Do subordinates share the organizational goals to be attained in solving this problem? If the answer is yes, then subordinates can effectively become more involved in the decision process than if the answer is no.

Do subordinates have sufficient information to make a high-quality decision? If the answer is yes, managers can be more democratic than if the answer is no.

The preceding questions posed by Vroom and Yetton are critical ones that managers should answer before attempting to arrive at the amount of participation or consultation that should be afforded to subordinates in the decision-making process. These questions also relate to many of the critical factors that determine proper leadership style. The commitment of subordinates to the problem, the time involved, sharing of goals, and the general level of cooperation and communication among the subordinates are all good measures of organizational climate and basic factors that determine the best leadership style.

A. Situational Leadership

According to Hersey and Blanchard the appropriate leadership style is largely determined by the maturity level of the employees being led.[18] Maturity levels vary along a continuum from low to high and fall into four basic categories specified M1 through M4 (see Figure 9.1).[19] M1's are characterized as being unable, unwilling, or insecure. M2's still lack ability but are more confident. M3's have the ability but lack confidence. M4's are both able and secure.

According to Hersey and Blanchard, appropriate style is a function of assessing maturity levels and coupling greater or lesser degrees of autonomy with appropriate job characteristics. M1's are managed most effectively in directive relationships (autocratic) with high task-low relationship assignments. M2's work best with high task-high relationship activities and a moderately directive leadership style referred to as selling. M3's work best with high relationship-low task assignments coupled with highly participative leadership. Finally, M4's exhibit high levels of performance with low relationship-low task assignments and maximum levels of autonomy from the leader. In combination, M3's need democratic approaches, which should be extended to include some laissez-faire characteristics among the employees who are primarily M4's.

Most professionals are either M3's or M4's and according to this model perform best with high involvement leadership styles. In fact, Hersey and Blanchard suggest that as followers reach high levels of maturity, the effective leader should respond by continuing both to decrease control over their activities and relationship behavior as well.[20] This leadership change is indicated by the bell

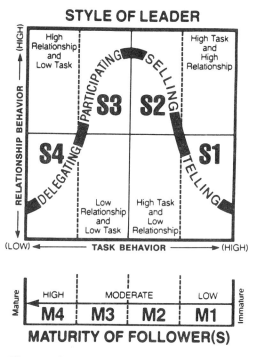

STYLE OF LEADER

Figure 9.1   Situation leadership. (Paul Hersey and Ken Blanchard, *Management of Organizational Behavior,* Prentice Hall, Englewood Cliffs, N.J. 4th ed., 1982, P. 152, Reprinted with permission.)

shaped curve contained in Figure 9.1 and an ideal leadership style for many professionals is high delegation contained in the S4 quadrant.

The professional work environment offers a distinct advantage to its managers because of the complex and challenging tasks, and both the job maturity (ability) and psychological maturity (willingness) of its members tends to be high. As Blank, Weitzel, and Green suggest psychological maturity makes a significant contribution to work satisfaction.[22] These conditions are conducive to participative approaches to leadership and increase potential for high levels of motivation. Professional work organizations are often characterized by uncertainty in work flow and task assignment and the degree of self supervision should be high and reflected by greater decentralization in the decision making process.[23] Also, close super-vision can accompany high self-supervision among professionals because managerial roles involve assisting professionals in main-taining task boundaries through a consultative style of manage-ment.[24] Thus, autonomy and closeness of supervision may function together to increase the work effectiveness of professionals. The evaluation and judgmental nature of many professional task assign-ments coupled with the need for task direction and boundaries tends to require frequent interaction between professionals and their supervisors.

VII. EMOTIONAL PROFILE OF THE LEADER

An additional factor that impacts on the choice of an appropriate leadership style is the value system, personality, and emotional profile of the leader. Research conducted by the National Training Laboratories and reported by Athos and Coffey identifies three emotional profiles.[25] A modified version of these profiles and their basic characteristics is contained in Figure 9.2. As indicated, these three profiles are the sturdy battler, the friendly helper, and the logical thinker. While no individual is totally classified as one pro-file or the other, many people express *preferences* for one over the other.[25] In view of the distinguishable characteristics that are asso-ciated with each, it is clear that emotional profile will influence to a greater or lesser degree an individual's approach to leadership and management.

It must still be emphasized that leadership can be learned (even though it is difficult) and a manager can be taught to change his or her approach to leadership, but the emotional profile of that specific manager can determine the degree of comfort (and effectiveness) ex-perienced in practicing a given style. There are other implications regarding emotional profile that are also important to understanding leadership. For example, specific managers who are predominantly "sturdy battler" types may succeed with autocracy in situations where leaders with different emotional profiles would fail as auto-crats. This difference is explained by the fact that sturdy battlers are often more comfortable and effective when assuming an autocratic role.

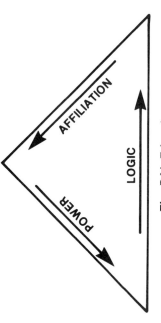

The PAL Triangle

The Friendly Helper

a. uncomfortable with tough emotions
b. comfortable with tender emotions — avoids conflict and freely expresses warmth and support
c. tends to evaluate others on the basis of supporting relationships
d. prefers democracy in leadership situations

The Sturdy Battler

a. uncomfortable with tender emotions
b. comfortable with tough emotions — often thrives on conflict
c. evaluates others in terms of their power and ability to control
d. often prefers autocracy in leadership situations

The Logical Thinker

a. uncomfortable with both tough and tender emotions
b. relies heavily on knowledge and accuracy
c. evaluates others in terms of their knowledge and expertise
d. is often comfortable with bureaucratic leadership

Figure 9.2 Emotional profiles that are associated with individuals performing leadership roles

Similarly, individuals who are predominantly "friendly helper" types often succeed in a wide variety of situations with democratic leadership because they are very sincere and comfortable with it. Friendly helpers thrive on warm, supportive relationships which are fostered by a democratic philosophy. Since autocratic leadership is often not seen as being warm and supportive, the friendly helper feels awkward in situations that call for "hard-nosed" boss-centered decisions or other "tough" action activities.

Finally, since bureaucracy is characterized by formal rules and regulations that are (or should be) based on logic, accuracy, and knowledge, the bureaucratic leadership style can be very appealing to "logical thinker" types. These leaders are most comfortable when a logical system exists which can be used to support their decisions; consequently, they are often prone to managing bureaucratically, whereas others with different emotional profiles are not.

Managers should determine their own emotional profile and analyze how it is affecting their leadership practices. Although it is common to find that effectiveness is greatest when using a leadership style that is congruent with one's emotional profile, this may only be true when the characteristics of the situation dictate the use of that style. If the characteristics of the situation suggest another approach, effectiveness will be reduced. Managers that are predominantly sturdy battlers should realize that they are prone to being autocratic; those who are friendly helpers are more likely to be democratic; and logical thinkers may tend toward bureaucratic leadership regardless of the situation. In important decision-making situations, these managers should make a critical appraisal of the extent to which their own emotional profile may be influencing them to apply an inappropriate leadership style, and realize that flexibility in the application of leadership style is important.

VIII. ONE-ON-ONE LEADERSHIP

More recent trends in the study of leadership have focused on the intense relationship that develops within organizations between a person and his or her immediate superior.[26] Leadership practices involve one to one exchanges that can vary in quality from minimum employment contract specifications to a full mutual sharing of positional and professional responsibility. As Graen and Scandura point out, the reality of the dyad is different from both the individual and group.[26] For example, when a professional successfully completes an assigned task, a contribution is made to professional achievement, to fulfillment of a personal contract with the leader (dyad) and to the effectiveness of his or her work group. Understanding both the complexities and impact of the dyadic relationship by managers of professionals can make a valued contribution to their leadership effectiveness. As previously stressed, professionals usually exhibit strong growth needs. Studies show that employees with high growth needs (professionals) respond to increased growth opportunities provided by their leaders through task assignment and support with improved levels of job satisfaction.[27] One study in which leadership intervention provided greater opportunities for challenge and new learning resulted in a 55 percent increase in productivity (quantity) for an employee group with high growth needs.[28] This favorable result is additionally enhanced by a substantial improvement in quality as well. Research involving the professional work environment shows the value of a strong dyadic career relationship to project and process affectiveness.[29] This research was particularly useful because it controlled for several possible confounding factors such as technical training, work background, technical competence of the staff, and user anxiety with clients.[29]

Vertical dyad linkages play an important role in leadership effectiveness. Exchanges of challenging work assignments for valued rewards can have a positive long term effect on individual performance and satisfaction. For example, a study of young professionals followed a group of managers for five years at AT&T. Their success was evaluated by salary scale and supervisory performance ratings. The researcher concluded that the more challenging a person's job was in his or her first year with the organization, the more effective he or she was five years later.[30] However, it is common for managers to assign simple, more routinized tasks to younger professionals and to bring them along rather slowly in their career. The dyadic relationship that consists of early challenging assignments coupled with leadership support and rewards can be the most effective approach toward managing professionals. In fact, a knowledge of dyadic relationships may offer the key to raising individual levels of performance. For example, dyadic relationships can help explain the value of mutual goal setting to performance improvement. Some researchers suggest that participation is a more critical factor in determining individual performance than goal acceptance. The important point appears to be that participation leads to understanding, specificity, and negotiation regarding performance goals. The ultimate acceptance of a goal is tied to complexities involved in the leader-follower dyad.[31] Mutual goal setting which offers considerable potential to managers of professionals to increase effectiveness is developed in more detail in Chapter 12.

IX. RELATIONSHIP BETWEEN POWER AND LEADERSHIP

Since power can be defined as the *capacity to change behavior*, many authorities on leadership believe that the power position of the leader with regard to subordinates is a critical factor in determining leadership effectiveness.[32] One of the distinguishing characteristics of the managerial position is the dependency relationship on others to perform the managerial job successfully. Many professionals such as physicians and accountants in non-managerial roles can rely most heavily on their own skills and expertise to be successful. However, once they become managers their personal effectiveness depends on the performance of employees who report to them. Successful managers cope with their dependence on others by being sensitive to it by establishing power over others.[33] They can then use that power to plan, organize, evaluate, etc., which, if successfully done, leads to an effective organizational unit characterized by high levels of motivation (Chapter 8). Dependency inherent in the managerial job makes the application of the dynamics of power necessary by the manager.[33] French and Raven have described five different power bases that are available to leaders in given organizational situations which are outlined below:[34]

> *Coercive power*: This is based upon fear and relates primarily to the ability of the leader to punish the subordinates for nonconformity.

Reward power: This is the opposite of coercive power in the sense that it relates to the ability of the leader to provide positive rewards, such as income or other benefits, to people who cooperate.

Legitimate power: This type of power relates to the position of the manager in the organizational hierarchy and is largely derived from the ability of the organization to support that manager in terms of his or her organizational position.

Expert power: An individual with this type of power is one who possess unique expertise or skills in particular areas that are regarded as important to subordinates.

Referent power: This is essentially the power of the personality and relates to the leader's ability to be admired because of one or more personal traits.

Each of these power bases is limited in scope by the nature of the organization and the person occupying a leadership position. For example, legitimate power is limited by the scope of the office as defined by the job description covering duties and responsibilities as well as the financial strength, prestige, and size of the organization. Expert power is usually restricted to those situations where expertise is valued by the subordinates; therefore, attempts to carry it into other situations usually are not successful. Reward power is often dictated by the financial strength and size of the organization as well as the autonomy given to the manager by top management. It follows that high level managers in powerful organizations usually have more rewards to provide than lower level managers in smaller organizations. The impact of a Civil Service System or a union on reward and coercive power requires little explanation. Professionals working for governmental agencies covered by Civil Service requirements are limited in their ability to discharge, promote, or grant other kinds of rewards or punishments to their subordinates. Many managers who are subjected to these artificial restrictions maintain that their ability to be effective leaders is greatly reduced.

Building on the work of French and Raven, Kotter argues that effective managers create, increase, or maintain four types of power over others.[35] These four types are as follows:

Sense of obligation: Involves managers doing favors for employees, being successful and creating a feeling that they (managers) should be allowed to influence.

Belief in the manager's expertise: Expert power which is established through visible achievement by the manager and is particularly important among professionals.

Identification with a manager: Charismatic in nature. Managers behave in ways that others respect.

Perceived dependence on the manager: Creating the feeling among subordinates that they need the manager's support for help or to avoid being hurt.

Figure 9.3 indicates the interaction involved between leader and follower which generates a pool of power beyond authority.

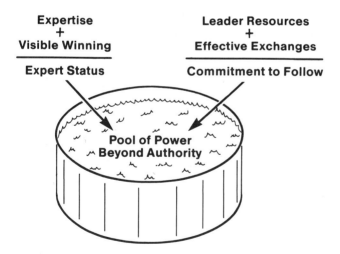

Figure 9.3   Formula for building leadership capacity. (Adapted from S.G. Green, Ph.D., *Creative Leadership*, presentation at the University of Cincinnati Executive Program, November 10, 1986.)

As can be seen from this relationship model, expertise coupled with winning decisions generate expert status. Leader resources which include remuneration as well as many other organization values, which are given for good performance increase commitment to follow. The end result is a pool of power beyond authority.

The important message for practical leadership from an analysis of power is simply that an effective manager needs power to influence subordinates. More powerful managers have greater freedom in choosing a leadership style. Managers of professionals should not only develop their bases of power, but they should be willing to use those power bases as needs arise. For example, regardless of leadership style practiced, if managers are unwilling to exercise punishment when subordinates do not cooperate, the managerial power base is being eroded. At the same time, a manager who rewards all employees the same, regardless of their level of performance, is weakening the reward power base and reducing total managerial power.

Specific studies of the professional work environment have found position power to be primarily determined by organizational climate rather than by type of organization.[36] Position power is usually not influenced by either matrix or functional organizational structuring, but can be strong in both structures with supportive overall climates. The effectiveness of leadership style is influenced by one's position power, the dyadic relationship, and the organizational climate. The characteristics of quality dyads and good and poor climates were delineated earlier in this chapter.

X. GOOD LEADERS ARE GOOD HELPERS

Every leader during the course of managing professionals must assume a helping role, but knowing the proper way to be helpful is a complex matter. A basic part of leadership is problem solving; but if the leader solves all subordinate problems, he or she keeps others dependent, does not develop subordinates, and is violating the principle of efficient time management (Chapter 5).

The specific role of effective helping should be to *teach* others to solve their own problems. Constructive helping directs a person toward self-help. However, much too often the motives for helping people are not directed toward self-help, but are aimed at some self-serving purpose for the leader-manager. Some of the questionable motives for helping are:

To obtain graditude or raise guilt
To make the subordinate happy
To give meaning to the leader's life
To show one's superior skill as a person
To control others or make them dependent

All of these particular motives for helping tend to breed defensive actions or attitudes on the part of the subordinate that are destructive to organizational effectiveness. If subordinates do not openly resent or become apathetic about help that occurs in this context, they may feel helpless and become very dependent upon the leader. Any of these conditions impedes the ability of the organization to move forward and utilize subordinates properly in the attainment of organizational goals. The manager of professional personnel will often find a challenging problem in knowing when, how long, and how intensely to help subordinates solve problems.

A. Pitfalls to Avoid in Building a Proper Helping Relationship with Subordinates

There are several pitfalls that should be avoided by managers who desire to build a constructive, helpful relationship with subordinates. Some of the most important ones are outlined below:

Avoid providing early advise to subordinates; instead assume a stance that is problem centered. Giving early advice is both inappropriate and ineffective for two reasons. First, it is assumed that the leader understands the subordinate's problem and has the correct advice, but this may not be true. Even with sound advice, the manager has solved the problem for the subordinate, which tends to make the subordinate more dependent. Secondly, even good advice may breed rejection. Most professional people want to solve their own problems rather than have the manager solve those problems for them.

Avoid excessive use of reassurance or "pat-on-the-back" approaches. The problem with these kinds of approaches is that their effectiveness is very short-lived. In essence, they deny that a problem exists when in reality this assumption may be incorrect. These approaches are commonly used by managers because they create good feeling, but their success record is poor. The subordinate can find himself in the position of learning, after being encouraged and told everything is going to be all right for a period of months, that he is suddenly in deeper trouble.

Avoid using punitive measures as a means of correcting deviant behavior or to get people on the prescribed course toward solving problems. Punishment tends to breed defensiveness and rejection; consequently, it often reduces the problem-solving ability of both the manager and the subordinate. Unless there have been specific instances where willful violation of rules and costly mistakes were made with questionable intent, one should avoid punishing subordinates for things that they do not understand or have not yet mastered. Many managers feel that correction of errors is the best disciplinary procedure they have available, and they seldom go into actual punitive measures. Correction of errors assumes that the subordinate does not understand how to deal with the problem and it sets in motion forces to teach the subordinate the proper way to deal with the problem at a future time. It is not until there is willful, costly violation to the organization by subordinates that strong disciplinary measures are taken.

Avoid making subordinates look bad in front of their peers. When employees are making mistakes which need to be corrected, discussion and attempts to solve these problems should be conducted in private, and not in front of other co-workers. Public ridicule is an ultimate example of criticism and lowering one's self-esteem in the eyes of others, which has been stressed as one of the biggest single mistakes an effective manager can make.

Avoid favoritism. If a superior is willing to help some subordinates but not others, both cooperation and motivation suffer. Constructive, supportive help should be available on an equal basis to all subordinates, and each of these subordinates should feel that the opportunity for such help is available to them when they need it.

Avoid bailing subordinates out of trouble too quickly. The overall objective of the effective helper is to get the subordinate to rescue himself or herself. This is the key to building a strong team characterized by self-confidence, self-esteem, and problem-solving skills (see Chapter 12). A certain amount of struggling on the part of the subordinate is often necessary and useful in attaining this objective.

The good helping relationship is built on the establishment of high levels of mutual trust in the leadership dyad. The steps outlined in Chapter 8 concerning handling employee problem behavior are particularly applicable. Although empathy is desirable, too much empathizing can be detrimental to an objective perspective of the problem. Once the help seeking employee accepts and fully understands the nature of the problem, the effective helper needs to provide available tools and support to expedite a solution. For example, professionals can often use secretarial help, typing assistance, or time away from the job, etc. This kind of support from their manager impacts favorably on their perceptions of their bosses, develops interpersonal problem-solving skills, and reduces conflict; all which contribute to building an excellent professional work environment.

XI. SUMMARY AND CONCLUSIONS

This chapter has identified and emphasized the importance of choosing an appropriate leadership style for managing professionals effectively. While innate characteristics influence the capacity to lead, many leadership qualities can be learned or acquired. This fact adds credibility to the study of leadership. Choosing an appropriate leadership style among professionals is a function of the manager, subordinates, and situation. Several aids have been provided that will assist managers in correctly analyzing the total leadership environment. Two basic guidelines are useful in making this analysis. First, it is important to be doing the right things rather than to worry constantly about doing things right. Second, the emphasis should be on being effective as opposed to being efficient.

Effective managers build a high quality dyadic relationship with their subordinates. In part, high quality is achieved by leveling with subordinates and minimizing both game playing and the use of formal rules and regulations as control devices. Straight talk is valued by most professional people and tends to keep a more realistic focus on the organizational environment and the objectives, which is often the key to leadership effectiveness. Good managers continually review and focus on objectives as well as the problems that subordinates are encountering in attaining those objectives. Development of a problem-solving attitude through proper helping and mutual support is the key to accomplishing meaningful results.

While this chapter has stressed that several variables affect the choice of style, a great many managerial situations in the professional environment dictate a democratic or high involvement approach. Professionalism and self-discipline are basic factors that suggest democracy. Also, democratic management that utilizes communication feedback principles can be very helpful in developing mutual trust with subordinates. Democratic leadership allows the boss to be perceived as helping his or her subordinates get the work done, rather than being perceived as being served by subordinates, which is an ineffective attitude to have permeating the entire professional work environment. Managers of professionals are often rated on their helpfulness in reaching goals for subordinates that relate to total organizational objectives, rather than on their own specific intelligence or skills as individuals. Managers who use superior intelligence and skill to make themselves look good, hoping that this goodness will rub off on subordinates, are much less likely to be perceived as effective managers than are managers who use intelligence and skill to build problem-solving skills and self-esteem among their subordinates.

The key to effectiveness resides in the organizational climate of which leader-member exchange is a very important component. Figure 9.4 relates climate characteristics and the quality of dyadic interchange to leadership effectiveness in professional work settings as developed in this chapter. While some elements of climate contained in Figure 9.4 are outside the control of the manager, there are many elements that can be modified and improved. The improvement of overall organizational climate should be a high priority goal of all managers.

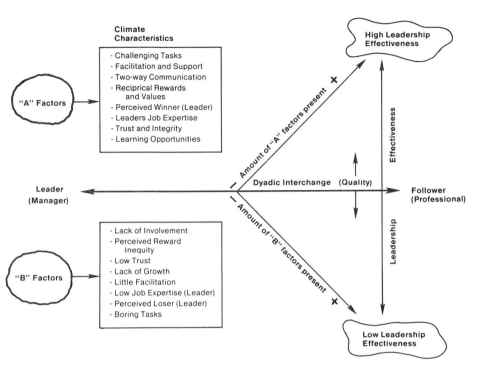

Figure 9.4 Leading Professionals: positive versus negative environments

REFERENCES

1. Simon Marcson, "Role Concept of Engineering Managers," *IRE Transactions on Engineering Management,* March 1960, pp. 30-33.

2. S. Lieberson, and J.F. O'Connor, "Leadership and Organizational Performance: A Study of Large Corporations," *American Sociological Review,* Vol. 37, 1972, pp. 117-130.

3. N. Weiner, and T.A. Mahoney, "A Model Corporate Performance as a Function of Environmental Organizationa, and Leadership Influences," *Academy of Management Journal,* Vol. 24, 1981, pp. 453-470.

4. J.E. Smith, K.P. Carson, and R.A. Alexander, "Leadership: It Can Make a Difference," *Academy of Management Journal,* Vol. 27, No. 4, 1984, pp. 765-776.

5. D. Campbell, *If I'm Charge Here, Why is Everybody Laughing?,* Niles, ILL.: Argus Communications, 1980, pp. 14-27.

6. Rensis Likert, "Motivation: The Core of Management," *American Management Association,* Personnel Series no. 155, 1953, pp. 3-21.

7. Rensis Likert, "Human Resource Accounting: Building and Assessing Productive Organizations," *Personnel,* May-June 1973, pp. 8-24.

8. Jacob B. Paperman and Desmond D. Martin, "Human Resource Accounting: A Managerial Tool," *Personnel,* vol. 54, no. 2, March-April 1977, pp. 41-50.

9. Desmond D. Martin and Philip Kintzele, "An Approach to Integrating Management by Objectives and Human Resources Accounting Concepts in Profit Making Enterprises," *Akron Business Economic Review,* Vol. 12, No. 2, Summer 1981, pp. 7-12.

10. Donald C. Pelz, "Influence: A Key to Effective Leadership in the First Line Supervisor," *Personnel,* Vol. 29, 1952, pp. 209-217.

11. Victor A. Thompson, *Modern Organization,* Alfred A. Knopf, New York, 1961, pp. 152-169.

12. Donald C. Pelz and F.M. Andrews, *Scientists in Organizations: Productive Climates for Research and Development,* University of Michigan Institute for Social Research, Ann Arbor, MI, 1976, p. 7.

13. Chester Barnard, *The Functions of the Executive,* Harvard University Press, Cambridge, Mass., 1938, pp. 161-163.

14. For a discussion of Lewin's work, see Ronald O. Lippitt and Ralph K. White, "The Social Climate of Childrens Groups," in *Child Behavior and Development,* (R.G. Barker), McGraw-Hill, New York, 1943, pp. 485-508.

15. T.A. Scandura, G.B. Graen, and M.A. Novak, "When Managers Decide Not to Decide Autocratically: An Investigation of Leader-Member Exchange and Decision Influence," *Journal of Applied Psychology,* Vol. 71, No. 4, 1986, pp. 001-006.

16. Hans J. Thamhain and David L. Wilemon, "Leadership Effectiveness in Program Management," *IEEE Transactions on Engineering Management,* Vol. EM24, No. 3, August 1977, pp. 102-108.

17. Victor H. Vroom and Philip W. Yetton, *Leadership and Decision Making,* University of Pittsburgh Press, Pittsburgh, 1973.

18. For a detailed discussion of situational leadership see Paul Hersey and Kenneth Blanchard, *Management of Organization Behavior,* Englewood Cliffs, NJ, Prentice Hall, 1982, pp. 150-192.

19. Ibid., p. 154.

20. Ibid., p. 155.

22. W. Blank, J.R. Weitzel, and S.G. Green, "A Test of the Situational Leadership Theory," Paper presented at National Meeting, Academy of Management, Chicago, IL, August 1986.

23. P.M. Mills and B.Z. Posner, "The Relationships Among Self Supervision, Structure and Technology in Professional Service Organizations," *Academy of Management Journal,* Vol. 25, No. 2, June 1982, pp. 437-443.

24. J. Slocum, and H. Sims, "A Typology for Integrating Technology, Organization and Job Design," *Human Relations,* Vol. 36, 1986, pp. 193-212.

25. A.G. Athos and R.E. Coffey, *Behavior in Organizations*: *A Multidimensional View,* Prentice Hall, Englewood Cliffs, N.J., 1975, p. 119.

26. For good analysis of dyads, see G.B. Graen and T.A. Scandura, "A Theory of Dyadic Career Reality," *Research in Personnel and Human Resources Management,* JAI Press Inc., Vol. 4, 1986, pp. 147-181.

27. A.A. Abdel-Halim, "Individual and Interpersonal Moderators of Employee Reactions to Job Characteristics: A Reexamination," *Personnel Psychology,* Vol. 32, 1979, pp. 121-137.

28. G.B. Graen, T.A. Scandura, and M.R. Graen, "A Field Experimental Test of the Moderating Effects of Growth Need Strength and Productivity," *Journal of Applied Psychology,* Vol. 71, No. 3, 1986, pp. 484-491.

29. J.R. Weitzel and G.B. Graen, "Extending Vertical Dyadic Linkages to Horizontal and Diagonal Dyadic Linkages: Dyadic Relationships in the Implementation of Computer Based Information Systems,"

Paper presented at the National Academy of Management Meeting, San Diego, CA, 1985.

30. E.E. Berlew and D.T. Hall, "The Socialization of Managers: Effects of Expectations on Performance," *Administrative Science Quarterly,* Vol. 11, 1966, pp. 207-223.

31. G.P. Latham, T.R. Mitchell, and D.L. Dossett, "The Importance of Participative Goal Setting and Anticipated Rewards on Goal Difficulty and Job Performance," *Journal of Applied Psychology,* Vol. 63, 1978, pp. 163-171.

32. Fred E. Fiedler, *A Theory of Leadership Effectiveness,* McGraw-Hill, New York, 1967, p. 142.

33. John P. Kotter, "Power, Dependence, and Effective Management," *Harvard Business Review,* July-August, 1977, pp. 125-136.

34. J.R.P. French, Jr., and B. Raven, "The Bases of Social Power," in *Studies in Social Power,* (Dowin Cartwright, ed.), University of Michigan Press, Ann Arbor, Mich., 1959, pp. 150-167.

35. John P. Kotter, "Power, Dependence, and Effective Management," *Harvard Business Review,* July-August, 1977, pp. 125-136.

36. Thamhain and Wilemon, "Leadership Effectiveness," in Program Management, *IEEE Transactions on Engineering Management,* Vol. EM 24, No. 3, August 1977, pp. 102-108.

37. Paul Hersey and Ken Blanchard, *Management of Organizational Behavior,* Prentice Hall, Englewood Cliffs, N.J., 4th ed., 1982, p. 152.

10

Change Processes in the Professional Environment

I. IMPORTANCE AND NATURE OF CHANGE

In his book, *The Adaptive Corporation*, Toffler argues that companies unable or unwilling to confront the challenges of a changing environment must inevitably wind up in the "Museum of Corporate Disasters."[1] One of the most perplexing problems that confronts managers of professionals is successfully introducing change in the organizational environment. Change is a *management problem*, because managers are usually the people who desire that changes be made for the purpose of increasing the ability of the organization to attain its goals.

The current business environment is so competitive that changes must be made on a fairly regular basis if the organization is to adapt and be effective (even remain in existence). In studies of organizational effectiveness, *adaptability and flexibility* continually show up among the top variables that impact on effectiveness as perceived by practicing managers.[2] Adaptability and flexibility are important parts of the change process. Managers in the professional environment are most concerned with change because the ability of the organization to adapt often rests with engineering, research and development, scientific and other professionals that are normally associated with an enterprise.

Change can be defined as any alteration in the established way of doing things. According to this definition, change does not necessarily have to involve technology or personnel. A simple modification of work location in the office or laboratory can cause similar management problems to those caused by larger or more apparent changes. For example, there have been instances where employees' desks were moved away from a window and productivity dropped sharply. Since the supervision and tasks assigned remained the same, the only thing that had changed was the arrangement of the desks in the room. Although in cases of this kind resistance has an impact on management problems, to the outside observer it is difficult to discern that any change has been made at all. Thus, it is not always major changes involving technology, formal organization, or task that increase management problems.

The movement of desks away from the window modified the social environment. Specifically, the windows were status symbols to the employees and perceived status was lowered among those employees who lost their preferred window location. Their performance deteriorated, and intragroup relationships suffered. Socialization is an important part of the professional work environment and managers of these groups need to examine the social impact of proposed change.

There are many facets to the change process ranging from the previously described rather simple disruption of social relationships to large scale strategic change that involves modifications or transformation of organization culture and managerial value systems. Tichy defines this larger type of change as non-routine, non-incremental and discontinued change which alters the overall orientation of the organization.[3] He argues that the task of managers regarding change is to deliberately and intentionally change the overall orientation of the organization. Overall orientation consists of organizational core values, mission, strategy and determines the way the organization operates including the alignment among the professional (technical), political, and cultural subsystems.

It is becoming increasingly clear that planned change is an integral part of high performance organizations. Peters and Waterman suggest that "transforming leadership," which they define as leaders that are value shapers and change oriented, is a basic dimension of effectiveness.[4] Similarly, Vail suggests that high performance is related to strong leadership and involves inducing clarity, consensus and commitment regarding the organizations purpose.[5] He says these necessary leadership skills can be learned and advocates the establishment of learning programs to provide them to key managers.[5] In summarizing the work on transforming organizations to excellence, Levy and Merry conclude that three leadership dimensions are important: 1) purposing, 2) innovation, and 3) people orientation.[6] Purposing provides organizational purpose and meaning, and innovation is deeply rooted in creativity and change. The people orientation involves open communication and protection of self-esteem emphasized in earlier chapters as well as high involvement management techniques that are developed in Chapter 12. These same authors identify three types of driving forces for change as follows:[7] First, internal forces which include strategic choices, creativity, new needs and belief systems and the tendency of organizations to grow. Second, external driving forces which include a variety of market changes that require adaptation for survival. Third, the interaction between internal and external driving forces which creates choices for change and precipitates further change. For example, when an organization creates a new product, this is likely to foster other changes within the organization. There is a continuous dynamic interaction among these forces that produces organizational change.

Managers must lead in an environment that is constantly changing. Employee commitment is needed to make change work, consequently, the people orientation is always an important part of successful change. Although professionals may be prone to accept change because of their level of education and accomplishment, these same characteristics may actually increase their resistance tendencies. The large investment in their own training and skill development will cause high sensitivity to how changes affect individual skill application and career development. Changes that are perceived to impact negatively in these areas are likely to meet strong resistance. Leaders of professionals need particularly strong skills in communication so that needed change is integrated into a future vision of success and growth for both the organization and professional. Additionally, these leaders need to understand the change process and how professionals are likely to react to it.

Strategic changes involve a transformation or modification of the value system within professionals. There can be a considerable time lag between managerially imposed changes and this inner change needed to make them effective for the organizational unit as a whole. Also, without strong leadership this needed inner change may never occur. Thus, managers of professionals face two major problems in making strategic changes for departmental and organizational adaptation. First, they must lead the way for strategic change. As Peters and Waterman point out, high performing leaders are true path finders.[8] Table 10.1 contains Peters' rules for managing change which can be very useful to making needed changes happen in the professional work environment. Note the emphasis placed on time, persistence, and status among these rules. Also, these are managerial rules as opposed to technical rules; namely, they require the application of managerial planning skills. Second, as previously mentioned in many parts of this book, the transition from doer to planner is often very difficult for the professional promoted into management.

It is important that professionals see structural change as a real benefit to themselves and their careers. Also, the leader needs to be perceived as technically competent, persistent, and in control. Unfortunately strong leadership does not always eliminate or reduce resistance to change. All professionals need to understand the nature of resistance to change so the harmful effects can be minimized. While it is commonly believed that there is a natural human tendency to resist change, there is little supporting evidence. A major point made in Toffler's *Future Shock* is that changes are taking place

Table 10.1   Rules for Managing Change

Rule	Interpretation
1. Spend time	Spending time exerts, in itself, a "claim" on the decision-making system.
2. Persist	Having more patience than other people often results in adoption of a chosen course of action.
3. Exchange status for substance	One of the most effective ways to gather support for program is to reward allies with visible tokens of recognition.
4. Facilitate opposition participation	Often those outside the formal decision centers overestimate the feasibility of change; encouraged to participate, they will often become more realistic.
5. Overload the system	Bureaucracies chew up most projects, but on the other hand, some sneak through; merely launching more projects is likely to result in more successes.
6. Provide garbage cans	Organizations endlessly argue issues to induce desired outcomes, put "throw-away" issues at the top of agendas (to absorb debate) saving substantive issues for later.
7. Manage unobtrusively	Certain actions can influence the organization pervasively but almost imperceptibly; moreover, the resulting changes will persist with little further attention.
8. Interpret history	By articulating a particular version of events, the leader can alter people's perception of what has been happening; whoever writes the minutes influences the outcome.

Source: T.J. Peters, "Symbols Patterns and Settings: An Optimistic Case for Getting Things Done," *Organizational Dynamics,* Autumn 1978, p. 6, reprinted with permission.

faster in America than we can adjust to them.[9] Our society is characterized by rapid change, and a cursory examination of observable events indicates that, in general, change is eventually accepted. The effective manager works to minimize the time needed for the acceptance of change, because resistance is usually costly to both management and employees.

II. THREE PHASES OF CHANGE

While there are several frameworks for examining resistance to change, an examination of the three phases or stages of the change process is particularly helpful. Since the primary concern of most managers is to reduce employee resistance and increase efficiency, it is important to realize that resistance can occur during any one of the three specific phases or stages that accompany every organizational change. Specifically, these three phases are the threat, impact, and after-effect of change.[10] The ability of the manager to plan for change, anticipate problems before they become costly, and understand the present stage of the specific change can be a major factor in determining managerial effectiveness.

A. Threat Phase

The threat phase of change is that time period during which a rumor moves through informal (grapevine) or regular management channels that suggest a change is possible or likely to be imposed. A threat phase may occur even though the change *never actually happens*. If employees *believe* that such a change will happen, they can start resisting it immediately. Employees may quit their jobs or lower their productivity long before a change ever actually takes place. These negative responses by employees are a result of the fact that they believe that a change is actually coming or contemplated. The length of time and significance of the threat phase is determined by the speed and the magnitude of the change. Changes that are made quickly obviously have a short threat phase, while changes that are large and require a considerable amount of planning usually have a threat phase of a year or more. Examples of these latter types of change include changes in building location, alterations involving technological improvements, or a major change in work procedures. These changes are usually perceived to be significant by employees, require long lead times, and consequently may have a long threat phase. Managerial ability to deal properly with the threat phase has a direct influence on both the nature and extent of resistance encountered. Involving professionals in change planning, being frank and honest about probable impact in answering questions, and not making misleading promises are important elements of the sound management of change.

B. Impact Phase

The second phase of change, which is commonly referred to as the impact phase, occurs when the organizational change is implemented. Often managers get through the threat phase without difficulty because the company has a good reputation for changes in the past or they have explained the nature of the change adequately. Once the change is introduced, however, serious problems may confront these managers. Why? Many times when professionals are actually trying a new process or building new work relationships, they find that it is actually more difficult than they first realized, and they then begin resisting the change. Also, employees may find that after the change is actually introduced, many of its aspects that they thought would be insignificant in the planning phase actually turn out to be much more threatening than was originally believed. This situation calls for appropriate managerial action designed to minimize the inefficiencies due to resistant behavior by employees. Increased attention needs to be given to communication with professionals so their true problems with the change can be fully understood and resolved.

C. After-effect Phase

The after-effect phase of change can involve resistance for several months, a year, or even longer after the change has apparently been introduced successfully. Employees sometimes accept the impact phase of change simply because it is a new stimulating activity that is different from their previous work assignments. Unfortunately, however, the newness wears off, and three or four months after a change has been introduced, workers may decide they prefer to have the "old way" back again. Resistance in the form of poor workmanship, increased conflict, or lack of tolerance for fellow workers may occur. Thus, the change process is usually long term, particularly for larger changes. In fact, the after-effects phase may occur over a period of several years from the time the change is first contemplated until it has been fully integrated and accepted into the organization.

Due to upward communication barriers that were discussed in Chapter 7, employees may not tell their managers the real problem. Since these managers do not associate sloppy effort or declining morale with a change made several months earlier, it is not surprising that the after-effect phase can be the most troublesome and difficult to resolve. When a change in subordinate effectiveness occurs for no apparent reason, the manager should seek an answer to the following question: *Have any significant changes been made during the past two years that could be influencing my subordinates negatively*? If the answer is yes, practicing communication skills (see Chapter 7) can be helpful in resolving the problem.

III. CAUSES OF RESISTANCE TO CHANGE

A common cause of resistance in the professional environment is *fear*; specifically, fear of what the change will do to the individuals that have to work with the change. Managerial action that increases understanding reduces fear and increases acceptance. As was seen in the case involving office window location, changes that are perceived by professionals to lower their social status in the organization tend to be resisted. Feelings of self-worth are often influenced by subtle changes, and employees vehemently resist changes that threaten their self-worth. The method used by specific managers in introducing changes can have as much of an impact on employee perceptions of self-worth as the changes themselves.[11]

It is also true that employees may have a genuine concern and feeling of *insecurity* which occupies their minds when changes take place that cause the environment to appear unstable. Under these circumstances, employees often do not fully realize the impact of their reaction on those around them. Methods that provide consideration of employee feelings are very helpful in minimizing these kinds of perception problems. As previously discussed, since professionals have a large personal investment in their training, they may be even more concerned than non-professionals about proposed changes. Questions often asked by professionals in these cases are as follows:

> How will these changes affect my ability to use my specialized training and acquired skill?
>
> How will these changes influence organizational attitudes concerning the importance of my work or profession?
>
> How will these changes impact on my promotional opportunities? What about professional growth and new learning?
>
> Will new changes increase formalization and inflexibility around my job? (see Chapter 11)

Changes that upset valued *social relationships* tend to be resisted. As indicated in Chapter 8, social needs are often very strong, and when changes are made that upset social relationships and frustrate these needs, they will be resisted. Employee needs for *security* are also strong. When changes are made that are perceived to be threatening either to an employee's physical or economic security, they will be resisted. Managers should ask themselves the following questions before an attempt is made to integrate change in work environment: What will this change do to (1) the status of the professionals affected by the change, (2) the social relationships of the professionals affected by the change, and (3) the economic and physical security of the employees? If the change has a negative impact on any one of these three variables, then management can predict with a high degree of certainty that these changes will be resisted.

Managers of technical and staff professionals such as engineers and health specialists often overlook the psychological effects of change that appear to be logical and are unprepared for the resistance that follows.[12] In addition, studies have shown that technical specialists often resist changes that do not originate in their own departments.[13] Apparently, these specialists view originating ideas as an index of departmental status and strive to protect the status image of their departments by rejecting outside ideas. This rejection can be troublesome becuase it usually is not based on the true value of the proposal. Successful managers will attempt to minimize this resistance either by eliminating its cause or by minimizing its importance to the employees. Emphasizing the value of cooperation with outside individuals and units to the ultimate well being of the professional group can be helpful in stimulating greater acceptance of outside ideas and proposals.

Change can be considered from two points of view, namely, the change agent or manager who implements the change and the people (professional subordinates) affected by the change. Much of the practical and theoretical emphasis has been focused on change agents and how they may best implement proposed changes. The implicit assumption often is that employees have little capability to accept or express positive responses toward planned change. This assumption may cause managers to anticipate resistance from employees which may lead to resistant behavior that would not ordinarily occur.[14] Specifically, managers may focus so strongly on probable resistance that employees respond as they feel they are expected to, namely, to resist the proposed change. These managerial assumptions are often both unwise and unwarranted particularly in professional work units.

IV. SPECIFIC METHODS AND TECHNIQUES FOR REDUCING RESISTANCE

Considerable attention has been directed toward proper ways of introducing change so that resistance is overcome. Many of these techniques have proven value in the professional environment. Often fear of losses in status, security, or destruction of social relationships are imaginary. In these cases, introducing employee participation into the change process can be vital in reducing resistance to the change. As discussed in Chapter 9, democratic leadership is

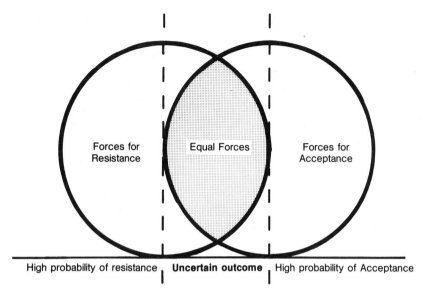

Figure 10.1 columns within figure:

Forces for Resistance | Equal Forces | Forces for Acceptance

High probability of resistance | **Uncertain outcome** | High probability of Acceptance

Figure 10.1   Influence of forces on subordinates that suggest acceptance of or resistance to proposed changes

helpful for managers when these kinds of situations are present. Resistance to change can be reduced if the manager can "sell through participation" the idea that employees will be better off as a result of making the change. As shown in Figure 10.1, unless the forces for acceptance are clearly greater than those for resistance, the probability of employees resisting the change is high. The extent and direction of these forces are determined by several variables. The more important of these are the manager, organizational climate, work group attitudes, employee value systems, and the change itself. The manager can often use participation among professionals to impact favorably on enough of these variables so these employees perceive that a net gain will result from making the change. If the manager is successful with participation, in the context of Figure 10.1, the forces favoring the change would exceed the forces against the change, and resistance will be alleviated as a managerial problem. In fact, participation may be both useful and necessary in implementing change in professional environments.

The process of gaining employee acceptance often involves creating a "we" attitude in making changes. This attitude can result from employee involvement through democratic management. Ideally, employees should feel that part of the substance of the change is their own idea. This is not as difficult as it may at first sound, because managerially promoted changes are usually desirable for the organization, and as the organization benefits, more rewards are available to the individual employee. Many times it is clear that a change is going to yield direct benefits to professionals, e.g., create better research facilities, new learning opportunities, more pleasant working conditions, or modernized technology. In these instances participation effectively reduces employee resistance, because the improved understanding increases the strength of the forces for acceptance.

Resistant employee attitudes do not automatically yield resistant behavior because attitudes of colleagues and the overall work group often keep employees from expressing their true feelings (peer pressure). Managers that can convince informal group leaders of the need for proposed changes can minimize the impact of resistant attitudes by specific employees. Professionals are unlikely to exhibit resistant behavior if it is not supported by the group in which membership is valued. As pointed out in Chapter 6, cohesive work groups can exercise great control over the expression of individual employee attitudes. In effect one of the strongest "we" attitudes that is potentially available to managers of professionals consists of the development of a favorable overall group attitude toward proposed changes.

Creating a "we" attitude involves the willingness to compromise on the part of management. For example, a manager discusses with a group of professionals the idea of introducing new technology into the work process and meets with some resistance such as a suggestion from the group that one piece of equipment should not be purchased as previously planned. This suggestion should be honored if practical. The "we" attitude emerges when the manager responds positively to these kinds of requests, because the manager is perceived to be both responsive and supportive through this sincere compromise effort and the professional subordinates see that they are impacting on the change process. Conversely, the manager who invites his subordinates in for suggestions on changes and gets several suggestions for correction and modification but ignores them loses both credibility and the valuable "we" attitude.

Several research studies including the classic Coch and French study of the late 1940s support the fact that change by decree is likely to meet with a great deal of resistance.[15] Coch and French had changes introduced by three possible methods in a manufacturing environment as follows: First, a group of subordinates were involved in the change on a total participation basis. Second, employees selected representatives from their group to meet with management and discuss the change. Third, the changes were introduced by decree or with no participation. In surveying the results of the three particular methods, these researchers found that there was less resistance exhibited by the group that experienced total participation. Apparently, a "we" attitude ensued which had beneficial effects. Introducing change by decree caused the most resistance among the three methods. Autocratic change usually destroys the "we" attitude and unless the change is clearly seen as favorable, employees will resist it.

V. ORGANIZATIONAL CRISES AND CUTBACK MANAGEMENT

Although many managers fail to plan for it and naturally avoid negative thinking, an increasing part of today's organizational life involves crises situations which includes force reductions among professional employee groups. One of the most frequent aspects of the change process is the occurrence of crisis situations. Crises often occur because managers fail to identify the need for change or do not implement changes in a timely fashion.

Slatter has identified four stages of crisis development and typical management response patterns as follows:[16]

1. Hidden Crises - In this stage managers are unaware of emerging major problems, and the need to implement changes.

2. Crisis denial - During this stage there are visible signs of crisis within the firm, but managers are unwilling to change. They often suggest changes that have already been implemented or state that existing problems are beyond their control or will be solved without any change. Thus need for action is denied. Managers may sincerely believe that they are on the correct path or they may feel they are taking a position necessary for they may feel they are taking a position necessary for self preservation. According to Slatter, managers often believe they will be blamed and may lose their jobs if previous actions are found to be wrong. Also, strategic change usually involves alterations in the management power structure, and managers who currently hold power are likely to resist needed change. Managers may take action to make the firm's financial position look better than it really is.

3. Organizational Disintegration - Since needed changes are not being implemented, the organization exhibits serious problems. While some change is likely to occur, it is often too little and too late. Existing decisions makers become more autocratic, and the full and impartial assessment of alternatives does not occur.

4. Organizational collapse - This stage is characterized by partial or total organizational failure. Effective decision making decreases and commitment to organizational goals declines. Managers become even more self oriented and the mobile employees leave the firm.

Slatter suggests that the earlier the developing crisis is confronted, less dramatic organizational change is necessary and the greater the chance of successful turnaround.[16] While some managerial action may occur during the "hidden crisis" stage, more often the crisis precipitates the needed changes. The presence of severe crises cause top management or boards of directors to lose confidence in existing leadership. This can lead to replacement of top executives which increases the probability of successful changes and turnaround for the firm. Once a firm's organization starts to disintegrate a new chief executive is necessary to bring about a complete change in organizational structure. Replacement at the top management level is consistent with the need for transformational leadership identified earlier in this chapter. Replacement of personnel at any level is one of the common and effective ways to implement change. While replacement is not necessarily practical in many cases, removal of professionals with negative attitudes is likely to be very effective.

The message to managers in the professional environment is to keep communications channels open both ways. Keep attuned to problems as well as successes. Try to uncover potential crises at the hidden stage and don't allow movement to crisis denial. In fact, crisis denial is a self defeating position that will likely lead to both personal and organizational failure. Changes may be needed that involve transfer, layoff, or dismissal of professionals. These kinds of organizational changes are often inappropriate for participation and subordinate involvement. For example, when a manager is faced with decisions involving employee layoffs (staff reductions) or disciplinary action against specific employees, it is usually not fair or useful to involve subordinates in these sensitive matters. In simple terms, increasing understanding and involvement through participation will not increase the forces for acceptance of these kinds of changes (see Figure 10.1). However, it is often helpful to obtain employee participation in the formulation of policies guiding layoff or disciplinary procedures prior to implementation.

VI. THE TASK FORCE CONCEPT

Major changes in the professional environment can often be integrated effectively with the use of the task force. This concept simply involves appointing a group of key subordinates and managers to study problems where changes are needed and to recommend the nature and content of changes to be made. Three important steps are necessary in making task forces work. First, select key group leaders for the task force. These employees should have the respect and support of their co-workers, and should have proven performance records. Second, use democratic techniques in managing the task force so all members will become involved and committed. Third, once the task force makes a recommendation for change, allow it to continue as a unit to play a key role in implementation and follow-up.

The positive results from following these steps will be that major changes are often integrated effectively into the organization with a minimum of conflict. Obviously, the change must be of significant size and impact so that the cost of formulating and operating the task force will be worthwhile. Many changes that involve new technologies, work procedures, or product lines or services, where the focus of employee activities must be changed, are particularly suited for task force assignment. If the task force is formed early during major changes, especially when the change is initially contemplated, the threat phase of the change is usually minimized or eliminated. The task force can gather data, field questions, and solicit input so that employees understand and become more involved in what is going to be done. This involvement is particularly important to professional employees, because their expertise can make an important contribution to a proposed change.

VII. WHAT TO DO WHEN PARTICIPATION DOES NOT WORK

In addition to cutback management and cases involving disciplinary action, there are other changes that, no matter how much participation is involved, the professional employee cannot see that an improved personal position will result from making the change. In these situations there are two avenues available to managers. One is to use other compensating factors to offset the professional's perceived negative impact of the change. Some possible compensating factors are discussed below.

First, increasing the *level of pay* to the employees affected and thereby reducing their dissatisfaction; second, increasing the amount of *fringe benefits* or privileges such as travel opportunities or vacation time; and third, making changes in the physical environment, such as improved facilities or adding to support staff. The amount of control the manager has over many of the above factors varies greatly from one organization to another and within a given firm. However, managers usually have some influence on one or more of these areas (often more than they realize), and the important point is to use it wisely. Compensating for the negative aspects of the change by increasing some of the hygiene factors or improving intrinsic job design is useful in offsetting negative attitudes about given changes. This approach costs money, and the cost has to be weighed against the benefits received. The key question for the manager to ask is as follows: *Are the costs of resistance going to outweigh the costs of providing these extra compensatory factors?* A positive or negative answer should determine the course of action.

A second approach to reducing resistance when change is perceived negatively and participation is not working is to introduce change on a tentative basis. When making changes on a tentative basis, technical managers should obtain employee agreement to try the changes, but if the changes turn out to be disruptive and dissatisfying, they also collectively agree to withdraw the change. If the tentative change concept is to work, managers must be able to reverse decisions regarding change. Consequently, if a change is made that management does not believe is reversible, it should not be made on a tentative basis. Both personal and managerial integrity is at stake in the change process, and to agree to do things and then not follow through reduces managerial effectiveness. Also, managers should not agree to make changes with employees that are impossible or make other promises simply to get acceptance of a change. Professionals will not respect a manager that says one thing and does another. Even proven methods of introducing change such as participation should not be undertaken unless the manager values participation and intends to utilize the input provided by the subordinates. The change situation should be analyzed carefully by the manager before changes are made, and then one of the particular approaches outlined in this chapter may be applied.

VIII. SUMMARY

If all desirable changes were readily accepted, resistance would not be a problem. Unfortunately, change is often resisted which results in increased costs as well as causing managers both psychological and technological problems of adjustment. Over the next several years many changes will occur in most organizations. Some will be small, but others will be of great magnitude. While some will be planned, others will be surprises. Managers need to pave the way for employee acceptance of these changes, because they are needed if American firms are to survive in newer globally competitive markets.

Professionals within the firm are likely to be the major contributors of new ideas that emerge in American business. These ideas which are vital ingredients for most firms may make the difference between success and failure. Specific change introduction techniques and the application of other methods to reduce resistance as developed in this chapter will be increasingly important components of the successful professional work environment. The more important points are summarized below:

1. Effectively handling planned strategic change may be the key to survival for many American firms.

2. Managers of professionals need to be strong leaders who play a "transforming role" and are "path finders" for their units.

3. While some characteristics of professionals suggest they are more likely to accept change than non-professionals, in several instances these same characteristics may lead to even stronger resistance.

4. Changes are not automatically resisted, but employees must perceive there are distinct advantages to making a change in order to avoid resistant behavior.

5. Since resistant attitudes by individual employees do not necessarily lead to resistant behavior because of environmental pressures, it is important for managers to work with group leadership in order to overcome specific employee resistances. If employees value their group relationships, which is common among professionals, they will be reluctant to resist changes that have overall group support. Informal group leadership can be an important ally of management in making changes.

6. The extent of employees' trust in management coupled with their own sense of security impacts strongly on acceptance or rejection of change.

7. Resistance to change can occur during any one of three specific phases of the change process.

8. Changes that are not understood often become clouded by employee perceptions of fear and uncertainty, which leads directly to resistant behavior.

9. Changes that threaten job skills or are perceived to impact negatively on job content or status factors important to the professional staff are likely to result in resistant behavior.

10. While participation in the change process is one of the most useful ways of reducing resistance, there are several types of change problems where it is ineffective. Management's provision for additional remuneration or making the change tentative can help reduce resistance when participation is not enough. In cases involving cutback management employee involvement may be dysfunctional and inappropriate.

11. The task force concept is an important vehicle for implementing change.

12. Managers should support promises with action, because management credibility is an important factor in determining the nature and extent of resistance among professionals.

REFERENCES

1. Alvin Toffler, *The Adaptive Corporation,* New York: McGraw-Hill Book Co., 1984.

2. Richard Steers, "Problems in the Measurement of Organizational Effectiveness," *Administrative Science Quarterly,* Vol. 20, 1975, pp. 564-558.

3. N.M. Tichy, *Managing Strategic Change,* New York: John Wiley and Sons, 1983, p. 17.

4. T. Peters and R. Waterman, *In Search of Excellence,* New York: Harper and Row, 1982, p. 82.

5. P. Vail, "The Purposing of High Performance Systems," *Organization Dynamics,* Autumn 1982, pp. 23-40.

6. A. Levy and V. Merry, *Organizational Transformation,* New York: Praeger 1986, p. 55.

7. Ibid., p. 236.

8. Peters and Waterman, Op. Cit. p. 82.

9. Alvin Toffler, *Future Shock,* Bantam Books, New York 1981, p. 259.

10. Irving L. Janis, "Problems of Theory in the Analysis of Stress Behavior," *Journal of Social Issues,* Summer 1954, pp. 12-25.

11. Bidu Shekhar Jha, "Resistance to Change - How to Overcome," *Industrial Management,* May-June 1977, pp. 21-22.

12. Keith Davis, *Human Behavior at Work,* McGraw-Hill, New York, 1977, p. 165.

13. Melville Dalton, "Changing Line Staff Relationships," *Personnel Administration,* Vol. 29, No. 2, March-April 1966, pp. 40-48.

14. Gary Powell and Barry Posuer, "Resistance to Change Reconsidered: Implications for Managers," *Human Resources Management,* Vol. 17, No. 1, Spring, 1978, pp. 29-34.

15. Lester Coch and John R.P. French, Jr., "Overcoming Resistance to Change," *Human Relations,* Vol. 1, No. 4, 1948, pp. 512-532.

16. Stuart St. P. Slatter, "The Impact of Crisis on Managerial Behavior," *Business Horizons,* May-June 1984, pp. 65-68.

11

Organizational Conflict and Stress

I. CONFLICT IN THE PROFESSIONAL WORK ENVIRONMENT

When an individual or group finds its goal directed activities are being blocked by other individuals, groups, or coalitions; conflict occurs. Early views of conflict in organizations were inherently negative and conflict was seen as a potential threat to overall effectiveness.[1] Many of these negative views are related to the additional burdens placed on communication and ensuing stress that results from dysfunctional conflict. However, all conflict is not dysfunctional, and managers are now becoming increasingly aware of positive outcomes that may be frequently associated with conflict. Among these are:

1. Conflict may improve decision making, i.e., force upper level managers to make difficult personnel replacement decisions that are needed but would not otherwise be made.

2. Conflict may force top management to take a more critical view of the organization; and, as a consequence, needed strategic change is more likely to occur.

3. Conflict can cause marginal employees to leave the organization. As more productive workers gain control of larger amounts of resources, less productive workers are encouraged to change their direction or job, and the firm is strengthened.

4. Some conflict contributes to a more interesting work environment.

5. Conflict may be an important motivational force that results in professionals seeking additional training and development in order to upgrade skills to remain or become more competitive.

Of course, not all conflict has positive outcomes for the manager and the organization. Conflict can be a leading cause of stress which may contribute to health problems for the individual employee. The complex problem of stress and individual deterioration in performance will be analyzed in detail later in this chapter.

Professionals, in research and development as well as several other staff functions are often relied on for a large measure of the creativity and innovation within the firm. Excessive conflict is likely to reduce their individual productivity levels in these important areas. High mobility associated with skilled professionals increases their sensitivity within the work environment which often reduces tolerance levels and raises turnover rates for this valued employee group. Consequently, managers in the professional work environment that are able to manage conflict constructively will substantially increase their managerial effectiveness. Managers need to be aware of systems within the organization that are designed to reduce levels of conflict as well as specific managerial techniques that can be effective in conflict management.

One of the major functions of good human resources management is to help managers establish procedures and policies for reducing levels of dysfunctional conflict. In recent years, conflict reduction systems have tended to include more formal representation procedures. A large number of grivances and disciplinary actions may indicate either the success or failure of these formal procedures particularly in their early stages. Similarly, they may also signal difficulties in the conflict resolution or problem solving systems within the organization. When these systems are not working well and dysfunctional conflict increases, the attitudes of salaried workers including many professionals is adversely affected.[2] Conflict as measured by grievance rates and disciplinary actions correlate with each other and impact on both behavior and attitudes.[2] High conflict intensity among professionals will usually result in poor organizational performance.[2]

A. Techniques to Reduce Conflict

As with so many issues in management, the basic means used to resolve conflict depends on the situation. Miles describes several conflict resolution strategies that are particularly applicable to the professional work environment as follows:[3]

1. *Alter the Context and/or Relationships* - Changing relationships can reduce conflict. For example, if two professionals are fighting about jurisdiction over specific tasks, the manager may be able to separate either the tasks or the two employees thereby reducing the conflict.

2. *Alter the Issues in Dispute* - In using this approach the manager's objective is to make the issues less personal to the parties involved. One way to accomplish this is to help employees focus on more important goals (superordinate) for the organization. For example, the manager of a sports team can show that winning the championship is most beneficial and important to all parties involved. Since existing interpersonal conflict is interfering with the attainment of this important goal, it is in the interest of each player to cooperate and resolve it. Professionals as well as other employee groups are likely to cooperate if cooperation is seen as promoting their own interests.

3. *Changing the Individuals Involved* - Of course conflict is often resolved when one or more of the conflicting parties is removed from the situation, preferably through transfer. However, if their attitude and/or performance is clearly detrimental to the organization, discharge may be appropriate. Although these alternatives are difficult to follow, they send clear messages to other professionals in the work group about how conflict is handled.

Potential conflict involving other employees is being affected by how current conflict is being managed. It is most important that managers of professionals take some action to resolve dysfunctional conflict. Issues involving conflict resolution are similar to most other issues confronting todays manager in that *preventing dysfunctional conflict is the most effective way to manage it.* There are several steps managers in the professional work environment can take that will help to prevent destructive conflict, as follows:

1. *Clarify Lines of Authority and Responsibility* - Professionally trained people are likely to be jealous of their work assignments. They are often seeking greater challenges and are likely to assume tasks that appear to be especially interesting. When task assignments are clear and organizational boundaries are well established the potential for conflict is reduced.

2. *Keep Lines of Communication Open* - As has been stated throughout this book, open lines of communication foster managerial effectiveness. Employees may not talk openly about their differences with others; particularly if these differences are personal in nature. Open communications increase the probability that managers can learn about potentially dysfunctional conflict early and then take steps to reduce it.

3. *Reduce Employee Interdependency* - Greater potential exists for conflict when employees are dependent on each other to perform their tasks. Autonomous

work assignments not only increase levels of motivation among professionals (Chapter 8), they also reduce the likelihood of conflict.

4. *Establish Predictability in the Reward and Disciplinary Process* - Any perceived favoritism in the distribution of rewards or the allocation of punishments may create conflict among subordinates. As developed in Chapter 8, managers need to base rewards on objective measures, preferably performance related, and enforce rules in a predictable fashion with relative consistency.

II. MANAGING STRESS

A. Stress and Strain Defined

Stress has been defined by McCormick[4] as "any aspect of human activity or the environment acting upon the individual which results in some undesirable cost to, or reaction upon, the individual." McCormick also defined human strain as "the 'cost' or effect or consequence on the individual, of stress."[4] Sources of stress can be physiological or psychological.

Sources of stress that emanate from work include high energy tasks (physiological); and information overloads (psychological). Sources of stress caused by the environment include excessive heat or cold, and noise or vibration (physiological); and confinement or a threatening hazard (psychological). Sources of stress related to the circadian rhythm include traveling distances that span several time zones (jet-lag) and sleep loss. This stress affects both the physiological and psychological condition of the human.

There are several measures of human strain. Physiological measures include the following:

Physical - Blood pressure, heart rate, sinus arrhythmia, pulse volume/deficit, body and skin surface temperature, and respiratory rate.

Chemical - Blood content, urine analysis, oxygen consumption/deficit, and calorie intake.

Electrical - EEG (electroencephalogram), EKG (electro-
cardiogram), EMG (electromyograph), and the GSR
(galvanic skin response).

Pyschological measures of strain include the following:

Activity - Work rate, number of errors, and the eye blink
rate.
Attitudes - Boredom, resistance to change, not cooperative, and strong preference to be left alone.

As previously indicated, dysfunctional conflict is a major source
of increased stress levels among professionals. Although limited
amounts of stress contribute to improved performance, stress overload may cause a noticeable deterioration in performance, as well
as increased absenteeism and turnover. Studies have shown that
higher stress combined with lower organizational commitment
contributes to voluntary termination of employment.[5] Since professionals often have work loyalties that extend well beyond their
present organizational affiliation, high turnover may result from
high stress. Two major factors contributing to stress among professionals are short lead times for work completion and close supervision.

A knowledge of a professional employee's customary behavior
patterns can help the manager to recognize changes that may indicate stress overload. Ivancevich and Matteson identify many of
these behavioral changes as follows:[6]

Working late more often than usual
Difficulty in making decisions
Significant decline in task performance
Problems in interpersonal relationships
Increased absenteeism

While these changes may occur sporadically during an extended
work period, if several occur at the same time or one (or a few)
with great intensity, corrective action is appropriate. The alert
manager often can spot problems in early stages which makes correction more effective and easier. It is important to note that while

all of the above behavior changes are undesirable, those that directly influence other workers compound poor performance. Stressful situations involving more than one individual should receive top priority for manager intervention. Much of the stress created within organizations is people generated. The authors have observed this so much that they have formulated a non-scientific and somewhat humorous definition of stress as follows: "Stress sometimes can be defined as the confusion created when one's mind overrides the body's natural desire to inflict physical injury on another person who truly deserves it!''

B. Individual Reactions to Stress

In addition to the desire to increase managerial effectiveness another important reason to handle stress properly and in a timely fashion is the possible connection between high stress and coronary artery and heart disease. Attempts to understand this relationship have led researchers to categorize individuals as either exhibiting Type A or Type B behavior.[7] Traits associated with Type A behavior include:

Excessive competitiveness
Impatience and never having enough time
Insecurity

When confronted with high stress, type A's react with a flight or fight response. If regularly activated, this reaction produces higher than normal levels of hormone production and cholesterol, and an increased tendency for the clotting elements of the blood to fall out and settle onto the walls of veins and arteries. Persons who experienced this behavior response were more likely to develop hypertension, headaches, ulcers, as well as increased vulnerability to other diseases. Two pioneering physicians who have done extensive research in this area, Meyer Friedman and Ray Rosenman indicate that in the absence of a type A behavior pattern, coronary heart disease usually does not occur before the age of seventy. However, for type A individuals coronary heart disease can easily erupt in the thirties or forties.[8] It is important for managers in the professional work environment to reduce this possibility both for themselves and their subordinates.

In contrast, Type B's are more relaxed, less hostile and do not feel constantly pressed for time. It has been estimated that 50 percent of the population is mostly Type A, 40 percent mostly Type B and 10 percent having equal traits of both.[8]

Stress occurs when a professional makes a cognitive appraisal that a significant imbalance exists between environmental demands and response capability. Appraisals of response capabilities are influenced by the extent the professional feels he or she controls the work environment. Those who feel a strong sense of control are called internals, and those who perceive little environmental control are called externals. Externals see luck or others as primarily control factors. Studies indicate that when internals and externals are exposed to tasks designed to be stressful, internals handle information more effectively and are better at using their experience on a task to improve their performance.[9] Managers who grant more autonomy and control to their professional subordinates will give them a stronger basis for coping with stress and reducing anxiety. Of course, there are many other positive benefits to the organization from involvement management, as mentioned in earlier chapters; these are developed more fully in Chapter 12.

Research also has shown a relationship between level of anxiety and coping response.[10] Two types of anxiety have been identified. State anxiety is a transitory, emotional experience which includes increased feelings of apprehension and arousal. Trait anxiety is the tendency to respond anxiously across a wide variety of situations.[11] State anxiety results in limited information processing capacity and sensitivity, and confused patterns of decision making.[11] Trait anxiety fosters an individual to feel personally inadequate and exaggerate potential threats. The negative consequences of each of these anxious states suggest that managers should attempt to reduce stress.

C. Psychological Disorders

The National Institute for Occupational Safety and Health (NIOSH) has developed a list of ten leading work-related diseases and injuries which includes psychological disorders.[12] There is increasing evidence that an unsatisfactory work environment may contribute to psychological disorders. The professional is not immune to this potential problem. Studies have shown that factors contributing to an unsatisfactory work environment may include work overload, lack of control over one's work, nonsupportive work, and machine-paced work. Psychological disorders that can result from such factors may be classified as: affective disturbances, e.g., anxiety, irritability; behavioral problems, e.g., substance abuse, sleep difficulties; psychiatric disorders, e.g., neuroses; and somatic complaints, e.g., headache, gastrointestinal symptoms. In addition to psychological disorders, stressful working conditions may have a systemic influence, possibly affecting the etiology and/or prognosis of other disease states, as suggested by recent studies of stress-related immunologic suppression.[13]

Although data bases currently available for determining the extent of work-related psychological disorders are limited, several indicators suggest that these problems impose substantial health and financial costs in the United States. A California study showed that claims for the development of "work-related neuroses" more than doubled during 1980-1982; claims for all other disabling work-related injuries during the same period actually decreased by about one-tenth.[14] A study of representative medical claims throughout the country showed that during 1980-1982 claims for "mental stress" that developed gradually, i.e., a chronic problem unrelated to a single traumatic incident or to any physical work-related disorder, accounted for about 11 percent of all occupational disease claims.[15] The American Psychiatric Association now lists "occupational stress" in its *Diagnostic and Statistical Manual* as a subcategory of the major diagnostic axis of "psychosocial stress."[16]

There are increasing data on the relationship between specific working conditions and psychological disorders. For example, in a NIOSH questionnaire survey of over 2,000 workers in 23 different occupations, strong occupational differences were found in psychosocial job stressors and in somatic and affective complaints. Ratings of boring, repetitive job tasks and role ambiguity were more prominent among several classes of blue-collar workers than

Table 11.1 The Social Readjustment Rating Scale

Life Event	Stress Value (Points)
1. Death of spouse	100
2. Divorce	73
3. Marital separation from mate	65
4. Detention in jail or other institution	63
5. Death of a close family member	63
6. Major personal injury or illness	53
7. Marriage	50
8. Being fired at work	47
9. Marital reconciliation with mate	45
10. Retirement from work	45
11. Major change in the health or behavior of a family member	44
12. Pregnancy	40
13. Sexual difficulties	39
14. Gaining a new family member (e.g., through birth, adoption, oldster moving in, etc.)	39
15. Major business readjustment (e.g., merger, reorganization, bankruptcy, etc.)	39
16. Major change in financial state (e.g., a lot worse off or a lot better off than usual)	38
17. Death of a close friend	37
18. Changing to a different line of work	36
19. Major change in the number of arguments with spouse (e.g., either a lot more or a lot less than usual regarding child-rearing, personal habits, etc.)	35
20. Taking on a mortgage greater than $10,000 (e.g., purchasing a home, business, etc.)	31
21. Foreclosure on a mortgage or loan	30
22. Major change in responsibilities at work (e.g., promotion, demotion, lateral transfer)	29
23. Son or daughter leaving home (e.g., marriage, attending college, etc.)	29
24. In-law troubles	29

(Table 11.1 *continues***)**

Table 11.1 (*continues*)

Life Event	Stress Value (Points)
25. Outstanding personal achievement	28
26. Wife beginning or ceasing work outside the home	26
27. Beginning or ceasing formal schooling	26
28. Major change in living conditions (e.g., building a new home, remodeling, deterioration of home or neighborhood)	25
29. Revision of personal habits (dress, manners, associations, etc.)	24
30. Troubles with the boss	23
31. Major change in working hours or conditions	20
32. Change in residence	20
33. Changing to a new school	20
34. Major change in usual type and/or amount of recreation	19
35. Major change in church activities (e.g., a lot more or a lot less than usual)	19
36. Major change in social activities (e.g., clubs, dancing, movies, visiting	18
37. Taking on a mortgage or loan less than $10,000 (e.g., purchasing a car, TV, freezer, etc.)	17
38. Major change in sleeping habits (a lot more or a lot less sleep, or change in part of day when asleep)	16
39. Major change in number of family get-togethers (e.g., a lot more or a lot less than usual)	15
40. Major change in eating habits (a lot more or a lot less food intake, or very different meal hours or surroundings)	15
41. Vacation	15
42. Christmas	12
43. Minor violations of the law (e.g., traffic tickets, jaywalking, disturbing the peace, etc.)	11

Source: Reprinted with permission from *Journal of Psychosomatic Research,* Vol. 11, 213-18, T.H. Holmes and R.H. Rahe, "The Social Readjustment Rating Scale," Copyright 1967, Pergamon Press, Ltd.

among white-collar professionals. The most satisfied occupational groups were physicians, professors, and white-collar supervisors. Groups experiencing the highest levels of job stressors and their resultant ill effects were assemblers and relief workers on machine paced assembly lines. NIOSH investigators also ranked 130 occupations by rate of admission to community mental health centers in Tennessee to determine the relative risk of psychological or stress-related disorders by occupation. Heading the list were jobs in *health care*, service occupations, and blue-collar factory work. These jobs tend to be characterized by stress-producing conditions such as lack of control over the job by the worker, repetitive work, shift work, and a responsibility for others.[17]

D. Life Changes and Stress

There is also documented evidence that a relationship exists between critical life events, ensuing stress and physical disease. Table 10.1 contains stress values for major life events (changes) as developed by Holmes and Rahe. An individual can estimate the amount of stress he or she is under by checking off each event on the list that has been experienced in the last twelve months. The sum of the point values for all events checked is the total stress score for that individual. Although it is impossible to make accurate predictions on an individual basis one interpretation of life change scores from this scale is as follows:[18]

Life Change Score for Previous Year		Probability of Illness Within Next Two Years
Less than 150	(low stress)	Low
150 − 199	(mild stress)	30%
200 − 299	(moderate stress)	50%
300 +	(major stress)	80%

In support of the above predictions, the following evidence is offered. A study of eighty-eight resident physicians at the University of Washington found that 93 percent of major health changes occurred within two years of life changes summing 150 points or more.[19] Sixty-seven persons experiencing sudden cardiac death were found to have life change scores three times higher than in earlier periods during the last six months of life.[20] Another study of surviving coronary patients had steady levels of life-change scores over 2 years, while those who failed to survive had high rate scores for life changes 7 to 12 months before death.[20]

These facts should convey an important message to professionals and their managers. Specifically, organization members undergoing major life change which yield high scores should adjust their levels to reduce attendant high stress. While each case needs to be handled on an individual basis, a few adjustments tend to be generalizable. Priorities need to be readjusted to provide additional time for relaxation. Some pressures can also be alleviated by following the guidelines for more effective delegation developed earlier in this book (see Chapter 4). Finally, a more realistic perspective of ones career is often needed. This new perspective includes change priorities mentioned above, a willingness to say no to many requests (both personal and job related), and, generally, acceptance of a less stressful life. Effective leader managers may spot stress overload among specific professional employees and recommend related changes to reduce anxiety and protect individual health. The resulting payoff can be two fold; first, the employees good health is preserved and second, organization performance is sustained. On this latter point, priority adjustment may reduce performance levels, but this reduction is likely to be more than offset by the avoidance of high rates of absenteeism, deterioration of quantity and quality of output, and the eventual loss of a valued professional.

E. Mergers, Acquisitions and Stress

It is clear from the Holmes and Rahe scale that loss of job or career change is a major source of stress. In many American firms a large number of mergers and acquisitions are occurring. When an existing firm is acquired (bought out) or merges with another organization many uncertainties are created in the minds of current employees about their jobs and careers. These uncertain outcomes may impact particularly on the professional staff. Professionals are often most sensitive to the strategic direction and orientation of a firm because of their large investment in education and training which contributes to an intense orientation toward career identity and involvement. New ownership and/or top management may change corporate strategy or direction both dramatically and quickly. These changes are likely to alter many professional work assignments or actually eliminate some of these jobs.

As mentioned earlier in this chapter and reinforced by Holmes and Rahe, uncertain outcomes that are highly valued are a leading cause of stress, and the uncertainties generated by mergers and acquisitions substantially raise stress among professional employees.

An attendant problem which may be associated with pending acquisition or merger is an extended period of organizational decline prior to takeover. Since organizations often use slack resources to resolve conflict and reduce stress, the absence of extra resources during hard times tends to raise levels of conflict and associated stress. One study involving professionals found that such dysfunctions as low morale, resistance to change, and loss of innovation and credibility clearly manifest themselves in periods of decline.[21] In fact, even in sustained periods of stability (stagnation) the dearth of growth generated resources within a given firm can provoke these same dysfunctional characteristics. Stress reduction among professionals associated with organization changes related to merger or acquisition can have high payoffs to the total organization.

F. Stress and Strain Reduction Techniques

Authorities on stress and strain reduction, recommend regular periods of exercise alternated with relaxation. Also at the end of each work day, employees should be encouraged to make a stress assessment of events that have occurred and individual reactions to them. These regular assessments will enable individuals to identify sources of stress, and the conditions where stresses are most prevalent. Specific steps can then be taken to eliminate these conditions or to otherwise alter them. Many medical experts recommend some organized sports activity each week in order to keep the cardiovascular system in good condition. Of course, in addition to differences in Type B personalities already developed, individual employees may react differently to stressors because of various other unique characteristics. A detailed review of nineteen studies examining evidence of sex differences in stress dynamics revealed women tend to report higher rates of psychological stress and that men are more prone to severe physical illness.[22]

Employees at higher management levels including many professionals report more stress from working long hours, having to spend leisure time on work, business travel, and the conflict of work and home demands than do their junior colleagues.[23] Most managers and professionals primarily concerned with career development experience a very high incidence of stress.[23] These stress levels even exceed those associated with senior level management.

While older people often experience greater stress around health issues, they are likely to experience less job stress than their younger colleagues. A possible explanation for this research finding is that older employees have developed coping mechanisms which increase their stress tolerance. Also, it is possible that a downward adjustment in job expectations occurs as one ages, thus reducing stress.[23]

Most important, the cognitive appraisal an employee makes of specific stressors will increase or limit their "automatic impact." Unfortunately, an increase in emotional arousal will not, necessarily, increase the likelihood of the person's initiating preventative behavior. Stress inoculation training is recommended to help the person translate emotional arousal into personal action.[24] This training focuses on developing the skills of participants to cope with stressors. According to Ivancevich and Matteson, participants must first learn to understand stress warning signals, and second to admit that they are under or over stressed. Finally, they need to develop concrete action steps for coping with their specific work situation, personality, and goals.[24]

One study of university students utilized three major stress reduction techniques in a controlled short term intervention experiment. These three techniques were progressive muscle relaxation; coping skills training involving the active instruction of clients in the identification of anxiety cues and the development of responses that will eliminate tension; and cognitive modification which is a technique designed to focus on the relationships between cognition and emotional behavioral, or physiological responses to stress.[25] The intervention involved several instructional sessions on these stress reduction techniques. The results of this study indicate that short term cognitive-behavior intervention programs are effective in reducing anxiety.[25] Also, sustaining effects of these interventions during real-life stressful events are demonstrated and the use of training aimed at acquiring behavioral coping skills to prevent relapse is supported. Finally, type A and B individuals were examined, and little difference was found in the stress reductions achieved by type As versus type Bs. Additional research has supported the effective use of these stress reduction techniques in the professional work environment.[26] Managers of professionals need a detailed knowledge of various stress reduction methods and their applicability.

III. STRESS AND BURNOUT

The effects associated with stress often leads to emotional exhaustion (severe strain) and lowered interest in ones job. Extended emotional exhaustion has a variety of consequences including fatigue, tension, withdrawal, and poor relations with spouses and children.[27] The negative results of these consequences has been specifically associated with those professionals who deal with clients. Among this large group are physicians, nurses, social workers, firefighters, and police officers.[28]

One detailed study of a medium sized police organization found that some of the stress in policing is the result of internal organization processes.[29] Of particular importance to managers of professionals is the finding that promotional opportunity was the most powerful predictor of both frequency and intensity of emotional exhaustion.[29] Specifically, career advancement and promotional opportunities reduce occupational stress among professionals. As Gaines and Jermier point out, as organizations seek to recruit more professionals with high achievement expectations, increased amounts of emotional exhaustion can be expected unless viable career tracks are established.[29] Since promotional opportunities are largely influenced by the size of the organization, managers of small professional units must look for other alternatives to combat this problem. Increasing challenge, learning opportunities, and flexibility are some of the alternatives that can be applied to reduce stress in professional work environments. Studies have shown that the presence of rules have no significant effect on professionals, but flexible rules positively correlate with the frequency of emotional exhaustion.[29] Thus, rules may be perceived as a helpful guide to a professional's work and career, but lack of flexibility in rules application often conflicts with the professionals' value system. There are many positive managerial steps that can be taken to make the organizational environment less stressful and more productive for today's professional. Fortunately, these steps are supportive of the leadership and motivational concepts developed earlier in this book. Rule flexibility, predictable work relationships, promotional opportunities and pay equity will *increase motivation and reduce harmful stress.*

IV. STRESS AND DECISION MAKING

The decision making activity associated with the managerial role is a contributor to additional stress. Thus, managers of professionals need to cope with all of the stressful situations already discussed in this chapter, and they also must adjust to decisional conflict and stress. Janis and Mann define a stressful event as any change in the environment that is likely to induce a high degree of unpleasant emotion such as anxiety or guilt.[30] These authors also indicate that several functional relationships exist between psychological stress and decisional conflict as discussed below.[30]

When a decision maker expects a given decision to leave many important needs and goals unfulfilled, stress is high. If a decision maker is firmly entrenched in a present course of action, but faces new, attractive alternatives to this existing situation, stress tends to be high. Stress is also high when a decision maker faces a threat of serious loss and perceived time to take steps to avoid such loss is too short to properly evaluate each possible alternative.

According to Janis and Mann, high stress situations are likely to result in faulty information processing which lowers the quality of the decision.[30] Conversely, in low stress situations, the decision maker may not give adequate thought and attention to the possible alternatives. Specifically, one or more of the important decision-making steps of systems analysis as developed in Chapter 5 may be neglected.

Human relations knowledge and skills are more important now than at any time in the past in order to be effective and to derive personal satisfaction from the managerial job. Identifying and relating to employee needs is often the cornerstone of increasing the value of the organization's human assets. Elements of the traditional approach to managing that tended to treat employees as malleable factors in the production process who could be molded easily into a productive segment of the organization is both outdated and impractical, and will not work with most professionals. In spite of the complexities of human behavior in the organizational environment, generally, and in the technical and creative environment, specifically, managers must continually strive to understand individual behavior.

It is clear that while much more is still to be understood about stress, a great deal is already known. Managers who devote considerable time and effort to learning more about management and stress will have a distinct advantage over their counterparts who are unwilling to make this effort. In fact, a willingness to improve skills in both directing and understanding people may be both useful and necessary in today's complex and competitive management setting.

V. SUMMARY

Conflict can be both positive and negative and it is more appropriate for leaders of professionals to manage it rather than attempt to eliminate it. Conflict can improve the organization by encouraging better decisions, making work more interesting and causing marginal performers to leave the organization. Several tips have been offered to more effectively manage conflict to help attain these benefits. However, intense conflict can have a very negative impact on professional work performance, particularly through the resulting stress. Stress often leads to emotional exhaustion and burnout among professionals which can result in a deterioration of performance, and increases in absenteeism and turnover. This chapter contained an overview of stress problems and suggests ways to reduce their negative impact.

It should be noted that in general, stress levels rise with uncertain outcomes that are regarded as important. Consequently, if managers can reduce the uncertainty associated with professional task assignments, stress levels will be lowered. Establishing effective two-way communication and using a predictable leadership style can be very helpful in reducing uncertainty among professional subordinates. Managers who continually provide educational opportunities to professionals will find lower incidences of negative stress. Additionally, two-way communication and education may signal professional employees that outcomes are not as critical as first perceived. Changed perceptions that reduce importance will lower stress levels, but there may be obvious dysfunctional consequences of reducing task importance among professionals.

Managers should avoid excessive formalization which is particularly dysfunctional among professionals. For example, clearly identifiable client relationship are often associated with important professional tasks. Physicians, nurses, and various types of staff advisors are good examples of professionals that continually work with clients. The resulting inflexibility associated with high formalization is likely to be perceived as interfering with client service. In many instances this perception is probably correct and in others the stress produced lowers professional effectiveness. Increased flexibility will have very positive payoffs for employees, management and the organization.

It must be emphasized, however, that formalization is not inherently bad. For example, it doesn't inevitably result in increased alienation among professionals.[31] Also, formalization produces positive effects as well, particularly for persons experiencing high personal stress. These effects include reducing role ambiguity and enhancing organizational identity among professionals.[32] The problem is that excessive formalization creates rigidity and increases role conflict. Since formalization can enhance identity and increase effec-make a conscious effort to achieve the right amount of rules and regulations for minimum stress and optimum performance.

Finally, all members of a professional work group should monitor their individual stress levels and be aware of their personality type. When this analysis suggests an incongruence is present corrective measures should be taken. The trend toward greater amounts of competition for existing professional jobs coupled with global pressures on many industries suggest stress levels are likely to increase substantially in the decade ahead. Usually, when individual stress levels rise, professionals need to shift emphasis from "self" to system (formalization) in order to sustain effectiveness.

REFERENCES

1. R.M. Steers, S.R. Ungson, and R.T. Mowday, *Managing Effective Organizations: An Introduction,* Baston Kent Publishing Co., 1985, p. 418.

2. H.C. Katz, T.A. Kochan, M.A. Weber, "Assessing the Effects of Industrial Relating Systems and Efforts to Improve the Quality of Working Life on Organizational Effectiveness," *Academy of Management Journal,* Vol. 28, No. 3, 1985, pp. 509-526.

3. R.H. Miles, *Macro Organizational Behavior,* Santa Monica, CA, Goodyear Publishing Co., 1980.

4. Ernest J. McCormick, *Human Factors in Engineering and Design,* 4th edition, McGraw-Hill Book Company, 1976, pp. 165-168.

5. S. Parasuraman, and J. Alutto, "Sources and Outcomes of Stress in Organizational Settings: Toward the Development of a Structural Model," *Academy of Management Journal,* Vol. 27, No. 2, 1984, pp. 330-350.

6. J.M. Ivancevich and M.T. Matteson, "Optimizing Human Resources: A Case for Preventive Health and Stress Management," *Organizational Dynamics,* Autumn, 1980, pp. 5-25.

7. B.H. Kleiner, and S. Geil, "Managing Stress Effectively," *Journal of Systems Management,* September 1985, pp. 35-41.

8. M. Friedman, and R.H. Rosenman, "Association of Specific Overt Behavior Pattern with Blood and Cardiovascular Medical Findings," *Journal of the American Medical Association,* 1959, pp. 1286-1296.

9. J. Ducette and S. Wolk, "Cognitive and Motivational Correlates of Generalized Expectancies for Control," *Journal of Personality and Social Psychology,* Vol. 26, 1973, pp. 420-429.

10. R.P. Archer, "Relationships Between Focus of Control and Anxiety," *Journal of Personality and Assessment,* Vol. 43, 1979, pp. 617-626.

11. R.L. Rose and J.F. Viega, "Assessing the Sustained Effects of a Stress Management Intervention on Anxiety and Focus of Control," *Academy of Management Journal,* Vol. 27, No. 1, 1984, pp. 190-198.

12. *Morbidity and Mortality Weekly Report,* U.S. Department of Health and Human Services, October 3, 1986, Vol. 35, No. 39, p. 613.

13. Kiecolt-Glaser, J.K., "Stress and the Immune Function," Measures of Job Stress: A Research Methodology Workshop, Workshop sponsored by NIOSH, New Orleans, Louisiana, 1985.

14. *California Workers Compensation Bulletin,* April 20, 1983.

15. *Emotional Stress in the Workplace—New Legal Rights in the Eighties,* National Council on Compensation Insurance, New York, 1985.

16. *Diagnostic and Statistical Manual of Mental Disorders,* 3rd ed., American Psychiatric Association, Washington, DC, 1980.

17. *Morbidity and Mortality Weekly Report,* U.S. Department of Health and Human Services, October 3, 1986, Vol. 35, No. 39, pp. 613-621.

18. T.V. Bonoma and D.P. Sleven, *Executive Survival Manual,* Boston: CBI Publishing Company, 1978, p. 59.

19. T.H. Holmes and M. Masuda, "Life Change and Illness Susceptibility," in J.P. Scott and E.C. Senay (eds.), *Separation and Depression: Clinical and Research Aspects,* Symposium American Association for the Advancement of Science, December 1970 (Washington, DC: AAAS 1973), pp. 174-175.

20. C.D. Jenkins, "Recent Evidence Supporting Psychological and Social Risk Factors for Coronary Disease," *New England Journal of Medicine,* No. 294, 1976, p. 1033.

21. K.S. Cameron, D.A. Whetten, and M.V. Kim, "Organizational Dysfunctions of Decline," *Academy of Management Journal,* Vol. 30, No. 1, March 1987, pp. 126-138.

22. T.D. Jick and L.F. Mitz, "Sex Differences in Work Stress," *Academy of Management Review,* Vol. 10, No. 3, 1985, pp. 408-420.

23. J. Marshall and C. Cooper, "Work Experiences of Middle and Senior Managers: The Pressures and Satisfactions," *Management International Review,* Vol. 19, No. 1, 1979, pp. 81-96.

24. Ivancevich and Matteson, et. al.

25. Rose and Viega, et. al.

26. E. Roskies, M. Spevack, A. Svikis, C. Cohen, and S. Gilman, "Changing the Coronary-Prone Behavior Pattern (type A) in a Non-clinical Population," *Journal of Behavioral Medicine,* 1978, pp. 201-216.

27. C. Maslach and S.E. Jackson, "The Measurement of Experienced Burnout," *Journal of Occupational Behavior,* Vol. 2, 1981, pp. 99-113.

28. B. Pearlman and E. Hartman, "Burnout: Summary and Future Research," *Human Relations,* Vol. 39, 1982, pp. 283-305.

29. J. Gaines and J.M. Jermier, "Emotional Exhaustion in a High Stress Organization," *Academy of Management Journal,* Vol. 26, No. 4, December 1983, pp. 567-586.

30. I.L. Janis and L. Mann, *Decision Making: A Psychological Analysis of Conflict, Choice, and Commitment,* The Free Press, New York, 1977, p. 50.

31. P.M. Podsakoff, L.J. Williams, and W.D. Todor, "Effects of Organizational Formalization on Alienation Among Professionals and Nonprofessionals," *Academy of Management Journal,* Vol. 29, No. 4, December 1986, pp. 820-831.

32. D.W. Organ and C.N. Greene, "The Effects of Formalization on Professional Involvement: A Compensatory Process Approach," *Administrative Science Quarterly,* Vol. 26, 1981, pp. 237-252.

12
Involvement Management: A New Trend

I. OVERVIEW

There is a trend among forward thinking managers to try to move their organizations in directions that will involve employees at all levels in important decision making processes. This approach to management is not new, it has received attention for over a half century. In the 1930s the Scanlon Plan was developed by Joseph W. Scanlon, then research director of the United Steelworkers Union and later a faculty member at MIT. The major purpose of the Scanlon Plan was to measure productivity improvement by a change in the computed ratio of total payroll dollars divided by the total dollar sales value of production, and distribute a share of the gains (usually 75 percent) to the employees. In addition, the Plan included a highly structured suggestion system and *labor-management committees* to effect improvements throughout the manufacturing operations.[1] Likert was also a strong advocate of participation and much of the research he directed at the Survey Research Center at the University of Michigan in the 1950s supported employee involvement. He authored two books in the 1960s that reported the results of many of these extensive research studies on supervision.[2]

In the 1960s and 70s McGregor's Theory X and Y became increasingly popular ways to categorize management styles. As pointed out in Chapter 8, Theory Y, an involvement management approach, was advocated by McGregor as an effective alternative to Theory X which he said represented the conventional approach to managing people. In addition to McGregor, general research studies during this period continued to identify democratic management as a major contributor to organizational effectiveness, and strong arguments were made for managing professionals in a participative manner. In the 1980s, management literature continued to extol the virtues of the participative organization. Peters and Waterman's popular best seller *In Search of Excellence* focused on the values of good people management and a participative philosophy. Miller's book on *Managing Professionals in Research and Development* discusses the challenges facing managers of professionals, particularly the professional's strong need for autonomy that must be *balanced* with the organization's need for control.[3] Many top level corporate executives are openly promoting increased participation. For example, Brian H. Rowe, Senior Vice President and Group Executive at General Electric Aircraft Engine Business Group, stressed the importance of participative management to his employees. He said:

> "Whereas five years ago I encouraged employees to form quality teams and focus groups . . . I now want to encourage . . . managers to manage in a participative style." Some fundamentals involved in this process were stated as follows: Treating employees with the utmost respect. (You'll be surprised how much reciprocal respect you'll receive.) Positive motivation rather than threats. Constructive handling of conflict. More critical and careful looks at what signals our actions give to employees. More opportunity for people to participate in decisions affecting them. Meaningful jobs. More growth for people (which does *not* have to mean a new job every

year to two—and could mean the opposite!) More cross-functional teamwork. The utmost personal integrity. Letting people know what is going on. Listening. Providing honest feedback."[4]

Lawler strongly feels that participative management is an old idea whose time has come.[5] As suggested in Chapter 9, appropriate management and leadership style is largely situational, and according to Lawler participative management suits the current work force, technologies and societal conditions better than any other alternative. He suggests several potential benefits for the firm that implements a participative or involvement management style or system within the organization.[5] Namely, it can create organizations where people think for themselves and manage their own work. This accomplishment reduces manpower needs, and increases job satisfaction for those who work. Another important benefit is a reduction in the already higher labor costs in the United States because existing workers are more fully utilized. Involvement and participative strategies are viable techniques for productivity measurement and improvement.[6] Thus the U.S. competitive position can be improved.

The recent emphasis on many participative management techniques including self-managing work teams, job enrichment, gain-sharing, and quality circles in the U.S. received considerable impetus from Japan's long term success with these management tools; and the dramatic impact their products have made in what were once exclusive U.S. markets during the last decade. Also, many studies of organizations that have increased involvement in decision making among employees have shown that favorable results ensued. A work redesign project increasing involvement among employees including professionals at a large financial institution during the 1970s was quite successful. For example, the organization was able to hold expenses of production constant over an annual period, at a time when average costs had been rising 15 percent annually. The result was a pre-tax saving in operating expenses of $220 million (110 million net profit) in 1976.[7]

This kind of evidence of positive results, coupled with America's concern over lagging productivity and Japan's surge in GNP, provided much impetus to quality circle and other team concept applications in U.S. manufacturing firms in the late 1970s and early 1980s. Best selling books including Ouchi's *Theory Z* and Pascale and Athos' *The Art of Japanese Management* also attracted many American managers to Japanese methods. In addition to this widely publicized Japanese influence, many American firms have begun using work teams to improve motivation and quality.[38] Work teams have a distinct European flavor and have been extensively used in European coal mines and automobile plants such as Volvo in Sweden for several decades. Although quality circles and work teams are commonly associated with manufacturing operations; their composition, purpose, and benefits are quite congruent with many professional work settings.

II. INVOLVEMENT TEAMS

Involvement teams have emerged in the United States in many forms as an important part of the search for increased productivity. These teams have taken several distinct forms ranging from small problem solving groups of hourly rated workers to well organized decision making teams of managerial and professional personnel. Also, self-managed production teams are becoming a more significant part of many manufacturing organizations. In addition to Japan's proven success with the group concept, documented evidence of increased individual motivation through participative ownership is an important positive influence. There is also a widespread belief that increased involvement leads to more effective decisions in most complex situations.

A. Quality Circles

One of the more popular applications of the involvement team concept occurring in the U.S. in the 1980s has been the Quality Circle (QC). Although it has been argued that circle concepts have existed in American management for some time, their widespread use has been associated with this recent period.

1. The Early Perspective

Quality circles were officially originated in Japan in 1962.[8] Their success is perhaps better understood with some explanation of the activities that preceded their official beginning. Prior to and following World War II, the Japanese generally produced poor quality products. In most cases "made in Japan" was a synonym for "manufactured junk." At that time U.S. engineers worked with the Japanese to improve production methods for selected products including high-quality communications equipment.[9] One of the engineers, Homer M. Sarasohn, suggested that W. Edwards Deming be invited from the U.S. to advise Japanese industry on quality problems. In 1950, Deming began to teach courses in statistical quality control to the Japanese. Later in 1954, Joseph M. Juran, another American, began to teach courses on the managerial aspects of quality.[10]

Rubinstein reported that quality circle concepts were used by a few U.S. firms in the late 1960s.[11] QC efforts didn't really get started in the U.S. until the mid 1970s. Early firms included Lockheed Missile and Space Division, General Motors Pontiac Division, 3M Corporation, and B. F. Goodrich Company.[12] The International Association of Quality Circles (IAQC) was formed in 1977.

2. The Structure of Quality Circles

There is no single statement that clearly defines quality circles. Conceptually, the quality circle is a blend of quality control and participative management. Quality circles usually consist of a small group (approximately 8 to 10 members) who do similar work and agree to meet on a regular voluntary basis to discuss their work/ quality problems. These groups analyze the causes of work related problems and recommend solutions to their management. Also, in areas within their purview, they take action to implement their recommended solutions. Circles are based upon the philosophy that organizational climate is a critical element in motivation and in the quality of work life. Employees are recognized as capable contributing members of the organization. Quality circle members are usually non-managers who share the same kinds of work, and consequently can interact meaningfully and confront the problems associated with performing their common tasks.

Each circle member is taught the elementary quality control techniques, basic approaches to problem solving and often group dynamics. There is also a circle leader who is usually the immediate supervisor of the circle members, and the success of the group is directly affected by his or her effectiveness. In addition to the immediate circle leader there is a facilitator who is responsible for the overall leadership of the circle program. The facilitator is responsible for training the members and leaders, and also forms a link between each circle and the rest of the organization. These groups work within the existing formal organizational structure and are not designed to compete for power with the traditional hierarchy.

3. Benefits of Quality Circles

Managers of professionals should be especially aware of the potential contribution quality circles can make to the work climate. Since scientists, physicians, nurses, engineers and other professionals often have high needs for both autonomy and involvement, specific circles can identify issues and bring solutions to frustrating problems in the work environment. In fact, participation in the circle itself is a unique form of involvement. The circle concept also provides an opportunity for managers to draw upon the skills of non-managerial specialists.

Since quality circles have been established in the U.S., several questions have been raised about their usefulness. One question that is continually being asked by both educators and practitioners is *whether or not quality circles are a fad or will they become a long term part of American management?* Recent declines in the growth rate of the IAQC casts some doubt on their long term prospects. Studies by Cox and Norris led to the conclusion that members of some American quality circles were actually less productive and had higher rates of absenteeism than did employees from the same organization who were not circle members. These same researchers also found no difference between the work performance, absenteeism and tardiness of members of quality circles before and six months after their joining the group.[13]

Although conclusions from the discussion above do not indicate a promising future for quality circles in the United States, there are other studies that are more encouraging. Responses to a detailed survey of 2000 members of the Organizational Development Division of the American Society for Training and Development (ASTD) supported the effectiveness of these groups. Sixty-three percent of the respondents indicated that quality circle programs were either moderately or extremely successful.[14] According to one author, the popular management press is full of stories about great savings produced by quality circles, and literally thousands of examples of better work methods and procedures suggested by employees as circle members are cited.[15] However, this same author indicates that most savings are "projected" because of the newness of the program and so actual costs of operating quality circles are often ignored.[16] Since each circle member undergoes training and good facilitators are expensive, these costs can be high. If company paid meeting time is also considered, costs of quality circle programs are very substantial.

Important conclusions drawn from the ASTD survey suggest that certain conditions need to be met if quality circles are to succeed in American organizations. Among these are:[16]

1. Management style and commitment are the most important determinants of quality circle usage and effectiveness.
2. Top management must understand the operation and usage of circles.
3. Effective training of circle leaders and facilitators coupled with provision for continued stimulation and follow up is critical.
4. Quality circles should not be used as a quick-fix for management problems.

Other researchers have also suggested that if circles are to be effective employees have to believe that their support and participation will benefit themselves as well as the organization and that participants must be well trained in group dynamics.[17]

A study of nine quality circles ranging in size from 3 to 12 members found that effectiveness of the circle correlated with the level of self esteem of its members.[18] A quality circle was designated as relatively successful if it had generated at least two solutions to problems that upper level management actually accepted and implemented and the Janis-Field scale was used to assess self esteem. Since professionals usually score higher than non-professionals on measures of self esteem, quality circles can be particularly applicable to professional work environments. This conclusion is further supported by research results that show that individuals with strong independence needs (a characteristic of professionals) are more positively affected by the opportunity to participate in making decisions than are employees with weaker independence needs that are more likely to be associated with non-professionals. For example, a study of 108 first, second, and third line managers in a large delivery company found that the opportunity to participate had little effect on people with weak independence needs. However, increases in participation opportunities among employees with strong independence needs resulted in more positive attitudes toward their jobs and increased their level of performance.[19]

Lindsay performed a major cross-sectional field study questionnaire of 3000 individuals who were members of the International Association of Quality Circles to determine practices and benefits of quality circles. Responses were received from 532 individuals that represented a wide variety of manufacturing, service, and government organizations which had or were planning QC programs. It was found that the majority of respondents had active QC programs (89 percent) and half of those who didn't had plans to start one within the next six months. Other descriptive findings were that 27 percent of the respondents' organizations that had been involved in QC's for more than three years, 56 percent reported regularly to VP level or above and 80 percent used steering committees which met regularly (usually weekly). Perhaps the most meaningful results were the confirmation of the philosophical base of QC programs being "People Building" and "Quality of Worklife", with dollar estimates for savings frequently being supplemented by use of non-quantified measures of effectiveness.[20]

In addition to learning about the characteristics of QC programs, the study was designed to obtain information about the financial success of the programs. The following respondent groupings were analyzed:[20]

1. Size relationships
2. Effect of organizational titles
3. Relationship between costs and savings
4. Factors relating to program success

The analysis relating to size showed that larger organizations tended to be non-manufacturing, to have the oldest QC programs and to have more staff specialist QC personnel than smaller organizations. Only the first item could be considered unusual. Considering the fact that the QC movement started in manufacturing firms in the U.S., it is surprising that the large organizations represented in the sample tend to be predominantly non-manufacturing. It may be that only a few large, well publicized programs now exist in large firms, where smaller firms may find it easier to develop and sustain QC programs. The second possibility is that there is a response bias at work. In reporting on organization size, some respondents may have used their own plant or division as a reference point, rather than the entire size of the firm or parent company.[20]

The analysis of organizational titles showed no significant effect of specialist or generalist job titles on either per member costs or savings. In a way, this is encouraging, in that it shows that well-trained QC practitioners can obtain outstanding results, regardless of organizational specialties.[20]

In testing relationships between costs and savings, it was found that savings increased in proportion to costs on a per member basis, although this was not on a dollar for dollar basis. Findings from an interesting sub-hypothesis were that the older programs did not show as strong a relationship between costs and savings as the younger programs. In fact, the result was not statistically significant at the 5 percent level for the older programs. This could possibly be explained by the larger size of older programs, yielding greater economies of scale and not having to commit a relatively large number of dollars to starting up the programs, in order to begin to get "payoffs" in savings. Another possible explanation for this result may simply be "burnout" among some programs, such that results are attained less consistently than in newer programs.[20]

Factors relating to program success showed once again that maturity of the program was directly related to financial success of the program, with the highest per member savings going to programs which were three or more years old. There were no significant differences in success based on manufacturing versus non-manufacturing firms, firm size or titles of specialists versus generalists who responded. In examining savings versus cost factors, controlling for financial success level, it was interesting to find that 75 percent of the highly successful programs cost less than $400 per member, but yielded 6 to 1 or better savings over costs.[20]

4. Summary

It is ironic that today many American firms are attempting to learn from the "Japanese way of management" when in reality most of the ideas and concepts were originally given to them by Deming, Juran, and other Americans. One important point that was initiated by the Japanese was involvement by *all* levels of personnel within the organization. For example, following World War II when Deming lectured about quality control (circles) in the U.S. only a few technical employees would typically attend. No managers or even first level supervisors were interested. At his first lecture in Japan technical employees attended along with supervisors, managers, and top executives! In recognition of Deming's great contribution to the economy of Japan, the Union of Japanese Science and Engineering instituted the annual Deming Prize awarded for advancement of precision and dependability of product. In 1960, he received the Second Order Medal of the Sacred Treasure (awarded only by the Emperor of Japan).

While the above analysis indicates circles are firmly entrenched in Japanese firms, an overview of the entire issue of quality circle applications in the United States is more tentative. Quality circles can be an effective part of American participative management, but a situational analysis should always proceed their introduction. It is important to relate the measurement/evaluation of the quality circle to its program objectives, and to communicate major results to all employees. The specific personal and work characteristics of professionals is favorable to the selective use of quality circles.

B. Work Teams

The emergence of work teams offers an excellent example of involvement management in practice. These teams are usually small work units (7 to 15 members) that are given considerable decision making and managerial responsibility over their work areas. In fact, they have been called "self managing work groups" or "autonomous work groups". They differ from quality circles in that these teams represent a braoder focus or philosphy of managing work than circles. Work teams can be developed with or without the actual use of quality circles. Their most distinguishing characteristic is their high degree of autonomy and freedom to plan and organize their work. These factors generate a feeling of "true involvement" among their members. In view of the basic nature of professionals, these teams have particular applicability to the professional work environment. In fact, work teams exemplify the S4 quadrant (delegation) in the Hersey-Blanchard situational leadership model (Chapter 9). As pointed out earlier, management styles characterized by high levels of delegation tend to be most appropriate for professionals.

The costs related to using teams are incurred primarily through the task and behavioral training given to the members of each group. Also since they meet frequently to coordinate and assess their progress, this time cost must be added when their relative contribution is being assessed.

According to Lawler, work teams make an important difference in the participative structure of organizations. Namely, participants gain more knowledge, skill, information, rewards, and power than they would have in a traditional organization.[21] Of course, these are conditions highly valued by most professionals. One research survey showed that a vast majority of firms using work teams experienced increased motivation and productivity.[22]

Work teams are used in manufacturing operations at Procter and Gamble, General Foods, Digital Equipment, and General Motors.

Managers who manage groups of professionals that have well defined units of work may find that developing a work team will provide substantial benefits to the organization.

III. ORGANIZATION WIDE INCENTIVES AND GAINSHARING

As discussed in Chapter 4 gainsharing plans are not new. One of the most successful which is still operating was initiated at the Lincoln Electric Company of Cleveland, Ohio in 1934. Several firms use plans adopted from the work of Joseph W. Scanlon also beginning in the 1930s. Both Scanlon and Lincoln believed that top management should share savings from productivity gains with the entire company work force.[23] As previously mentioned, in the Scanlon plan a labor cost norm is established for a base period, and this norm is expressed as a percentage of the total sales value of products delivered. When cooperative efforts reduce this percentage, a percentage of the savings is shared with employees as a bonus. This is a high involvement plan because Scanlon felt employees at all levels in the firm should participate. In order for these plans to function all employees must work closely to improve the efficiency of the organizations, consequently there is genuine participation. Review committees are formulated that represent points of view throughout the firm to scan suggestions for performance improvement. Although these plans are plant-wide and are often directed at increasing performance levels among non-professionals, a working knowledge of their structure can be beneficial to managers of professionals as well.

As repeated throughout this book, professionals are likely to respond favorably to a work environment that recognizes and rewards their individual accomplishments. Gainsharing plans do this, and can integrate well into smaller work environments. Managers in small firms that employ numerous professionals and want to raise overall levels of performance should investigate gainsharing plans as a potentially useful tool. There are many research studies that show favorable results for organization wide incentives. For example, Eggers Industries uses such a plan in their Wisconsin plant which realized a 26 percent reduction in labor costs during its first two years of operation.[24] However, all results are not favorable, and management needs to be both extremely competent and committed to employee participation for these plans to work.

IV. MANAGEMENT BY OBJECTIVES AND EMPLOYEE INVOLVEMENT

Since the advent of participative management several decades ago, many managers have identified the problem of balancing delegation of authority to employees with the need for rational control. More specifically, what assurance is present that lower level decision making will stay on a prescribed path that will contribute to the attainment of organizational purposes?

Management by Objectives or MBO as it is popularly called offers a potentially effective solution to this very real problem of balancing participation with the need for hierarchical control. Although Drucker is often credited with "inventing" management by objectives, many of Drucker's precursors wrote about the need for objectives as a foundation of management. These individuals include Henri Fayol (1916), James O. McKinsey (1922), Ralph C. Davis (1937), and Chester I. Barnard (1938). When asked if anybody he knew practiced MBO before he wrote about it, Drucker mentioned Sloan of GM, Pierre DuPont, and Donaldson Brown.[25] However, it was Drucker's work with Harold Smiddy, Vice President of General Electric's Management Consultation Services and chief architect of GE's decentralized structure, between 1950 and 1954 that placed objectives on center stage and made them the core of an emerging management discipline.

MBO is based on two fundamental premises: First, the clearer the idea one has of what one is trying to do, the greater the chance of accomplishing it; and second, progress can only be measured in terms of what one is trying to make progress toward. This approach to management establishes clear cut objectives throughout the organization and then evaluates participants on how well they attain them. Objectives are based on mutual agreement between superiors and subordinates, and seem to offer great promise to managers who are attempting to increase their unit's effectiveness. Also, since most professional units must compete for funds with other units that consistently seek dollar increases in their operating budgets, the development of clear cut performance objectives can be a useful bargaining tool to help assure attainment of a "fair share." This management tool has been either partially or totally adopted in many areas of both private and public enterprise. Since MBO has superiors and subordinates at all levels setting goals together and working to achieve these goals in a cooperative fashion, it has produced highly satisfactory results in many organizations.

A study of 300 American personnel managers of firms employing 1000 or more were asked to rank six widely known management tools according to their perception of the ability of the proper application of these tools to increase organizational effectiveness.[26] These six tools and their respective mean value rankings by the 165 personnel managers that responded are as follows:

1. Management by objectives (2.4)
2. Human relations training, as part of formalized management development (3.0)
3. Management information systems (3.1)
4. Skill training, as part of the personnel program (3.6)
5. PERT, critical path scheduling (4.0)
6. Human resource accounting (4.9)

Management by objectives was clearly the preferred tool among personnel managers which reflects the sustained popularity of MBO since its inception in the mid 1950s. Both the high rankings of MBO and human relations training may in part reflect the strong people orientation of the type of professionals surveyed. Also, this finding may in part reflect more recognition or knowledge of this tool by personnel professionals than some of the others. For example, if production or engineering professionals were asked this same question, one might expect both management information systems and PERT to be given considerably more importance, both due to greater knowledge and perceived applicability to their function.

Since research indicates that human resource accounting is not widely practiced, it is not surprising that it would rank last among these six tools.[27]

In addition to the influence of people orientation on the favorable perceptions of personnel managers toward MBO, it is likely that these same attitudes influence perceptions concerning the way goals are set among superiors and subordinates in their respective organizations. Over 90 percent of these managers see that goals are established only after some solicitation of input or some agreement is attained among the parties involved. Less than 10 percent of these managers see goals being set autocratically by management decree. These perceptions might be quite different among managers with typically less people orientation such as line production managers, maintenance managers, or plant superintendents.

These findings are important to managers of professionals because personnel managers often strongly influence the basic management philosophy of the organization. It is clear that these managers tend to favor MBO and mutual goal setting and will likely encourage unit managers to move in that direction.

A. Components of MBO

Management by objectives as a system involves four basic components. First, the establishment of clear cut objectives for the mission of the organization as a whole and the organizational units involved. This is usually accomplished by key managers working with policy guidelines established by top level executives with the concurrence of governing boards or ownership.

Second, the establishment of objectives for each manager and subordinate that when attained will contribute to the overall objectives of the entire enterprise. These objectives are established by a process in which the superior and the subordinate meet and jointly identify the common goals of the unit, define the employee's major area of responsibility in terms of results expected, and develop or write a plan to accomplish these results. At this time, some agreement should be reached with regard to measuring criteria for evaluating performance, a specific time period of the attainment of the objective or part of it, and an agreement that at some future date a performance review session will be completed. Specifically, the objectives can be defined as what the subordinate is agreeing to accomplish in a certain period of time. Usually, this accomplishment is an end result or a performance that specifies what is to be done and how it will be measured. *All objectives must be measurable.* If it is not quantifiably measurable, it is not an objective. Often a unit has prime objectives or overall accomplishments that the unit as a whole wishes to attain over a given time period. In addition, supporting objectives exist which if accomplished will contribute to the attainment of the overall primary objectives. In this context most subordinate objectives are categorized as supporting objectives because they are narrower and contribute specifically to the attainment of primary objectives.

The third element in the MBO process is the periodic occurrence of performance review in which the superior and the subordinate meet and discuss what has in fact been accomplished, and explanations for any failures that may have occurred. Appraisal interviews should encompass both qualitative and quantitative aspects of a given performance in accordance with priorities that have previously been established, the difficulty of the objectives, and the extent to which deadline considerations have been met. The role of the manager of professionals in a performance appraisal interview should be to act primarily as an advisor and helper rather than that of critic or judge. The discussion should be maintained in a problem-solving context with the basic objective of the interview directed toward improving future performance rather than criticizing past performance. A problem-solving context will minimize defensiveness and increase the probability that constructive action will take place benefiting both the organizational unit and the individual employee.

A fourth and final component of the MBO process concerns the distribution of rewards. Each manager should endeavor to provide rewards to those employees who continually attain or exceed their objectives as planned. One study of professionals in a hospital showed that nurses' job performance was significantly influenced by an administrative climate that established performance objectives for individual staff nurses and provided rewards based on the nurse's accomplishments.[28] Additionally, a performance-reward climate tied to clear performance objectives served to legitimize and reinforce the head nurses formal leadership role. Conversely, in the absence of a strong performance-reward climate, assertiveness behavior on the part of the head nurse had an inverse effect on job performance.[28] The actual distribution of rewards such as promotion and merit salary increases should occur *after* the performance appraisal interview has been conducted in order to minimize individual defensiveness.

V. MBO VERSUS TRADITIONAL MANAGEMENT

Figure 12.1 illustrates how MBO differs from traditional organizational approaches to management, by comparing a typical classical approach to management with the more behavioristic approach of MBO. Note that conventional management authority is vested in the positions themselves within the organization. This situation is

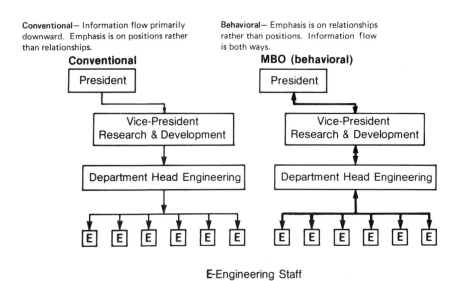

Figure 12.1 A comparison of conventional management with MBO

	Traditional Management	MBO
School of Management	___ Classical	_____ Behavioral
Emphasis	_____ Positions	____ Interrelationships
Authority	_____ Downward	___ Two-way
Planning	_____ Sporadic	____ Consistent
Decisions	_____ Autocratic	____ Cooperative

Figure 12.2 A comparison of traditional management with MBO

depicted by the heavy lines which enclose the squares which represent the position levels in the hierarchy. Likewise, the authority arrow flows from the top down, emphasizing the dictatorial approach, in which there is little room for collective objective setting which capitalizes on the talents of subordinates. However, note how the identical organization changes with the distinct shift in emphasis to MBO. Heavy lines indicate that now the emphasis is in the level *between* positions, the level where objectives are jointly set by superiors and subordinates (involvement). The authority arrow has a head at the top as well as at the bottom, indicating the communication feedback process which superiors can use for better and stronger decisions.

As Figure 12.2 indicates, MBO offers considerable advantages in the important areas of authority planning and decision making when compared with traditional managerial methods. Of particular note to managers of professionals is the emphasis on two-way communication and cooperative decision making, because these are critical elements of involvement management and supportive of professionals' needs.

VI. MBO CAN HELP INTEGRATE INVOLVEMENT AND CONTROL

Some managers are reluctant to incorporate any participative management system because it might erode their authority; MBO permits authority to actually be strengthened by developing consent among those being directed. Since subordinates are in agreement with the superior on the objectives to be reached and how they will be measured, a much greater commitment to accomplishment is the likely result.

While the benefits of MBO are usually evident from the start of any program designed to implement the process, they have been summarized and categorized in many different ways. These categorizations tend to conform to the organization where MBO is being implemented. A convenient grouping shows 15 advantages—five each for the organization, the supervisor, and the subordinate in a professional work environment as follows:

For the organization
    Clear goals
    Forces planning and control
    Surfaces conflicts
    Obtains commitments from supervisors
    Draws upon first-echelon expertise
For the manager of professionals
    Forces effective delegation
    Increases time for managing
    Two-way communication
    Better evaluation criteria
    Obtains commitments from subordinates
For the professional employee
    Improves direction and guidance
    Provides autonomy
    Allows participation
    Forces feedback from above
    Improves morale

According to research conducted by Andrews and Farris on the effective management of scientific and engineering professionals, granting substantial freedom to subordinates can act as a partial substitute for skilled supervision. However, their data show that for freedom to be effective the superior must consult with his or her subordinates *before* making these decisions.[29] Earlier research by Pelz and Andrews concluded that freedom should be provided in an environment of direction and stimulation so that subordinates do not engage in trivial problems and stagnate.[30] The implementation of MBO by the manager can provide the type of environment where there is both freedom and a strong sense of direction. For example, as professionals become involved in mutual goal setting with their superiors, great amounts of freedom can be granted to these subordinates to accomplish goals. A sense of direction is built into mutual goal setting but the work environment is still relatively free. Mills found that a direct relationship exists between experiencing ambiguity and job tension, job dissatisfaction, personal ineffectiveness, and unfavorable attitudes toward work associates among professionals; and suggests that a program of MBO is appropriate for reducing both ambiguity and conflict.[31]

Once understood, MBO is often welcomed by both managers and subordinates alike because it is a management system based on cooperation, communication and participation by all levels in the organization, and all organizational participants can realize benefits. In fact, MBO is essentially a system wherein supervisors and subordinates participate in objective setting, work toward the objectives, and realize satisfaction as goals are reached. MBO systems are likely to put increased pressure on managers to be more effective. A study conducted in four separate branches of a large non-union retail organization in the midwest found that once goal setting and feedback were implemented, salespersons were continuously providing the performance relevant information to their supervisors.[32] Apparently this resulted from their attempt to meet commitments on performance goals, which tended to enhance their supervisor's ability and commitment to carry out his or her support and maintenance responsibilities.

This same research concludes that any organizational process that encourages the level of employee commitment in the goal setting and feedback procedure potentially should have a positive payoff.[32] Managers of professionals should continuously attempt to induce employees to help set performance goals, and increase the level of publicity surrounding goal setting behavior.

VII. MAKING MBO WORK FOR PROFESSIONALS

Once the basic elements of the MBO process are understood by the manager of the organizational unit contemplating its use, there are several steps that must be taken and pitfalls that must be avoided if the process is to be constructive. MBO is clearly not an answer for improved managerial effectiveness in every professional organization. In fact, improperly or inappropriately applied it may actually lead to lower effectiveness. In his review of 185 case studies, surveys, quasi-experiments, and true experiments, Kondrasuk found some evidence but not conclusive proof for the effectiveness of MBO.[33] He argues that we need better research on MBO effectiveness particularly well-controlled experiments especially longitudinal ones in field settings. One of the problems is that often only parts of MBO are employed in the organization and a true MBO system is not used. In establishing management by objectives there must be a commitment from the top management team, preferably the top management of the company in which the professional unit is located. It is not necessary that all organizational units utilize MBO, frequently they do not, but it is necessary that top management supports the efforts of the particular organizational unit in question before installing an MBO system. The authors have helped several professional organizations install MBO programs, and this experience indicates that when MBO is not supported by top management, it will lose its momentum after initial steps are taken to implement it, and eventually is very likely to fail. These experiences include hospitals, public service organizations, and private industrial and service firms. It is important for the head of the professional unit to ensure that all managers in the unit are trained on the nature, purpose, and use of MBO. This training should explain the criteria and measurement standards for a good objective, the importance of mutual goal setting, and appraisal interviewing. A *good objective is stated as an end result* and not as an activity. Usually a good objective begins in writing with the word *to* followed by an action verb, and specifies one key result to be obtained by a specific target date. Thus, it is measurable in terms of cost and time. Good objectives are realistic, attainable, understandable, and consistent with other organizational objectives and resources.

Ideally, when an objective is finalized, it should be put in writing to minimize conflicts of interpretation or understanding on the part of the parties involved. One of the major problems in writing objectives is that they tend to be stated in terms of an activity. For example, if a college professor stated that his or her objective was to effectively educate students, in the context of MBO that is an activity and not an objective. It is not measurable as stated, it does not have a specific time requirement, and it says nothing about resources or parameters. Specifically, this professor could develop objectives by breaking his or her job down and indicating what constitutes effectively educating students. Key objectives could be specified in the amount of time set aside to meet with students, prepare course outlines, improve student course evaluations, involve students in sponsored research, and by agreeing to write an article for a scholarly journal. These latter points are measurable, consistent with organizational objectives, and stated primarily in terms of end results. If all of these objectives were accomplished, the overall activity of effectively educating students would have a high probability of being achieved.

A. Objective Setting

Each division or upper level manager should develop clear-cut high level objectives (goals) for the organizational unit. These objectives should be effectively communicated to lower level managers, and their input solicited before these top level objectives are finalized. One study involving the use of MBO in an engineering unit found that a major problem or complaint of some middle managers was the lack of higher level management objectives.[34] Managers should also take action steps to ensure that each subordinate or lower level manager in that unit understands the complexity of developing good objectives and is aware of the techniques that can be used to aid in the process.

Prior to concluding objective-setting sessions with subordinates, it is important that each manager and subordinate have substantial agreement on the duties of the job and the priorities attached to those duties. One technique that is useful in attaining this end is for each party involved to prepare separate lists of important job tasks in a prioritized order. Next, the superior and subordinate should discuss the listing to see what areas of disagreement and agreement exist. In this way they are in an excellent position to reach a congruent relationship with regard to job responsibilities and duties. Once this congruence is attained, the manager and the subordinate are ready to establish goals together. It is particularly essential among professionals that "mutuality" occurs, namely, the manager must be flexible enough to modify some objectives on the basis of subordinate input. Without mutuality, the professional employee will feel that he or she is being dictated to, and many of the problems associated with autocracy and loss of autonomy and responsibility emerge. The presence of mutuality is a fundamental ingredient that makes MBO an involvement management program.

B. Potential Barriers

A major obstacle to making MBO successful is that many managers regard it as simply a numbers game, and tend to place excessive emphasis on quantity rather than quality. Appropriate use of communication feedback from subordinates can be effective in counteracting this difficulty. Additionally, agreement with the subordinate on job content and priorities can help to eliminate overlapping responsibilities between units and individuals. Managers must be willing to delegate, and they must encourage subordinates to assume responsibility. Effective delegation in using management by objectives also minimizes paperwork, which is often seen as an obstacle to adopting MBO. Any supportive activities that the managerial staff can assume which minimizes the paperwork for lower level managers and professional employees will encourage the MBO process to be fruitful for the entire unit.

Managers in research and development and some health professions, such as rehabilitation medicine, face a particularly tough problem in the successful formulation and development of objectives with their employees. Typically, no agreement exists with regard to the measurement of "scientific" performance. Moreover, an examination of the studies on measurement of scientific performance reveals little agreement among investigators as to what constitutes scientific output or what measures should be used to reflect it.[35] Among the more commonly used measures is to apply a variety of techniques to assess the quantity and quality of written output. The ability of the researcher to meet given time constraints is also regarded as important. Whether MBO is used or not, many authorities on research management agree that an attempt to establish objectives for research units is a useful and often necessary managerial task. Similarly, it is difficult to determine the effectiveness of physical therapists in the treatment of many stroke cases. The severity of the stroke, age, physical condition, and attitude of the patient substantially affect the timing and result of the treatment. If the manager evaluates a therapist's performance solely on the basis of an end result, the outcome may be misleading or regarded as unfair. Professionals in rehabilitation medicine are also likely to resist attempts to put time limits on treatments or to establish other types of criteria that are perceived as reducing their autonomy.

C. The Behaviorally Anchored Rating Scale

While is it difficult to establish clear-cut performance objectives for scientists engaged in pure research, physical therapists, or for other professionals who are exploring problems or essentially dealing with the unknown, some current tools may be useful in the appraisal process. One useful approach to appraisal in these situations is for the manager to work with professional employees in the development of behaviorally anchored rating scales. This appraisal tool involves the development of scaled statements that describe effective and ineffective specific job behaviors associated with getting results. These behaviors can be constructed by categorizing and systematically scaling a manager's report of critical incidents of effective or ineffective job performance. When specific behaviors are identified, it is assumed that a distinction can be made between more effective and less effective ways of doing the job.

Kearney provides specific guidelines on how to construct behaviorally anchored rating scales as follows:[36]

1. Supervisors and subordinates identify activities critical to effective job performance, namely, performance
   dimensions.
2. Specific statements based on observations of both effective and ineffective job performance are drawn

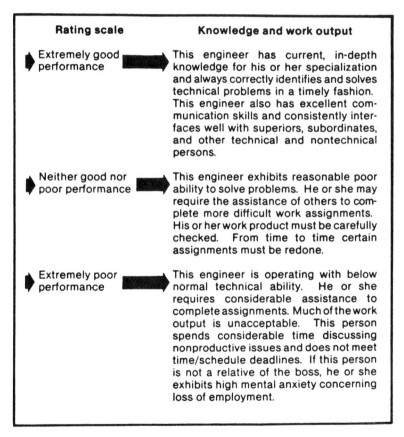

Rating scale	Knowledge and work output
Extremely good performance	This engineer has current, in-depth knowledge for his or her specialization and always correctly identifies and solves technical problems in a timely fashion. This engineer also has excellent communication skills and consistently interfaces well with superiors, subordinates, and other technical and nontechnical persons.
Neither good nor poor performance	This engineer exhibits reasonable poor ability to solve problems. He or she may require the assistance of others to complete more difficult work assignments. His or her work product must be carefully checked. From time to time certain assignments must be redone.
Extremely poor performance	This engineer is operating with below normal technical ability. He or she requires considerable assistance to complete assignments. Much of the work output is unacceptable. This person spends considerable time discussing nonproductive issues and does not meet time/schedule deadlines. If this person is not a relative of the boss, he or she exhibits high mental anxiety concerning loss of employment.

Figure 12.3 Simplified behaviorally anchored rating scale for a design engineer

from these dimensions. Attention is given to job actions that reflect favorable or unfavorable performance.

3. These statements are then assigned by the manager or job holder to the appropriate dimension. Mutual agreement among participants is important in making this assignment.

4. These statements are then scaled from 1 to 9 on an effective-ineffective continuum.

Performance can then be measured against these dimensions as part of MBO or part of basic performance appraisal. While this technique can be helpful to all managers, it is particularly useful to managers where end results (goals) are difficult to quantify. A simplified behaviorally anchored rating scale for a professional design engineer is shown in Figure 12.3.

D. Implementing MBO: Concluding Thoughts

Once objectives are established through a process of mutual agreement with subordinates and specific time periods for attainment of these objectives are accepted, performance interviews should be conducted at the appropriate times. For professionals, this time period is usually once each year.

The application of effective communication skills as developed in Chapter 7 is particularly helpful to conducting constructive appraisal interviews. Appraisers should focus on the problem, direct the communication at improving performance, appear to be interested, offer constructive and helpful suggestions to appraisees, and above all protect employee self-esteem.

In the early stages of making MBO work, there may be some periods of disenchantment with the process. Since MBO involves some new processes in interviewing and objective development that have not been used before, managers and subordinates become uncertain about the necessity or usefulness of these extra efforts. This disenchantment is normal. Some managers and professionals feel threatened by agreeing to accomplish end results in specific time periods. This type of threat or pressure can be minimized by mutual goal setting where the concerns of the professional employee are fully shared and supported at goal-setting sessions. If good performers are clearly rewarded by management, the entire professional group will see that it is adventageous to both set goals and accomplish them.

It is useful in the initial stages of management by objectives to move rather slowly and build on past successes, because an attempt to move quickly can overwhelm all employees involved. Extra paperwork, interview time, and attempting to establish a complete set of objectives can be so threatening to these employees that the system fails because of the lack of cooperation. The total organizational unit must work together (high involvement) to make MBO work. Thus, upper level managers must provide an environment where threats are minimized and the action is taken at a pace that subordinates can adjust to.

Management by objectives is not a panacea, but it can be a useful tool in improving managerial effectiveness and increasing involvement among professionals. While it is not easily applied, there is considerable evidence to suggest that most professionals can benefit from a well-planned and functioning management by objectives program.

VIII. SUMMARY

As the title and content of this chapter suggest, involvement or participative management is being utilized by more and more organizations. Certainly it is not a new concept, and many managers have accepted its precepts for many years. What is new is the large scale attempt on the part of so many organizations to apply it, and the fact that this trend reaches heavily into many manufacturing firms that have a long tradition of autocratic decision making.

For many of these firms, this change is not as easy one. A large number of older managers must change their thinking about the values of participation. Trust and openness are vital to making high involvement management work. A knowledge of the communication and leadership skills (Chapters 7 and 9) is particularly beneficial to democratic managers and successful methods of introducing change (Chapter 10) are also needed. Fortunately, newer managers are likely to be more supportive of the management philosophies that are based on two-way communication and employee involvement.

There is no one best approach that can be generally applied, but managers of professionals have the advantage of having subordinates that have both high levels of self-esteem and motivation. As Bennis and Nanus point out, successful participative management requires leaders who move employees toward self motivation.[37] The professional work environment contains the ingredients for successfully involving employees in important organizational affairs. One of the managers key tasks is to match the most appropriate involvement tools to his or her work environment. If this is accomplished, the payoffs will be high to both the individual manager and the organization.

REFERENCES

1. For additional discussion of the Scanlon Plan see Mitchell Fein, "Improved Productivity Through Worker Involvement," *Annual Industrial Engineering Conference Proceedings,* 1982; Brian E. Moore and Timothy L. Ross, *The Scanlon Way to Improved Productivity,* John Wiley & Sons, 1978; and C.F. Frost, J.H. Wakely, and R.A. Ruh, *The Scanlon Plan for Organization Development,* Michigan State University Press, 1974.

2. For a detailed analysis of many of Likert's findings see R. Likert, *New Patterns of Management,* New York, McGraw-Hill Book Company, 1961; and R. Likert, *The Human Organization,* New York, McGraw-Hill Book Company, 1967.

3. For a detailed discussion of the problems of managing R & D professionals see Donald B. Miller, *Managing Professionals in Research and Development,* San Francisco, Josey Bass, 1986.

4. Brian H. Rowe, *From the Front Office,* GE/AEBG, March 1986, pp. 3-4.

5. Edward Lawler III, *High Involvement Management,* San Francisco, Josey Bass Inc., 1986, p. 1.

6. Nicholas A. Damachi, Richard L. Shell, and H. Ray Souder, "Managerial Propensity to Use Participative Strategies for Productivity Measurement and Improvement," *Industrial Management,* Vol. 26, No. 3, May-June 1984, pp. 23-27.

7. R.W. Walters, "The Citibank Project: Improving Productivity Through Work Redesign" in R. Zager and M.R. Rosen eds. *The Innovative Organization: Productivity Programs in Action,* New York, Permagon Press, 1982, pp. 109-124.

8. Frank M. Gryna, Jr., *Quality Circles: A Team Approach to Problem Solving,* New York: AMACOM, 1981, pp. 10-12.

9. Kenneth Hopper, "Creating Japan's New Industrial Management: The Americans as Teachers," *Human Resources Management,* Summer 1982, pp. 16-17.

10. Frank M. Gryna, Jr., op. cit.

11. Sidney P. Rubinstein, "QC Circles and U.S. Participative Movements," *ASQC Technical Conference Transactions,* Washington, DC, 1972, pp. 391-396.

12. Frank M. Gryna, Jr., op. cit.

13. J.F. Cox and D.R. Norris, "Measuring Quality Circle Effectiveness," *Proceedings of the American Production and Inventory Control Society,* 1983, pp. 178-181.

14. M. O'Donnell and R.J. O'Donnell, "Quality Circles - The Latest Fad or a Real Winner?", *Business Horizons,* May-June 1984, pp. 48-52.

15. Lawler, *High Involvement Management,* p. 60.

16. O'Donnell and O'Donnell, op. cit.

17. R. Wood, F. Hull, and K. Azumi, "Evaluating Quality Circles: The American Application," *California Management Review,* Vol. 26, No. 1, 1983, pp. 37-53.

18. Joel Brockner and Ted Hess, "Self-Esteem and Task Performance in Quality Circles," *Academy of Management Journal,* Vol. 29, No. 3, 1986, pp. 617-623.

19. Ervin Williams, *Participative Management Concepts, Theory and Implementation,* Atlanta, Georgia State Univ. Press 1976, p. 102.

20. William M. Lindsay, *Measurement of Quality Circle Effectiveness*: *A Survey and Critique,* Unpublished M.S. Thesis, College of Engineering, University of Cincinnati, 1986.

21. Lawler, *High Involvement Management,* p. 108.

22. T.G. Cummings and E.S. Molley, "Improving Productivity and the Quality of Work Life," New York, Praeger, 1977.

23. For more detailed discussion of both these plans see Dale S. Beach, *Personnel*: *The Management of People at Work,* New York, Macmillan Publishing Co. 1985, pp. 501-513.

24. M. Dulworth, "Employee Involvement and Gainsharing Produce Dramatic Results at Eggers Industries," Washington, DC, U.S. Department of Labor 1985.

25. Ronald Greenwood, "Management by Objectives: As Developed by Peter Drucker, Assisted by Harold Smiddy," *Academy of Management Review,* Vol. 6, No. 2, 1981, pp. 225-230.

26. Timothy T. Serey and Desmond D. Martin, "The Impact of Selected Management Tools on Organizational Effectiveness," College of Business Administration, University of Cincinnati, Cincinnati, Ohio, April 1979.

27. Jacob B. Paperman and Desmond D. Martin, "Human Resource Accounting: A Managerial Tool?" *Personnel,* March-April 1977, pp. 41-50.

28. J.E. Sheridan, D.J. Viedenburgh, and N.A. Abelson, "Contextual Model of Leadership Influence in Hospitals," *Academy of Management Journal,* Vol. 27, No. 1, 1984, pp. 57-78.

29. Frank M. Andrews and George F. Farris, "Supervisory Practices and Innovation in Scientific Teams," *Personnel Psychology,* Vol. 20, No. 4, Winter 1967.

30. D.C. Pelz and F.M. Andrews, "Autonomy Coordination and Stimulation in Relation to Scientific Achievement," *Behavioral Science,* Vol. XI, 1966, pp. 89-97.

31. Robert H. Mills, "How Job Conflict and Ambiguity Affect R. & D. Professionals," *Research Management,* Vol. XVIII, No. 4, July 1975.

32. J.S. Kine, "Effect of Behavior" plus "Outcome Goal Setting and Feedback on Employee Satisfaction and Performance," *Academy of Management Journal,* Vol. 27, No. 1, 1984, pp. 139-149.

33. J. Kondrasuk, "Studies in MBO Effectiveness," *Academy of Management Review,* Vol. 6, No. 3, 1981, pp. 419-430.

34. Joseph P. Martino, "Managing Engineers by Objectives," *IEEE Transactions on Engineering Management,* Vol. EM23, No. 4, November 1976, pp. 168-174.

35. S.A. Edwards and M.W. McCarrey, "Measuring the Performance of Researchers," *Research Management,* January 1973, pp. 34-40.

36. William J. Kearney, "Behaviorally Anchored Rating Scales-MBO's Missing Ingredient," *Personnel Journal,* January 1979, pp. 20-25.

37. Warren Bennis, and W. Nanus, *Leaders,* New York: Harper and Row, 1985.

38. For a discussion of the quality issue see: P.L. Townsend and J.E. Gebhardt, *Commit to Quality,* New York, John Wiley and Sons, 1986; and W. Edwards Deming, *Out of the Crisis,* Cambridge, Massachusetts Institute of Technology, Center for Advanced Engineering Study, 1982.

13

Managerial and Organizational Effectiveness: An Epilogue

I. BASIC COMPONENTS OF ORGANIZATIONAL EFFECTIVENESS

As indicated previously, the purpose of this book is to provide managers of professional staff with tested management and behavioral concepts and techniques that can be applied to increase both managerial and organizational effectiveness. The authors believe that a significant proportion of an organization's effectiveness can be measured by its performance in six specific areas:

Overall productivity (a ratio of input to output)
Quality of products and services
Planning and the presence of clearly stated goals
Adaptability and flexibility (quick reaction capability)
The quality and effectiveness of intra- and interorganizational communication
The choice of an appropriate management style

One study of a large representative sample of personnel professionals found substantial agreement that productivity, adaptability, and clearly stated goals are the three most important variables affecting organizational effectiveness within their firms.[1] This finding was reported for both the present and a ten year projection into the future. Additionally, a detailed report on jobs in the 1990s suggests that in order to stay competitive industrial democracies such as the United States must emphasize productivity and continue to develop and utilize a highly skilled work force.[2]

A. Effectiveness Begins with Good Planning

In order to achieve performance in these areas, the manager must plan and organize well. The basic elements of good long- and short-range planning were discussed in Chapter 2. It is important to note that throughout this book emphasis has been placed on the significance of *separating planning from doing and the facilitative role of the manager.* Short- and long-range plans should be based on clearly understood and stated goals for both the unit being managed and the overall organization. Specific plans should be established that help remove barriers to goal accomplishment among subordinates.

As developed in Chapter 6, professional employees have differing and often unique needs that warrant special consideration in good managerial planning. Participative management can be extremely helpful in both discerning the nature of these needs and responding to them. In giving consideration to individual needs, managers should remember that equity is a vital part of effective planning. A given subordinate's perception of equity or inequity is usually judged only in relation to how other people are being treated in the same situation. Plans should attempt to establish predictable relationships for subordinates once they understand the situation. Individual differences can be accounted for in the context of different situations without upsetting equity. For example, a manager's plan to transfer employees among jobs can differentiate among subordinates on the basis of skills, health, or special interests as long as these criteria are clearly understood by the subordinates involved. Thus, effective communication is vital to successful implementation of plans and organizational effectiveness.

Managers of professionals should plan for both contingencies and conflict among employees. A certain amount of conflict is both normal and healthy, and it is unrealistic to have a goal of creating a managerial environment that is totally free of conflict (Chapter 11). But in recent years it has become increasingly important to establish some kind of procedural "due process" which will enable employees to communicate concerns about inequitable treatment. This is particularly important for professionally trained individuals. For such a system to work, all employees must have the right to use it, and provision for a third, impartial party to "hear" unresolved cases is necessary. While these elements have been common parts of collective bargaining agreements for many years, they are only recently being used in nonunionized settings. Since high perceived equity among subordinates improves levels of cooperation with both peers and managers and tends to increase motivation (Chapter 8), managerial attention to both equity and due process in the planning process will enhance organizational effectiveness.

B. The Future of Planning

Since planning is fundamental to effectiveness, some discussion about the future of planning is worthwhile. Planning activities and the involvement of management will be affected not only by the scope and detail of the existing plan but also by improvements that occur in systems, techniques, and technology. One such tool which holds promise for planning improvement is *decision support systems* (DSS). The principal objective of these systems is to provide management with a clear picture of the organization's current state and to stimulate its future under various hypothetical environments.[3] The impact of such a system on planning is in the development of simulation models and the testing of tactical and strategic changes which are being proposed.[4]

Artificial Intelligence (AI) and expert systems will also have a role in the future of strategic and operational planning. By transferring much of the human intelligence and insight into the computer, models can be developed to assist in the acutal formulation of plans. The main advantage of an AI system for planning is its ability to review data. Artificial intelligence will thus enable a firm to model the entire planning system in parallel, review the results via computer, and more strategically select the appropriate course of action. AI *will not replace* human judgement but *will assist* in improving decisions and greatly reduce the time for the process. The time savings will allow for greater concentration on the actual implementation of the plan.

One set of characteristics which has been outlined for the planning systems of the 1990s is outlined below:[5]

> Structured but less formal
> Focus on the plan and its development process
> Plan drives the budget and not vice versa
> Involvement of all levels of management
> A balance between market, financial, and operations
>   issues
> A broadened perspective
> Longer planning horizons
> Pervasive discourse on plans
> Driven and managed top down with feedback at all levels

As the 1990s approach the trend towards these characteristics can be seen in the most innovative companies.

C. Organizational Structure: A Major Tool of Effectiveness

As suggested in Chapter 3, good organizing and structuring is essential for both efficiency and effectiveness. In fact, the quality of a given manager's organizational structure has a lot to do with the level of employee adaptability and flexibility which is attained. Needless to say, adaptability and flexibility are particularly crucial to almost all businesses because today most are subject to rapid and often unpredictable change. Good organization should enable the business to respond effectively to environmental requirements and facilitate the realization of employee potential.

In order to develop an effective organization, managerial knowledge of principles, alternative structures, and the elements of sound line-staff relationships as developed in Chapter 3 is essential. It is often useful to define and group tasks, and allocate assignments based on employee preferences whenever possible and practical. The manager of professional employees should be aware of techniques that assist the integration of goal setting and organizational structure. One such technique, MAPS (multivariate analysis, participation, and structure), has been proposed for this purpose.[6] Ralph Kilman concludes from his studies that MAPS generates sufficient confidence from its applications that its ethical use can be supported.[6] While it is beyond the scope of this book to explain in detail this rather complex tool, a brief discussion will follow concerning its applicability and usefulness. The MAPS method considers both the nature of the tasks to be accomplished and the preferences or interests of specific employees in performing this work.[7] This technique is similar to management by objectives in that organizational members interact with their managers in objective setting and task identification. Multivariate analysis is then used to cluster interrelated tasks. Once preferences for given task clusters are known, multivariate statistical techniques can be used to assign employees to the organizational subunits that best fit their interests and preferences. In view of the high needs for autonomy and strong preferences for specific task assignments associated with professional workers, the MAPS method offers potential help to the manager who is trying to build an effective organizational structure.

While attention was given in Chapter 3 to selection of new personnel, managers more commonly face the problem of allocation and assignment of work among existing personnel on a periodic basis. The MAPS method is useful in this latter problem as well as in the assignment of tasks to new employees. It provides a framework for matching two critical elements of good structuring, namely tasks and people.

For a number of years many management authorities, including Drucker, have suggested that a decision should be made at the lowest level in the organization that is closest to the scene of action.[8] Minimizing the number of organizational levels tends to lower the levels where decisions are made, and also simplifies the organizational structure. Simple structures are easier to understand and foster more effective communication than complex ones. Consequently, as long as a given structure will do the job, keep it as simple as possible.

II. CHANGING ATTITUDES AND VALUES OF AMERICAN WORKERS

Changing values and attitudes precipitated by cultural change have added to the complexity of the managerial task in recent years. During the past two decades, worker attitudes toward welfare and leisure have undergone significant change. For example, earlier studies concluded that most workers associated hard work with both getting ahead and raising self-esteem.[9] During the past several years non-professional employees in increasing numbers no longer subscribe to this belief. Accepting welfare is no longer considered demeaning by many people, and hard work is not seen as leading directly to advancement. The professional, however, usually has quite different views. He or she will likely believe that working hard on high priority tasks will lead to success.

The differences discussed above are at least partially described by the changing profile of the average American worker. For example, Naisbitt and Aburdene point out that in the 1950s the average worker was like the following:[10]

white males were 62.5 percent of the work force.
white male breadwinners had a wife and children to support and worked full time in an office or factory.
he either belonged to a union or would join one.
he was about 45 and would retire at 65 and was motivated by job security and steady pay.

By June 1984, white males had become the minority in the work force, only 49.3 percent. Naisbitt and Aburdene go on to say that today's average worker looks like this:

a 34 year-old baby boomer with two children and a working spouse.
plans to work past retirement and is willing to accept some risk in exchange for possibly being rewarded for superior performance.
does not belong to a union and would not consider joining one.

is increasingly likely to have some sort of flexible work
   schedule.
increasingly, that "average worker" is a woman.

As pointed out in earlier chapters, rewards for professionals
should be linked to performance, but many managers continue to
relate individual performance appraisal to vague traits or seniority
rather than to actual goal-related accomplishment. Recent trends
in the use of MBO-type performance appraisal systems, including
behaviorally anchored rating scales, offer some encouragement as a
potential solution to this problem (Chapter 12). Employees who
realize that personal reward is attained through good job performance will usually contribute to organizational effectiveness.

A. New Credentials Requirements

Unfortunately, in many instances credentials needed to qualify for
employment have been increased by management, but job content
has remained relatively unchanged. Jobs that required only a high
school diploma or less in the 1950s required a college degree in the
1970s as a basic educational qualification.[11] This condition has
continued since that time. Because the job content is no more challenging, many employees become frustrated with their job assignments. Many, but not all, organizations with professional workers
are no exception to this problem. A number of jobs currently exist
that require a technical degree or graduate education which could
be performed by a less educated technician without difficulty, but
there must be a careful balance. For example, if a business has the
need to integrate new technology into their operations, professional
employees with advanced level degrees would probably be appropriate. In the case of product manufacturing, almost any company
can build quality products when *cost* is not a factor. Conversely,
most companies can build inexpensive products when *quality* is
not a factor. The highly educated and experienced professional
employee can make the difference to develop and produce quality
products, competitively priced, for the world market place. Obtaining the correct balance between cost and quality is a difficult

task and should not be left to employees with marginal education and experience.

The management challenge is to determine job requirements and properly match workers to those requirements. For example, in analyzing the managerial practices of General George C. Marshall and G.M.'s Alfred P. Sloan, Drucker emphasizes that both these successful leaders personally picked lower level officers and managers in their respective organizations.[12] Moreover, their great managerial success is largely attributed to their superior ability to select and place people in the right jobs.[12] In addition, management should upgrade jobs where possible, and be aware of the impact of the rising educational level of the work force on job satisfaction and motivation.

B. An Educated Professional Work Force is Not Automatically More Productive

High levels of educational attainment and professionalism have also generated a more mobile work force which has reduced the importance of company loyalty to many employees. The practical implication of reduced loyalty is that managers who do not continually strive to make their work unit environment responsive to employee needs may find that they are losing their most valuable employees to competing organizations. Years of service or other factors relating to a given employee's history with the company may turn out to be quite irrelevant.

While techniques for building the right work environment have been given special attention throughout this book, it is important to remember that increasing *time pressure* and/or *minimum control* over one's job activities create major problems for most professional employees. These problems are not new. They have existed for over twenty years. Martin Patchen's comprehensive study of the Tennessee Valley Authority, which employs many professional personnel, found that these employees attach great importance to control over work methods and a work environment that is characterized by low amounts of time pressure.[13] As time requirements are intensified, employees tend to take less pride in their work; namely, they hurry to complete the assigned tasks and concentrate less on how well tasks are done.[14] Today's professionals regard reduced time pressure, autonomy, control over work methods, and communication feedback on performance as essential elements of a good working environment. Each of these elements can be considered a proper component of an enriched job. It is good practice for the manager of professional employees to analyze both current job designs and managerial practices for the specific units that fall within his or her realm of accountability. Although at first glance or reading the above analysis may lead one to conclude that reduced time pressure will result in more free time for workers to engage in nonproductive tasks, the authors' experience with numerous companies over the past twenty years does not support that conclusion. In general, reduced time pressure leads to greater productivity and sustains positive (long-run) managerial relationships with professional employees. Involvement management concepts (Chapter 12) provides a vehicle to achieve these results.

III. CAREER DEVELOPMENT IN THE PROFESSIONAL ORGANIZATION

Aspiring young professionals are vitally interested in personal growth and career advancement. One study of 277 municipal employees examined the relationship between career involvement and adaptability. This study's findings suggest that extensive career planning is related to higher salaries, more career involvement, and adaptability.[15] One career planning model asserts that the establishment of career goals by employees leads to increased efforts to achieve these goals, which results in more career involvement. If these goals are successfully attained, employee performance and self-esteem are increased.[15] There is growing evidence that specific attention to career planning is important both to the manager and the employee. Although advising young people on how to manage their careers is difficult, managers of professional employees are often confronted with this task.

Some of the useful advice that these managers can offer new subordinates and may find applicable to their own situation, especially if they are new managers, is contained in the following list, which is adapted from the separate work of Webber, Jennings, and Buskirk.[16]

1. Make an accurate self-appraisal of the real criteria that are being used in evaluating your performance. Try to accurately appraise your own performance against these criteria, and concentrate your time and effort on improving perceived performance deficiencies in these critical areas.

2. Keep yourself up-to-date in your field. This process includes continually reading current literature, and being aware of seminars and presentations on new and important topics. Technology awareness is important to most professionals.

3. Strive to be an active influence in organizational decisions, and try to gain positions with high visibility where your performance can be observed by higher management.

4. Develop good relationships with superiors who are highly regarded in the organizational hierarchy.

5. Seize opportunities by nominating yourself for positions that involve advancement. On the other hand, do not be afraid to turn down a promotion for which you are not qualified, or a job in which you assess that your chances for success are very low.

6. A managerial position involves a series of dependency relationships. If you find these relationships repulsive, you may not be cut out to be a manager.

7. Written job descriptions are often either too narrow, outdated, or both, so do not be afraid to move out beyond the job description in performing your duties. In fact, many times successful job performance requires such action.

While the above suggestions help prepare professionals and new managers for advancement, it is important throughout this process that each employee has established written objectives (performance plan) that have been set through mutual discussion with the boss. The number of objectives set should be kept at a small manageable number; three to six are suitable for most jobs. Accomplishments should be closely monitored against the performance plan and a summary made available to the boss at the end of the evaluation period.[17] Career development is a high priority objective for younger professionals, and, when it is conducted well by both management and employee, the resulting payoff is substantial to both individual and organization.

A. Importance of the First Job Assignment

The characteristics of the first job assignment are important to the manager, professional employee, and organization. Employee turnover is often highest during the first year or so of employment among qualified employees, and proper handling of early assignments by superiors will often reduce turnover among more valued new employees.

Managers should realize that the first career assignment is a time of great apprehension for most new recruits. He or she may feel that this assignment is the real test of the value of acquired skills in a professional educational program, and failure at this job will mean that the value of their educational investment in time and money is subject to question. Needless to say, this possibility represents a strong potential threat to both the satisfaction and self-esteem of the new employee. Thus, the manager should recognize these apprehensions and offer support to new professionals during their critical first year.

Since many organizations regard first-year assignments as *relatively unimportant probationary periods for new employees*, managers may not have upper management support in their special handling of the new recruit. For example, some organizations do not make important job assignments to employees with less than one year of service; consequently, new employees' fears of failure during the first year may be exaggerated. Since research alluded to in Chapter 9 shows a positive correlation between challenging first year assignments and later success in an employee's career, the advisability of simplistic unimportant early work assignments is questionable. The manager who understands the importance of challenging the new professional, and the differences between the overall managerial perceptions versus the new employee's perceptions of the significance of first-year assignments can be helpful in both developing the professional and improving organizational effectiveness.

B. Avoiding Professional Obsolescence

While the period of time involved in which professional obsolescence will occur varies by organizational structure and technology demands of the business, it is generally agreed that unless new knowledge is continually made available to professional employees, they will become obsolete. Many firms have learned from experience that highly educated employees become a liability to the firm unless new learning which is equivalent to their current state of knowledge is generated in 12 to 18 years from their date of initial employment. Specifically, if a recent graduate enters the organization with a Ph.D. in 1988, by the year 2000 or shortly thereafter he or she should acquire new knowledge equal to what was acquired in pursuit of the doctorate. For example, the majority of college graduates in the 1960s did not have a *single* course in computer programming or systems development. Yet more recently it would be difficult to envision any graduate of a professional curriculum that has not had computer orientation. As the rate of technology development and implementation increases, *the need for new learning and training becomes even more important.* A supportive personnel/human resources department can be very helpful in coordinating continuing education and training programs. Each program should be tailored to the specific needs of the given firm. A word of caution . . . training planners and directors should avoid the two common pitfalls of "copying" programs from other firms or "spoon feeding" participants.

    An organizational climate that creates the desire to learn should be provided by the manager of professional employees. Two essential ingredients of this environment are first, specific rewards for successful completion of training and education programs given to participants, e.g., opportunities for advancement and assignment of more challenging work; and second, recognizing employees who improve or do outstanding work on their current jobs. These factors are generally consistent with modern approaches to motivation (Chapter 8).

The issue of a dual career is also related to the professional obsolescence program. Does the person who becomes a manager devote virtually all of his or her time to managerial problems and spend little or no time on new developments in the field? The logical answer to this question is no, because keeping up-to-date in the field is an important part of the managerial task. As Drucker points out, professionals do not easily accept as their boss either someone with credentials in a field they do not respect or one who is not "top flight" in their own profession or in a related field held in high esteem.[12] An ideal managerial climate continues to reward those managers for outstanding professional work, and encourages individual managers to attend seminars and other presentations that relate to the development and updating of their technical knowledge. While the manager's time for professional development is limited, some time should be selectively allocated for this activity. Properly managing one's time is essential, and the efficient manager can benefit from mastering the fundamentals of time management (Chapter 5).

IV. WHAT'S AHEAD FOR LABOR RELATIONS?

The ability of management to sustain cooperative relations with all employees is essential for organizational success. Many changes are occurring in the American labor movement that will affect the professional work environment. As has been widely publicized, unions are in a declining position in the United States.[18] The labor force is changing in ways that decrease the probability of future organizing successes. For example, substantial increases in female, highly educated, and younger workers are all important factors in this decline. Also, so many of the characteristics among strong unionized work groups between the decades of the 1930s and 1950s are not widespread among professionals. Employees who have invested large amounts of time and money in their professional development are not prone to engage in activities that promote an averaging of individual rewards so the group as a whole can receive more. Unions tend to narrow wage gaps between top and bottom and increases are more likely to be across the board than in non-union settings. Unions usually place a high value on seniority which is often discouraging to the aspiring younger professional employee.

In view of the prevalence of cutback management (Chapter 10), and attendant pressures on unions which result in bargaining strategies to minimize losses rather than to maximize gains, it is not surprising union appeal is limited. When these conditions are coupled with the value system usually found among professionals, future organizing attempts are likely to fail.

An appropriate question that managers of professionals might ask themselves is as follows: *Is this declining trend in union activity and pressure long term or temporary?* While many signs suggest that it is long term a few words of caution are offered. Professionals offer a large emerging group of employees that specific unions could tap for membership growth. Traditional union leadership has not been characterized as possessing a "professional" value system. However, the dramatic increase in the number of professionals, as well as that of current union leaders who are aging and retiring, could bring change.

New professional leadership within unions that promulgates a value system congruent with most practicing professionals could enhance union appeal. Some authorities have specifically suggested that professional employees can easily become disenchanted with their working conditions and become prime candidates for unionization.[19] The best way to prevent this occurrence, assuming managers do not want union restrictions facing them, is to continually address the needs of professionals affirmatively as developed throughout this book.

V. INFORMATION SYSTEMS AND COMPUTER APPLICATIONS IN THE FUTURE

Successful organizations today obtain much of their managerial and organizational effectiveness and efficiency by the proper utilization of computers. The cornerstone of manager performance is a properly designed information system. Without this, managers and other key employees are unable to accomplish a multitude of necessary tasks in a knowledgeable, timely fashion. The most successful organizations in the future will be those that are able to take advantage of ongoing computer technology developments.

A. Management Information Systems

The management information system (MIS) of the future will be a logical plan linking various parts together to form a consolidated system. The two key phrases in this statement are *logical plan* and *to form a consolidated system.*

Most management information systems of today evolved (or are evolving) from completely independent functions. For example, in many firms Product Engineering had their own system as did Production and Inventory Control, Manufacturing Engineering, and Quality Assurance. Each system operated independently of the others, with some duplication of services and overlapping data bases. Many times confusion and complications mounted as the varying systems continued to expand. To control this increasing bureaucracy and cost, many companies have integrated these systems into a unified MIS.

The future MIS will evolve from a logical plan to distribute information pertinent to all areas of the organization from a common base of data and knowledge. An example to illustrate a future MIS would involve a corporation using just-in-time delivery for production. During daily operations on the automatic inspection line, a vital part starts to be rejected constantly. This information is distributed on a real-time basis to various areas. Manufacturing is notified that there is a problem with a vital part. Engineering is given the specifications of the rejected part for investigation. Purchasing receives information to contact suppliers for more parts to cover the amount rejected. Sales receives notification that assemblies requiring these parts will be delayed and to contact the customer. Management is also aware of the problem and can keep a close watch for further developments. All of this would be accomplished through the use of a comprehensive management information system.

B. Overview of Computer Applications

The next generation of computers and information systems will find a variety of applications. These computers will upgrade information technology in the areas of industrial automation, office automation, and in the retailing and service industries. All users of computers, including systems analysts and engineers, will be greatly affected by future generation machines. Each of these applications is feasible today on the basis of technology which has been demonstrated in research settings. Advances in integrated information-management systems, computer architectures, and human-machine interfaces are required for these applications to become realizable.[20]

The past several years have seen a vast increase in the use of CAD/CAM systems and robots in industrial settings. Future factories will also see increased applications in inventory management, product-cost estimating, and in expert systems for design purposes. The components necessary to implement these ideas include software systems which will be vital in linking the information related to product design and manufacturing. Available also, will be libraries of modular control routines that will enable intelligent robots to be used in low-volume production settings.[21]

Computer technology is presently available to handle the management of most office information. The next generation of systems will permit human-machine interactions through voice input commands, intelligent voice output, and natural language processing. Expert systems will be available to assist in develolping computer applications and also for helping retrieve information relevant to the user's immediate needs. Communication in the office will be enhanced by systems which link together telephone lines, office computers, and video networks. This will also open the door for improved long distance communications which will include widely distributed electronic mail and phone video message systems.

A great abundance of applications in information service industries are awaiting the new generation of computers. Expert systems could be utilized in several areas, including searching of property and court records, tax and financial planning, and analysis and information systems for use in repairing such things as cars and appliances. Hardware and software systems that are already in existence must be integrated together for these ideas to be implemented into working products.[21]

The development of future computers will see an increase in the automation of the computer industry itself. The computers being developed today will be doing much of the design work on the generation of machines that follow them. Hardware and software is being developed to automate program design and for use in debugging and maintaining programs. Expert systems will also be used for the fault diagnosis of computer hardware. The ultimate computer of tomorrow will be a machine which will completely maintain itself and even, on its own, design a machine to take its place.

C. Information Systems and Manufacturing

The future of information systems for use within a manufacturing facility is a topic which is rapidly changing with technology. In the industrialized countries, the labor force is changing from goods producing, basic manufacturing to service activities including information-oriented software production. As this takes place, the need for high quality and understandable information will increase. The changes being made in the technology and sciences of manufacturing are leading to automated factories (factories of the future) run by a multitude of machines with minimal human interface.

These factories of the future are essential if the United States is going to maintain a manufacturing base and be able to compete in the world marketplace. To analyze the information needs of automated factories of the future one must be familiar with the basic types of information inputs which will be available.

The anatomy and thought processes of humans are being incorporated in the next generation of robotics and automated machines. A comparison of the human body to advanced technologies is given below:

bones robot arm or other automated equipment elements

brain microprocessor/computer

consciousness	program execution/operation, real-time processing
feet	guidance systems, obstacle recognition, support devices
hearing	audio input, language understanding
joints	hinge or universal joint
judgment	logic circuits, decision making
knowledge	data, expert systems, artificial intelligence
learning	data input, pattern recognition and interpretation
memory	storage devices
nerves	electronics, conductors, semiconductors
reasoning	heuristic trials, deductive processes
sight	vision and image processing
skeleton	machine structure
speech	audio output, voice synthesis

During the early 1980s, there were approximately five to six thousand robots in use in the United States, with population anticipated to increase to over one hundred thousand by the year 1990.[22] Industrial robots can provide continuous production at lower costs. Combined with vision systems, tactile sensing, sonar, object recognition, and computers, the robot will become more advanced (intelligent) and more useful.

In addition to more comprehensive information systems, the future will also see advances in factory equipment. While most development will be in computer architecture and processing techniques, there will be many developments in machine tools and process control equipment. One example is the need to develop a secure data storage device for use on machine tools and factory equipment. During recent years Japanese tool builders have used magnetic bubble memory devices, which are built into the machine controls. However, these devices may not be reliable in metal manufacturing operations due to possible magnetic interference. As manufacturing techniques become more automated and complex, larger and more secure memory devices should be incorporated in most factory equipment.

D. Information Use in Factory Operations

The fundamental information needs of the future factory will basically remain the same. Factory managers will still need to know performance indicators; manufacturing information, such as tooling data, machine operation, maintenance, cost data, power consumption, downtime; and general management information involving all operating functions. For the actual manufacturing shop floor there will be a need for interpretation of such data so that it may be appropriately applied. Interestingly, this is how data is used in manufacturing today. However, the factory of the future will have interpreters that are no longer human, but machines such as industrial robots, microprocessors, object recognition devices, and a multitude of other high-tech devices.

The transfer of information will occur as a series of binary numbers, generated by electrical (or optical) pulses. One such example has been in place for several years at the Mazak Machine Tool Corporation in Florence, Kentucky. A small scale factory of the future, Mazak utilizes a binary code on part pallets, which is in turn interpreted by the machine tool for part processing data, tool selection, and inventory/work in process control. The central factory computer tracks this data and generates reports for management, in addition to performing actual machine control. While not entirely automated, Mazak is an example of a manufacturing firm applying advanced technology.

While all computers operate in a similar machine code, there has been a proliferation of computer operating systems and languages. As the application of computer factory control increases so does the need for standardization of a factory programming language. One which is easily understandable to programmers and operators is natural language. This is needed so that robots, machine tools, material handling, and object recognition or inspection devices can operate in harmony. There is also a need for a high level programming language, based on common words, that will allow an operator to generate all the required programs from the manufacturing floor. The combination of part design and process planning is just one aspect of computer aided engineering. This new field is responsible for linking the basic factory operations via a common data base, applying group technology, simulation programming, and advanced technologies.

Information will still be used by humans, in addition to machines. As John Naisbitt, author of *Megatrends*, suggests: "Information technology brings order to the chaos of information pollution and therefore gives value to data that would be otherwise useless. If users, through information utilities, can locate the information they need, they will pay for it."[23] The responsibility of professionals in manufacturing and their managers in the future will thus be to effectively locate, interpret, and apply the information available, to enhance production and to supply the necessary data for continued high quality cost efficient operations.

E. Information Systems and the Service Sector

The future challenge to the service sector is to effectively apply technology. With more computers being accepted into society the importance of information science has increased considerably. However, management must be concerned with the operation of equipment and more importantly software, to ensure that the total system is acceptable to users. Information system designers in the future should be concerned with problem solving and management, and with the interface provided to humans. The increased application of automation to the office environment and the importance of knowledge worker productivity has brought increased concentration on improving ergonomics and workstation design.[24]

Along with the trend to design improved workstations has come the concept of bioware. Bioware can be thought of as the area of *biological interpretation of data*; in other words, how will the human do it? This area of development is responsible for the term *user friendly*, and has resulted in improving the human-computer interface.

The nature of traditional information jobs, such as accounting and finance, have been the leaders in the use of computers within the office environment. Because of increased automation, several traditional jobs will likely see diminishing employment. As machines communicate with each other there will be less human involvement, and as may be expected, less opportunity for error. Advances in office automation have seen many changes within the clerical support staff, and have caused concern over areas such as radiation from cathode ray tubes, lighting, physical comfort, and productivity.

The advances in computer technology for office automation will be based on the same devices that have spawned industrial automation: the microprocessors. While computers decrease in size they have been increasing in power, and it is the power that service personnel will use.

Designers are being treated to the advent of the computer aided design station, secretaries to the computer integrated workstation, and factory technicians to portable computers. These devices have revolutionized these and similar careers creating many professionally oriented jobs that often require workers to have advanced training. When a microprocessor is incorporated into the workstation, the user has gained stand alone power while maintaining a link to the central computer. This link allows the user to free the central computer for more complex tasks while leaving routine operations to the workstation control device.

F. Human Resource Considerations

As the number of businesses purchasing small computer systems continues to increase, the programmer will become more involved with the production and application of software. The small business cannot afford a computer service technician, so increasing numbers of technicians will be supported by computer retailers and manufacturers. However, as computers proliferate and grow older an expanded service industry will likely evolve; the computer repair shop, similar to today's TV and electronic repair shops.

Today, most computer operating personnel consider themselves professionals. These individuals, along with programmers and service technicians, normally work 40 hours weekly, but not on regular schedules. Programming must sometimes be done according to equipment availability, often at night or on weekends. Repair personnel generally are on call twenty-four hours a day according to various schedules and rotations. Irregular work schedules for personnel working with computers are likely to increase in the future.

A National Science Foundation report stated a few years ago "there is a shortage of computer manpower which is expected to persist for the foreseeable future, but only the educational institutions have a real crisis."[22] Factors which support this conclusion include:

1. Students with graduate degrees pursue business/industrial employment versus education
2. Loss of faculty to business/industry is twice as high as any other occupation
3. Lower enrollment in engineering disciplines
4. University funding cuts

Faculty mobility has been influenced by both working conditions and salary. Students with relevant experience upon graduation have been able to obtain positions paying above average starting salaries. In the U.S. several universities have attempted to adjust to demand; 80 percent have increased loads, 50 percent have increased course offerings, and 66 percent utilize more graduate assistants in an increased capacity. All of these measures make teaching less attractive and have the long term effect of discouraging new prospects. Teaching must be made more attractive and salaries raised for real improvement to occur.[25]

As computer applications increase in production, insurance, or other new fields, experience and education in those fields will be required. This means that the computer professional who expects to succeed in production needs both production know-how and computer experience.

A recent trend is for the computer professional to move upward in management, instead of forever being bound to the computer room. This will require additional management skills and experience.

The following conclusions can be drawn with regard to employment and education in computer related fields:

1. The computer eliminates clerical jobs but creates higher level technical jobs. This causes some job displacement, because new openings require more skill and education.

2. As the number of working women increase in the total worker population, the number of women working in the computer field will increase.

3. Enrollment in computer-related college/university courses will continue to increase.

4. Professionals engaged in design will concentrate on software, hardware, communications, and whole office systems. Development of workplace modules combining work surfaces, seating, telephone telex, computer terminal, microcomputer, and photocopier will emerge.

5. MIS will become more cost effective and more relevant to decision-making. Until very recently, computers have been of little help in decision-making. This is probably because most systems analysts have little experience in managerial decision-making and because decision-making is more of an art than a science.

As system analysts learn how to assist top management in the decision process their status within the organization will likely increase. Several decades ago, the original marketing approach utilized for selling computers was based on reduced manpower; however, the opposite was most often true. The current approach stresses processing and automation capabilities. The future challenge to computer experts is to reduce the paper flood, to provide timely, pertinent information to improve the efficiency of the organization, improve decision-making, and increase profitability.

VI. WHAT'S AHEAD FOR PROFESSIONALS?

As suggested at many points throughout this book, the evidence clearly indicates that America's work culture is becoming increasingly professionalized.[33] A large percentage of the workforce wants to be considered professional. From the perspective of both the individual professional and management, this trend offers both opportunities and challenges. In addition to increased professionalism the workforce in the future will be more heterogeneous and exhibit considerable change in lifestyles and values. Today's organizations should not feel compelled to set societal values or provide workers with their sole sense of membership within the community. Instead organizational activities should be adapted to accommodate a culturally diverse workforce.[26] One way to accomplish this is for organizations to move back to urban centers which offer greater accommodation for varied professional groups. Additionally, departmental activities may be organized to make employees without families feel acceptable.[26] Also, modern telecommunications should be used to lessen excessive professional and executive travel. A climate that tolerates mistakes nurtures professional development and effectiveness because mistakes often are an important part of creativity.[26] The need for managerial change is reinforced by the Aspen Institute for Humanistic Studies report which concludes that management practices have not kept pace with changes in both the nature of work and in the values that people bring to their jobs.[2]

In addition to the difficulties mentioned, people who will be managing organizations during the 1990s and into the next century will be facing a number of other problems in a difficult environment. The fundamental challenges for professionals in management will center on a sound grasp of the relevant technology, communication skills, and a capacity for effectively relating with *and* motivating people. While the effective manager today requires these abilities, the need for communication, technology understanding, and human interface skills is predicted to increase for the successful manager in the future.

A. Problem Identification

The major problems (and opportunities) confronting managers in the future may be grouped into eight categories as outlined below:

Lagging productivity
Quality/cost concerns
Economic difficulties
Social concern and reform
Environmental requirements

Government regulation and controls
Product liability
Energy availability and cost

1. Lagging Productivity

The United States Bureau of the Budget several years ago provided a general definition of productivity as follows: "Productivity estimates compare the amount of resources used with the volume of products or services produced."[27] In manufacturing industries the common measure of productivity recorded by the federal government relates unit of product output to labor-hours input, a measurement index that is *not* appropriate for highly automated factories that may employ very little labor. A more meaningful measure would relate the output to all required inputs, i.e., material, capital, information, and labor.

According to the U.S. Department of Labor, productivity in the private economy grew over the post-World War II period at an approximate annual rate of 3.1 percent. This average rate of increase is for the period from 1946 through 1974. Examination of the data reveals a slightly higher rate of 3.6 percent in the earlier postwar period. This dropped to 3.0 percent during the early 1960s, and in the 1970s dropped to 2.4 percent. This lower level of productivity improvement has continued during the 1980s.

Productivity growth is an essential factor in the continued economic well being of the United States. One of the primary benefits is increased worker income. Over the years real compensation to the worker has risen at about the same rate as labor productivity. In addition, the consumer benefits through increased goods and services at affordable costs. Prices usually increase the least in those areas where productivity is rising and the most where productivity is lagging. Achieving improved productivity is important in determining the growth of real earnings and our standard of living. Improved productivity is also critical to reverse the decline of U.S. manufacturing industries, a problem confronting our economic system.

2. Quality/Cost Concerns

All organizations—manufacturing, government—have a need to produce quality goods and/or services. Given the presence of first rate foreign and domestic competition, most low quality and high cost producers will not be successful. The manager's goal should be to sustain *a consistent and competitive level of quality*, while maintaining a cost structure that realizes an acceptable financial position.

The manufacturing sector perhaps has the most severe need for producing high quality cost competitive products, particularly those firms in the world market place. Examples of U.S. industries that have failed to meet the quality/cost standards of global competition include steel, automobiles, machine tools, semiconductor chips, fiber optics, cameras, and consumer electronics. These are just some of the markets that the United States is either losing or has totally lost its dominance. More manufacturing industries in the future are likely to feel the destructive blow of foreign competition.

Several U.S. businesses have attempted to solve the quality/cost problem by minimizing or phasing out their manufacturing. They may be pursuing various profit making activities ranging from design through distribution but are not performing the added value of manufacturing. This reliance on "off-shore" capabilities to produce U.S. products has realized profits for the short-run but could ultimately eliminate several businesses as well as severely impact the U.S. economy and our standard of living.

The increase of service sector jobs will likely continue to replace the loss of manufacturing jobs. However, service sector jobs produce *much lower* average incomes. Traditionally the service sector productivity gains have been substantially less than manufacturing and this trend is expected to continue. Quality of output is perhaps only slightly less important in services than in manufacturing.

The successful manager (and business) of the future will have established and met high quality and cost containment objectives.[34]

3. Economic Difficulties

From a managerial perspective, balance of trade and the federal deficit will have influences on most businesses during the years ahead. Lagging productivity and quality/cost concerns have been central issues in the U.S. balance of trade position. The problems, however, properly managed can be opportunities for specific firms. For example, correctly determining what products or items should be "out-sourced" or not manufactured in the U.S., versus determining how to produce high quality low cost products in the U.S. near major markets, can realize economic gains. Thus, skillful management will make the difference for manufacturing firms and most businesses in the future.[28]

The growth of the U.S. economy has historically paralleled the growth of manufacturing. If the manufacturing sector continues on its present decline, it may curtail or even cause a reduction in the overall economy. It's interesting to note that a strong growing manufacturing base is what enabled the United States economy to afford an increased demand for services. We can not survive only on service industries.

It is a fact that expansion of the U.S. service industries during recent years has outpaced all earlier projections. According to U.S. Department of Labor statistics, the wholesale and retail trades, finance, communications, transportation, and personal services added approximately 10 million jobs to the U.S. economy between 1979 and 1986. Unfortunately, about 1.5 million manufacturing jobs were lost during this same time period. Since 1960, services have grown from about 60 percent of the gross national product to more than 68 percent in 1985. More strikingly, Labor Department projections indicate that services will provide approximately 90 percent of *all* new jobs during the next 10 years.

The loss of manufacturing in the United States along with the purchase of oil continues to increase foreign imports and reduce our ability to export, thus negatively impacting the U.S. balance of trade.

According to David A. Stockman, former Office of Management and Budget Director, when President Reagan leaves office in 1989, the federal government's spending will have exceeded its income by $1.5 trillion. The next president will inherit a debt nearly triple that accumulated by all former presidents since George Washington. In 1980 other nations owed U.S. creditors $150 billion. It is

predicted that in 1989, the U.S. will owe the rest of the world up-
wards of one-half trillion dollars.[29]

No one can be sure of the consequences of the balance of trade
situation and the staggering federal deficit. However, it is clear
that managers in the future will have to be alert to changing times
and draw upon all human and physical resources to maintain successful business operations. Only the most fit will survive.

4. Social Concern and Reform

Social concern and reform has impacted the modern worker. In recent years the work force has taken on a different profile. As previously discussed in this chapter, workers are better educated, and
they have greater social awareness than the generation that preceded them. Typical worker concerns include underemployment,
unemployment, and the need for environmental improvements.

Social concern and reform is also creeping into business. Not
since the days of Franklin D. Roosevelt and the New Deal has the
field of corporate governance been so active in generating proposals of reform. As Warner Bennis stated several years ago, "everybody's in the act, it seems—not just Ralph Nader, who nags, has-
sles, and litigates on behalf of corporate social responsibility or the
ubiquitous Lewis D. Gilbert, who presses for reform and sues corporations to make them more responsible to the shareholder."[30]

The social concern and reform trends are likely to continue
for individuals and corporations. Consequently, the manager of
the future must be able to integrate these complex changing views
into his or her leadership role.

5. Environmental Requirements

Environmental requirements will continue to be a major concern
of managers, as previously mentioned, in part because of the chang-
social views of many individuals and corporations. Requirements for
improved air quality, wastewater treatment, and solid/hazardous
waste disposal will continue to intensify, and will be factors to consider in many management decisions concerning new products, processes, and physical facilities.

One of the problems associated with environmental improvements is that most of the required equipment is not cost effective in the short run. That is, while most plant modifications leading to environmental improvements require substantial capital investment, they *do not provide any greater productive output.* The manager of the future will focus on attaining the proper balance of return on investment and environmental conformance.

6. Government Regulation and Control

Government regulations and controls are projected to increase over the next several years, especially in the areas of environmental concerns, consumer product safety, and worker health and safety. Government agencies such as the Environmental Protection Agency and the Occupational Safety and Health Administration will continue to impose restrictions and requirements on most industries, both product manufacturing and service organizations. Managers of the future must be able to effectively and efficiently meet these requirements.

7. Product Liability

There continues to be a proliferation of product liability suits across the United States following the adoption of the law of strict liability in tort. Product liability suits have covered a wide range of alleged inferior product designs and defective product manufacturing cases. In addition to corporations being named, managers, project engineers and other professionals have also been personally cited in a number of suits. Liability suits have also intensified for service organizations. It is predicted that the ultimate threat product liability poses to industry will surpass the threat posed to the medical profession by malpractice.

The rationale for product and service liability is acceptable to all persons. Certainly if someone is injured by a defective product or service, then the product's designer/manufacturer/provider should be held accountable. However, the prevailing interpretations of the law and the resulting cases against many organizations leave several unanswered questions and unexplained outcomes. If this problem is not fairly resolved with major legislation changes, the difficulties for managers in the future will likely be a monumental problem.[35]

8. Energy Availability and Cost

In the future managers will likely be faced with the problem of obtaining necessary energy for business operations at an affordable cost. While the world may not yet have an energy shortage, there is a looming crisis. Part of the problem is that at times certain energy demands exceed available supplies (remember the 1970s?), and we may be moving toward the point where total demand *will* exceed supply. Perhaps the most serious aspect in the short term is the deepening monetary crisis. During recent years, the U.S. balance of payments has been substantially affected because of monies expended for imported oil.

VII. CONCLUSIONS AND IMPLICATIONS

In summary, the years ahead will be increasingly problem laden and more complex from a management point of view. The successful manager will be able to transform these problems into opportunities. The need for developing effective management skills and abilities will continue at an increased level. No doubt, the professional worker will become a more valued human resource but there will be *increased competition* in almost all fields for the top jobs. Successful executives will be continually looking at specific professionals who have the skills to help give their respective firms the competitive edge in a global market place. As Brandt points out, staffs of established companies need to be *mixed and stirred* as the year 2000 approaches, or those companies will not be around in the 21st century.[31] Of particular importance to professionals, Drucker suggests that the organization of the future will have far fewer managers and many more specialists than are found in today's firms.[32] In addition to the insight and ability to change problems into opportunities, the manager of tomorrow must be able to accomplish more with less resources. In some ways it seems the future is now!

REFERENCES

1. Desmond D. Martin, W.F. Lewis, and T.T. Serey, "Personnel Managers' Perceptions of the Determinants of Organizational Effectiveness," *Akron Business and Economic Review,* Vol. 16, No. 3, Fall 1985, pp. 19-23.

2. Aspen Institute, "Work and Human Values: An International Report on Jobs in the 1980s and 1990s," New York: Aspen Institute for Humanistic Studies, 1983, pp. 9-58.

3. Edward J. Leary, "Decision Support Systems Aid in Management of Operations, Resources and Finances," *Industrial Engineering,* Vol. 23, No. 9, September 1985.

4. H. Ray Souder, William Leigh, and Richard L. Shell, "Using a Relational Database in Industrial Engineering Projects," *Industrial Engineering,* Vol. 23, No. 6, June 1985.

5. D. Scott Sink, "Strategic Planning: A Crucial Step Toward a Successful Productivity Management Program," *Industrial Engineering,* Vol. 23, No. 1, January 1985.

6. For a detailed discussion on MAPS design technology, see Ralph H. Kilman, "On Integrating Knowledge Utilization with Knowledge Development: The Philosophy Behind the MAPS Design Technology," *Academy of Management Review,* July 1979, pp. 417-426.

7. Ralph H. Kilman, "An Organic Adaptive Organization: The MAPS Method," *Personnel,* May-June 1974, pp. 35-47.

8. Peter F. Drucker, *Management Tasks, Responsibilities, Practices,* Harper and Row, New York, 1973, p. 545.

9. "Report of a Special Task Force to the Secretary of Health, Education, and Welfare," *Work in America,* The MIT Press, Cambridge, Mass., 1973, p. 10.

10. John Naisbitt, and N. Aburdene, *Re-inventing the Corporation,* Warner Books, 1985, pp. 80-81.

11. "Report of a Special Task Force to the Secretary of Health, Education, and Welfare," *Work in America,* The MIT Press, Cambridge, Mass., 1973, p. 138.

12. Peter F. Drucker, "Getting Things Done: How to Make People Decisions," *Harvard Business Review,* July-August 1985, pp. 22-26.

13. Martin Patchen, *Participation, Achievement, and Involvement on the Job,* Prentice-Hall, Englewood Cliffs, N.J., 1970, p. 234.

14. Ibid., p. 235.

15. Sam Guild, "Characteristics of Career Planners in Upwardly Mobile Occupations," *Academy of Management Journal,* September 1979, pp. 539-550.

16. For an excellent discussion of career advice, see Ross A. Weber, "Career Problems of Young Managers," *California Management Review,* Vol. 18, No. 4, 1976, pp. 19-33. See also E.E. Jennings, *Routes to the Executive Suite,* McGraw-Hill, New York, 1971; and R.H. Buskirk, *Your Career: How to Plan It, Manage It, Change It,* Cahners, Boston, 1976.

17. H. Bean, "Preparing for Promotion Pays Off," *Business Horizons,* January-February 1984, pp. 6-13.

18. For a detailed analysis of current trends in the labor movement, see R.B. Freeman and J.L. Medoff, *What Do Unions Do?,* New York: Basic Books, 1984.

19. D. Chamot, "Professional Employees Turn to Unions," *Harvard Business Review,* May-June 1976, pp. 119-127.

20. H. Ray Souder, and Richard L. Shell, "Tomorrow's Computers Promise Faster Speeds, Greater Challenges," *Data Management,* Vol. 23, No. 2, February 1985.

21. R.J. Douglas, "Need and Uses," *IEEE Spectrum,* November 1983, pp. 41-45.

22. R.F. Cotellessa, (Chairman), *Report of the Information Technology Workshop,* National Science Foundation, October 1983.

23. John Naisbitt, *Megatrends,* Warner Books, 1984.

24. Richard L. Shell, O. Geoffrey Okogbaa, and Thomas Huston, "The Work Station of the Future for Knowledge Workers," *Industrial Engineering,* Vol. 17, No, 8, August 1985.

25. *Science Indicators/The 1985 Report,* The National Science Board, U.S. Government Printing Office, 1985.

26. P. Gardner, "Creating a Corporate Culture for the Eighties," *Business Horizons,* Vol. 28, No. 1, Jan.-Feb. 1985, pp. 59-63.

27. *Measuring Productivity of Federal Government Organizations,* U.S. Bureau of the Budget, Government Printing Office, 1964.

28. Richard L. Shell and Joseph A. Steger, "Cooperative Research in Manufacturing," *Urban Resources,* Vol. 3, No. 1, Fall 1985.

29. David A. Stockman, *Postscript,* Harper & Row, 1986; and *The Triumph of Politics,* Harper & Row, 1986.

30. W.G. Bennis, "RX for Corporate Boards," *Technology Review,* Vol. 81, No. 3, December 1978-January 1979, p. 12.

31. S.C. Brandt, *Entrepreneuring in Established Companies*: *Managing Toward the Year 2000,* Homewood, IL, Dow Jones, Irwin, 1986, p. 78.

32. Peter F. Drucker, "The Worst Thing Is to Modernize," *U.S. News & World Report,* February 2, 1987, p. 23.

33. For a discussion of trends among professionals see J.A. Raelin, "The Professional as the Executive's Ethical Aide-de-Camp," *The Academy of Management Executives,* Vol. 1, No. 3, August 1987, pp. 171-182.

34. For a discussion of technology and innovation see Richard Foster, *Innovation*: *The Attacker's Advantage,* New York, Summit Books, 1986.

35. James F. Thorpe and William H. Middendorf, *What Every Engineer Should Know About Product Liability,* New York, Marcel Dekker, 1980.

Index

A

Acceptance theory, 71
Achievement, 194, 195
Acquisitions, 283
Adaptability, 251
Adaptive corporation, 251
Advancement, 195
Affiliation, 194
Albermarle vs. Moody, 62
Allowances
  development of, 84
  process, 84
  waiting, 84
Alternative creators, 111
American Society for Training
  and Development, 299
Anxiety
  state of, 278
  trait, 278

Appraisal interviews, 308
Art, defined, 10
Artificial intelligence (AI), 327
AT&T, 238
Authority, 274
  of character, 73
  defined, 71
  functional, 73
  informal, 71
  staff, 73
  types of, 72
Autonomy, 140, 190, 193, 212,
  235, 303

B

B. F. Goodrich Corp., 297
*Bakke vs. the University of
  California*, 62
Balance of trade, 351, 352

359